This study in literary theory, written by one of the foremost younger Marxist critics in England, explores some of the most tenacious and taxing problems in contemporary aesthetics. It starts with a survey of ideological factors which have shaped past and present literary criticism, which includes the first extended critique of the work of Raymond Williams to have appeared in the Anglo-Saxon world. It then proposes a Marxist critical method capable of dealing with 'literary modes of production' and 'general', 'aesthetic' and 'authorial' ideologies. Eagleton integrates certain semiological findings into a materialist reflection on the relations between literary text and ideology, and poses central questions about the scientific character of criticism. He also develops a concrete critique of social and aesthetic 'organicism' in English literature from Arnold to Lawrence. The book ends with a chapter on the—too often evaded—problem of what is meant by literary 'value' in studies of literature. *Criticism and Ideology* represents a notable theoretical departure within contemporary Marxist aesthetics.

Criticism and Ideology

A Study in Marxist Literary Theory

TERRY EAGLETON

VERSO

London · New York

First published by NLB 1976

© Terry Eagleton 1975, 1976

Verso Edition 1978
Second impression 1980
Third impression 1982
Fourth impression 1984
Fifth impression 1985
Sixth impression 1986
Seventh impression 1988

Verso
UK: 6 Meard Street, London W1V 3HR
USA: 29 West 35th Street, New York, NY 10001-2291

Printed in Great Britain by
The Thetford Press Limited, Thetford, Norfolk

Cloth ISBN 902308 92 0
Paper ISBN 86091 707 X

Contents

Preface

Any English Marxist who tries now to construct a materialist aesthetics must be painfully conscious of his inadequacies. It is not only that so many issues in this field are fraught and inconclusive, but that to intervene from England is almost automatically to disenfranchise oneself from debate. It is to feel acutely bereft of a tradition, as a tolerated house-guest of Europe, a precocious but parasitic alien. The essays which follow labour under these embarrassments. They are perhaps most marked in the final chapter on the problem of literary value, which seems to me little more than a provisional clearing of the ground on which a genuine discussion of these matters could be conducted; but they are also apparent in the excessively cryptic and elliptical language of Chapter 4 (a revised and expanded version of an article which first appeared in *New Left Review*), which in trying to compress a complex span of literary history into a single framework lapses inevitably into inexact formulation, metaphorical gesture, partial and reductive reading. I should add that this was the first section of the book to be written, and that it stands to some extent under the judgement of the two preceding chapters, where (undoubtedly at the cost of schematism and simplification) I have striven for more rigorous formulations. But I have felt it best to let the book stand as it is, replete with errors and omissions which are both the result of my own limitations and, perhaps, inevitable in a work which has little as yet in England to support it.

I am deeply grateful to a number of people who have given me valuable advice and encouragement in writing this book. I must thank in particular Perry Anderson, Francis Barker, Mike Ewart, John Goode, John Harrison, Quintin Hoare, Francis Mulhern,

8

Paul Tickell, Alan Wall and George Wotton, all of whom have generously spared time from their own work to criticise the manuscript. I also have a long-standing debt to the many past and present members of the Marxist criticism collective in the University of Oxford, who in an improbable institution have pioneered a context within which this kind of discourse has become continuous, absorbing and productive. It is certain that without their devotion to the problems of a materialist criticism, this book would never have been written. There are similar groups and individuals throughout the country with whom I have discussed these issues, and to whom I also owe thanks.

T.E.

In Memory of My Father
FRANCIS EAGLETON

What we do best is breed
Speech to dispel the fear
Which blinds men to their need,

Be to the mute a tongue,
Become the living voice
Of comrades quelled by wrong.

I

Mutations of Critical Ideology

It is difficult to see criticism as anything but an innocent discipline. Its origins seem spontaneous, its existence natural: there is literature, and so – because we wish to understand and appreciate it – there is also criticism. Criticism as a handmaiden to literature – as a *shadowing* of literature, a ghostly accomplice which, to adopt a phrase from *Four Quartets*, prevents it everywhere. Yet 'prevents' bears upon us here in its common as well as its classical meaning. If the task of criticism is to smooth the troubled passage between text and reader, to elaborate the text so that it may be more easily consumed, how is it to avoid interposing its own ungainly bulk between product and consumer, *over*shadowing its object in the act of obediently 'ghosting' it? It seems that criticism is caught here in an insoluble contradiction. For if its task is to yield us the spontaneous reality of the text, it must permit no particle of its own mass to mingle with what it mediates; such mingling would signal the unspeakable crime of 'appropriation'. Yet how is it to do this without consigning itself to that mode of natural existence which is the life of a parasite? How is it to avoid that form of self-transparency, that humble conformity to the life of the text, which is mere self-abolition? All criticism should confess its limitations; but bourgeois criticism rarely seems more confident than when it speaks of its own redundancy – when it insists, self-laceratingly, on the partial, intrusive, provisional nature of its own propositions. Subtle and delicate though they may be, such propositions are finally as straw before the inexhaustible godhead of the text itself. Yet it is one thing to parade the superfluity of one's discourse, and another thing to keep silent. Criticism may be a crippled discourse, but it is too late for it simply to dismantle itself; there is too much at stake, materially and academically, for that.

The radical self-doubt of criticism is such that it is not even able to say whether it is an 'amateur' or 'professional' pursuit. It cannot, surely, be *professional*, for nothing is more natural than reading. It is simply a matter of turning the pages until you get to the end – turning them, naturally, with a peculiar attentiveness, but an attentiveness which, though it can be nurtured and informed, cannot ultimately be taught. Yet it cannot be amateur either, for it is unthinkable that the labour-intensive industry of literary enquiry – schools, University faculties, publishing houses, literary bodies – turns on a mode of cognition more akin to wine-tasting than chemical experiment. When English literary studies were first academically institutionalised in Britain, this dilemma was 'resolved' by a judicious blending of the two modes. English literature was a non-subject in a palpable sense: the English gentlemen who occupied the early professorships at the 'ancient' Universities no more needed a course of specialised training in how to read their own literature than they needed a course of training in how to give orders to their domestic servants. Yet they were, after all, professors of English, and the cavalier frivolity they displayed towards their calling could not go wholly undisguised. The simple solution available to them was to study English literature but to pretend that it was something else – to systematically mistake it for the 'classics'. No more professionally reputable cloak could have been discovered. One had, naturally, one's private opinions about Crabbe as one had about Catullus, but the study of English letters could not conceivably consist in vulgarly airing one's private predilections in public. Such public airing, as Yeats remarked, belonged to shopkeepers – as it happened, historically, to the son of a shopkeeper, F. R. Leavis. 'Amateur' predilections were preserved, but preserved in isolation from the professional business of knowing *about* literature – a traditional combination of positivism and subjectivism still potent in contemporary criticism.

Such a posture inevitably provoked its reaction. Academically powerful but historically superannuated, the aristocratic and haut-bourgeois 'pioneers' of a discipline they palpably disbelieved in were ripe for dislodgement by the ideologies of a social class entering the 'ancient' Universities for the first time, able to accomplish the objective tasks set for criticism by contemporary history as their ideologically bankrupt predecessors could not. A petty-bourgeois liberal humanism, academically dispossessed and subordinated yet in intellectual terms increasingly hegemonic, occupied the bastions of reactionary criticism from within as a dissentient bloc. Vehemently radical in its onslaughts on the 'academic establishment', the unity of whose aesthetic and ideological assumptions they trenchantly exposed, this petty-bourgeois nonconformist humanism installed itself as the champion of precisely those literary mutations which the ideological moment demanded, and undauntedly rewrote the whole of English literary history in its image. No more militant, courageous and consistent project is to be found in the history of English criticism.

Yet we are not dealing here with a simple clash of 'class-ideologies'. What is in question, rather, is the contradictory mode of insertion of the *Scrutiny* ideology into the dominant aesthetic and ideological formations. To designate the movement 'petty-bourgeois' is not in the first place to refer to its social origins, for they (though they have a certain relevance) were inevitably diverse; it is rather to denote the contradictions of its ideological universe. 'Radical' and occasionally populist in its formulations, feared and mocked by the ruling academic caste, *Scrutiny*'s historic function (complex and changing though it was), was at one level reasonably plain: it was to bring about that drastic reconstruction of forms, values, discourses and lineages within the aesthetic region of ideology which, at a point of serious historical crisis, would play its part in revitalising and reproducing the dominant ideology as a whole. Indeed, it was much more than a question of merely refashioning the aesthetic region of ideology: it was a matter of effectively *substituting* that region for ideology as such. The ideological vacuum occasioned in English society by the partial collapse of certain traditional sub-formations (notably religion), and the historically determined absence of others (notably a fully-fledged sociology), demanded filling; and it was this task which, in the tradition of Matthew Arnold, *Scrutiny* attempted. Like Arnold, then, it was at once 'progressive' and 'reactionary' – vigorously alert to the moment of the 'modern' and its new ideological demands, but able to meet them only with pathetically obsolescent and idealist 'solutions': the 'organic community' of a mythicised English past, the 'University English school' as the spiritual essence of the social formation. It is here, precisely, that one index of the essentially petty-bourgeois character of *Scrutiny* is evident. For if that puritan, nonconformist tradition was (in the determinate absence of a revolutionary heritage) the only possible force which in its moral combativeness, intellectual seriousness and social realism could 'progressively' refashion the structures of a stagnant, socially irrelevant academicism, it was by the same token a subordinate, historically disinherited lineage, driven back onto nostalgic 'artisanal' images of a pre-capitalist past, embracing the 'modernist' (*The Waste Land*) but also repulsing it (*Ulysses*) from a 'traditionalist' standpoint. *Scrutiny* 'progressively' revaluated literary traditions, but did so because it saw such traditions as the privileged repository of 'human' values brutally overridden by the development of contemporary capitalism. It acted, accordingly, as the impotent idealist conscience of a capitalism in the process of definitively transcending its liberal-humanist phase.

The historical marginality and 'spiritual' centrality of *Scrutiny* resolve themselves in a single category: élitism. Here, once more, the petty-bourgeois character of the movement is revealed. For élitism, as Nicos Poulantzas has argued,[1] is a structural trait of the petty bourgeoisie. Committed by its nuclear social and economic conditions to a framework of overarching authority, to 'standards' and 'leadership', the petty bourgeoisie rejects at once the democratic 'anarchy' it discerns below it and the ineffectualness of the actual authority posed above it. This was precisely *Scrutiny*'s situation. Though *empirically* decentred, largely excluded from the ruling academic caste, it nevertheless laid claim to *be*, spiritually, the 'real' élite. On the one hand, *Scrutiny* was a progressive *vanguard* thrown into militant conflict with the academic establishment – a conflict for which it mobilised elements of the 'radical' and liberal ideologies of subordinate groups and classes. It effected what Raymond Williams has called, in another context, a 'negative identification' with such social forces,[2] to the point where at an early stage it even entertained (in speculative, academic fashion, naturally enough) the 'desirability' of 'some form of economic communism'.[3] But the 'vanguard' was also, notionally, the 'élite', already disseminating standards from its spiritual power-positions within the literary establishment. That confusion of 'vanguard' and 'elite' was the

1. See his *Fascism and Dictatorship* (London, 1974), pp 254–5.
2. *Culture and Society 1780–1950* (Harmondsworth, 1963), p. 178.
3. *Scrutiny*, March 1933.

precise effect of *Scrutiny*'s inherent contradiction, as an ideological force locked in complicity with the very society it spiritually castigated.

It was, indeed, that complicity which notoriously prevented *Scrutiny* from formulating the theoretical bases of its critique. *Scrutiny*'s naive sensuous empiricism, epitomised in the act of 'practical criticism', was a 'progressive' testing of aesthetic categories against the immediacies of lived experience – a dissolution of generalities in the 'lived' as ideologically potent as Eliot's dislocation of articulate meanings into poetic concretion. But it was, on the other hand, the confession of a mere incapacity: the blankness of a critique ideologically prohibited from achieving the potentially more subversive level of theoretical discourse. To combat 'ideology', *Scrutiny* pointed to 'experience' – as though that, precisely, were not ideology's homeland. Yet the 'philosophy' of *Scrutiny* went beyond sensuous empiricism, and necessarily so. Just as, for Eliot, such empiricism proved ideologically insufficient, demanding its sublation into doctrinal Christianity, so *Scrutiny* stood in objective need of a metaphysic whose intuitive force was in inverse proportion to its theoretical articulateness. Such a metaphysic was provided by the work of D. H. Lawrence. Lawrence's idealism did not undercut sensuous empiricism: on the contrary, it lent it nothing less than ontological status. Furnished with this metaphysic, then, *Scrutiny* was able to lambast the varieties of utilitarian empiricism from the standpoint of an absolute idealism, while at the same time assaulting 'absolutist' systems (including, naturally, Marxism) from the viewpoint of a thoroughly 'English' liberal empiricism. The position was invulnerable in direct proportion to its irrationality. Since the metaphysical underpinning slipped by definition through the net of language (so that to demand its demonstration was to reveal oneself in that very act as unregenerate) it was shielded from scrutiny; but it was, by the same token, theoretically sterile. All one could do was point to which phenomena represented 'life', and which did not; there was by definition no possibility of real development within the case, self-limiting and self-referential as it was. It could only be a matter of restating that case again and again, each time with gathering stridency and abstraction, as the liberal-humanist values of a particular phase of industrial capitalism entered into deeper contradiction with that capitalism's developed forms. The logical upshot of this contradiction was then a transvaluing of liberal humanism itself, into the banalities of tory reaction.

Scrutiny's monumentally significant critical achievement produced, in turn, its reaction. That criticism was a pursuit which engaged questions of fundamental value came as an attractive, intuitively valid proposition to students concerned to relate 'literature' to 'life'; yet some of the claims entailed by that buoyant humanism, when pondered in the small hours of the morning, seemed slightly grandiose. There was the question, for example, of those individuals who had no access to the supremely civilising discipline of literature – individuals who certainly formed the social and historical majority, but who were not remarkable for their readiness to rape and plunder, or who, if they were, could not confidently be said to be thus disposed because of their ignorance of Henry James. And there was the even more disturbing question of those individuals who, while undoubtedly deep in literary culture, seemed to find no incompatibility between that and such activities as superintending the murder of Jews. The liberal humanist vision accordingly brought to birth its own negation, tied to it as its very shadow – the rhetorical disillusionment of critics who, sharing the very structure of its assumptions, had nowhere to move on its partial collapse but into postures of patrician reaction masquerading as bleak historical realism. With the partial breaching of the bourgeois humanist fortress, criticism is increasingly driven to transcend its empiricist, intuitionist practices and adopt some 'long perspective' – some problematic which, while more or less compatible with empiricism, is less vulnerable to pious hope and errant subjectivism. *Genre*, stylistics, theology, psychoanalysis, structuralism: tentative though these projects are in contemporary England, the system-building is now on.

And, of course, historical materialism. There is no doubt as to the ideological determinants of the resurgent interest in Marxist criticism which we have witnessed in the West at least since 1968. It is the task of Marxist criticism (as indeed with all the critical methods I have briefly listed) to recognise its own historical determinants, but to demonstrate that its validity is not identical with them. In the case of Marxism, however, this demonstration is especially difficult. For historical materialism stands or falls by the claim that it is not only not an ideology, but that it contains a scientific theory of the genesis, structure and decline of ideologies. It situates itself, in short, outside the terrain of competing 'long perspectives' in order to theorise the conditions of their very possibility. This, doubtless, seems a somewhat unfair, deftly convenient advantage to claim over the adherents of such alternative methods. Nor is Marxist criticism rendered any more popular by its simple incompatibility with empiricist and intuitionist techniques; it is less pliant than other 'long perspectives' to the sideways insertion or separate preservation of those ideologically paramount values.

Criticism is not an innocent discipline, and never has been. It is a branch of Marxist criticism to enquire into the history of criticism itself: to pose the question of under what conditions, and for what ends, a literary criticism comes about. For criticism has a history, which is more than a random collocation of critical acts. If literature is its object, it is not its sole point of genesis; criticism does not arise as a spontaneous riposte to the existential fact of the text, organically coupled with the object it illuminates. It has its own relatively autonomous life, its own laws and structures: it forms an internally complex system articulated with the literary system rather than merely reflexive of it. It emerges into existence, and passes out of it again, on the basis of certain determinate conditions. Not all literature needs criticism to prevent it; but there may come a moment, nevertheless, when poetry has to be apologised for. In constructing the history of criticism we are not tracing the exfoliation through history of a linear, if irregular, process: it is the history of *criticisms* which is at issue. We are seeking the determinants of the particular historical 'spaces' which make the emergence of such an object possible in the first place, and which determine its relations to other synchronous discourses. The science of the history of criticisms is the science of the historical forms which produce those criticisms – criticisms which in turn produce the literary text as their object, as the 'text-for-criticism'.

The moment when a material or intellectual practice begins to 'think itself', to take itself as an object of intellectual enquiry, is clearly of dominant significance in the development of that practice; it will certainly never be the same again. What thrusts such a practice into self-reflexiveness is not merely an internal pressure, but the complex unity it forms with adjacent discourses. Writing history, criticising or psychoanalysing, studying political economy, falling bodies or acts of promising are not 'natural' activities, the random upshot of 'human curiosity'. They occur within historically determinate spaces of self-reflexion, spaces whose mutual conjuncture marks out the possible objects of knowledge, and so of control, of an ideological formation. This is not, need one say, to *reduce* all such practices to the ideological: the validity of gravitation is not relative to the ideological structure of eighteenth-century England. It is, rather, the product of a scientific discourse produced from within ideology, and plays its role within that ideological formation. Such self-reflexive moments do not necessarily mark the birthplace of a *science*. When history begins to 'think itself' as historiography, material production as political economy, quotidian behaviour as philosophy or psychology, the rupture thus established between thought and reality is not the guarantee of a knowledge, though it is the pre-condition of one. It may well be a merely 'provisional' rupture, an opening through which the practice unites more intimately with itself. That this is so, indeed, is particularly evident in the case of criticism. For criticism's self-separation from its object is a kind of feint – a mere prelude to reuniting with it more completely. Its analytic distantiation of its object is the parody of a knowledge – a means of 'possessing' it more closely, dissolving itself into oneness with it. The end of criticism is to efface itself before the text, vicariously naturalising its own troubled 'artifice' by its power to elicit the 'naturalness' of the text itself. In a spiral of mutual reinforcements, the literary text naturalises experience, critical practice naturalises the text, and the theories of that practice legitimate the 'naturalness' of criticism. As a meta-literary practice, a *metaphor* of the text, criticism writes large the text's inability to think the conditions of its own possibility, reproducing that incapacity under the guise of a knowledge. Under the form of an illumination, criticism renders natural the text's necessary self-blindness. The formal relation between criticism and text resembles the relation between the tribal bard and the king to whom he recounts historical victories, or the relation between bourgeois political economist and capitalist manufacturer. In each case, the 'separation' between discourse and reality is the mere ghost of one: the function of the discourse is to be no more than the self-consciousness of its historical situation. This, precisely, is the function of criticism – to furnish the terms in which the text can know itself, rather than the terms in which what the text does not and cannot know can be disclosed.

The point where poetry has to be apologised for arises classically in English literary history with Sir Philip Sidney's *Apology for Poetry*. The poetry which Sidney defends is, of course, an institution inseparable from explicit ideological values – the values of a courtly classical humanism hostile to such lapses of taste as the mixing of social classes in drama. Literature for Sidney is a potent ideological instrument for inculcating those virtues appropriate to the hegemonic class of which he is spokesman; it is for this reason above all that it must be protected from the criticisms of an assertive bourgeois puritanism. Sidney's text marks a fading moment of ideological buoyancy, an achieved synthesis of courtly and puritan elements; but the incipient pressures which call forth an *apology* for poetry will erupt soon afterwards, in the economically unstable, religiously fraught 1590s, to call that ideological synthesis into increasing question. It is only after that eruption has grown to revolutionary crisis and subsided on the other side of civil war that the next major criticism, the so-called 'neo-classical', is called into being. Once more, criticism becomes a crucial ideological instrument – but now in the struggle to stabilise an ideological formation which will seal the contradictory unity of those social classes which compose the hegemonic bloc. In the drive for order, proportion and propriety, the demand for socially cohesive categories of Nature and Reason, the need to reduce and systematise social life to a series of ordered practices, history once again selects criticism as both paradigm and instrument of such a project. In the need to incorporate new classes and fractions of classes into cultural unity, to establish a consensus of social taste, construct common traditions and disseminate uniform manners, criticism becomes one fulcrum of a whole set of ideological institutions: periodicals, coffee-houses, aesthetic and social treatises, classical translations, guide-books to manners and morals. Again, it is only with the gradual erosion of this formation, in the revolutionary turmoil which closes the eighteenth century, that a distinctive corpus of criticism once more emerges into prominence. In the 'emancipated', egalitarian, populist and individualist aesthetics of Romanticism, criticism once more becomes a privileged terrain on which the class-struggle is ideologically conducted. It is equally important in the shaping of a new conservatism, as the later work of Coleridge attests – in the deriving from art of organicist images of society which will pass as a vital heritage into the nineteenth century.

It is not my intention to trace that passage here; I discuss some aspects of it in Chapter 4 of this book. Nor has the intention of these brief comments been to suggest that criticism is no more than a reflex of its ideological moment. Criticism belongs to the aesthetic region of ideology, a region with its proper degree of autonomy of the whole. But the emergence of a criticism (Renaissance humanist, neo-classicist, Romantic, liberal humanist) signifies a certain conjuncture between that region and others – a conjecture in which the aesthetic region assumes an unusual degree of dominance within the whole ideological formation. It is not that the aesthetic becomes *the* dominant region of the ideology; it is rather that it is 'foregrounded' as a privileged bearer of the themes over which that formation broods. It is not, naturally, as though the aesthetic is stripped at such moments of its proper trappings to become 'raw ideology': there is no such phenomenon. On the contrary, even though literary aesthetics begin at such times to speak of more than themselves, to form frequently overt alliances with the political, ethical and religious spheres, they do so in terms of their own internal debates, demands and traditions. Their ideological efficacy remains an *aesthetic* one, and in this, indeed, lies their power. For the aesthetic is for a number of reasons a peculiarly effective ideological medium: it is graphic, immediate and economical, working at instinctual and emotional depths yet playing too on the very surfaces of perception, entwining itself with the stuff of spontaneous experience and the roots of language and gesture. Precisely on this account, it is able to naturalise itself, to proffer itself as ideologically innocent, in ways less easily available to ideology's political and juridical regions. The relative subordination of the aesthetic within the history of ideologies is to be explained, not by its inherent paucity, but by other factors within social formations – most notably, the material and ideological forces which dictate the exclusion of the masses from art.

The 'history of criticism', then, is an aspect of the history of a set of specific ideological formations, each of which is so internally articulated as to privilege certain critical practices as a peculiarly overdetermined instance of its other levels. The science of the history of criticism is the science of the historical determinants of this over-determination of the literary-aesthetic.

To return from these general considerations to English literary criticism in the twentieth century is inevitably to think, once more, of that powerful ideological moment represented by *Scrutiny*. Yet in the 1930s in particular, *Scrutiny* had a rival in the form of a fragmentary, notably uneven body of materialist criticism. That so much of this writing is now of merely historical interest is one aspect of our present dilemma, even though one name at least has survived from that era. Who is the major English Marxist critic? Christopher Caudwell, *hélas*. It is in such pat question and answer that the problem of a Marxist criticism in contemporary Britain is most deftly posed. For though Caudwell is the major forebear – 'major', at least, in the sheer undaunted ambitiousness of his project – it is equally true that there is little, except negatively, to be learnt from him. Not that we can learn only from the English, or that Caudwell's limitations were just his own. Insulated from much of Europe, intellectually isolated even within his own society, permeated by Stalinism and idealism, bereft of a 'theory of superstructures', Caudwell nonetheless persevered in the historically hopeless task of producing from these unpropitious conditions a fully-fledged Marxist aesthetic. His work bears all the scars of that self-contradictory enterprise: speculative and erratic, studded with random insights, punctuated by hectic forays into and out of alien territories and strewn with hair-raising theoretical vulgarities. If Caudwell lacked a tradition of Marxist aesthetics, it is a measure of that absence that we, coming after him, lack one too.

It may come about, however, by a curious historical twist, that Marxist criticism may develop not through continuity with what went before, but precisely by having bypassed it. When Raymond Williams came to write in the early 1950s, the ethos of Thirties criticism, compounded as it was of vulgar Marxism, bourgeois empiricism and Romantic idealism, could yield him almost nothing; Caudwell, he remarked sardonically in *Culture and Society 1780–1950*, was for the most part 'not even specific enough to be wrong'. Marxism *had*, inevitably, influenced Williams: indeed Marxism and *Scrutiny* supplied between them the formative influences on his early

22

development. *Scrutiny* had to be rejected as a whole position because of the élitism to which it led; Marxism for what are perhaps more interesting reasons:

'As for Marx, one accepted the emphases on history, on change, on the inevitably close relationships between class and culture, but the way this came through was, at another level, unacceptable. There was, in this position, a polarisation and abstraction of economic life on the one hand and culture on the other, which did not seem to me to correspond to the social experience of culture as others had lived it, and as one was trying to live it oneself'.[4]

The closing formulation is curious: no one, surely, ever took the base/superstructure distinction to be a matter of *experience*. Yet it is precisely this insistence on experience, this passionate premium placed upon the 'lived', which provides one of the centrally unifying themes of Williams's *oeuvre* – which supplies at once the formidable power and drastic limitation of his work. I have commented briefly on some of the critical consequences which followed upon the questioning of the liberal humanist case, but one I have omitted: the emergence of what one might term a 'Left-Leavisism', of which Williams's work has been the major exemplar. For it is surely obvious how the negative judgement on Marxism delivered in the above quotation crystallises itself in obliquely Leavisian terms, at the very moment in the text when that case is itself under fire. Williams's enterprise has been, in the most fertile sense of the phrase, a life's work: not merely the work of a lifetime, but an *oeuvre* whose intricate internal logic and complex structural unity are the product of an argument deeply anchored in the experience of an historical individual. It is a method well enough revealed in his literary style – an elaborately formal, resoundingly public discourse in which an abstractive habit has become an instinctual reflex, a conjuring of weight out of emptiness which lacks all edge and abrasiveness. Concrete particulars are offered in such modified, mediated and magisterial a guise as to be only dimly intelligible through the mesh of generalities. Yet at the same time his ponderous pauses and stiffly rhetorical inflections, his ritualising of a cluster of key terms to the point where they seem less public concepts than private inventions,

4. Introduction to *From Culture to Revolution*, ed. Terry Eagleton and Brian Wicker (London, 1968), p. 28.

suggest the movement of an unmistakably individual voice. What appears at first glance the inert language of academicism is in fact the stage of a personal drama, the discourse of a complex, guarded self-display. A closed private idiom is cast into public oratory: the speaking voice slowly weaves its authoritative abstractions at the same time as it shocks by its sheer idiosyncrasy, its mannered yet candid trust in its own authenticity. It is a style which in the very act of assuming an unruffled, almost Olympian impersonality displays itself (not least in its spiralling modifications) as edgily defensive, private and self-absorbed. It is a mode of self-confession which is simultaneously a self-concealment – the style of a thinker intellectually isolated to the point of eccentricity, driven consequently to certain sophisticated gambits of self-defence and self-justification, but none the less resolutely offering his own experience as historically representative. Such a discourse rests on a rare, courageously simple belief – Wordsworth and Yeats come to mind as *confrères* – that the deepest personal experience can be offered, without arrogance or appropriation, as socially 'typical'. It is in some ways the voice of the social critics examined in *Culture and Society 1780–1950*; and indeed the key to that work is that Williams offers himself, not consciously or intrusively but implicitly and with every title to do so, as the latest figure in the lineage he traces, a character within his own drama.

Williams's achievement, then, has been to pursue the implications of felt personal experience to the point where they have organically emerged as methods, concepts, strategies; and this, naturally enough, is what one would expect from a socialist thinker who has always been first and foremost a literary critic nurtured in the Cambridge school. Like Caudwell, Williams was severely deprived of the materials from which to construct a socialist criticism – indeed it is a grimly ironic mark of that deprivation that the social tradition to which he was forced to resort in *Culture and Society* was one of almost uniform political reaction. The English Marxism available to him was little more than an intellectual irrelevance; indeed if a Marxist criticism comes about in English society, one might risk the paradox that one of its sources will be the fact that Williams had in his own time to reject it. What he did, then, he did almost single-handedly, working from his personal resources, without significant collaboration or institutional support. The product of that unflagging, unswerving labour was the most suggestive and intricate body of socialist criticism in English history – criticism for which no English comparison is even remotely relevant, but which must be referred for comparative assessment to the aesthetic production of a Lukács, Benjamin or Goldmann. It is enough to say that any Marxist criticism in England which has shirked taking the pressure of Williams's work will find itself seriously crippled and truncated. Williams has been the English pioneer, and like every pioneer must now submit to criticism from those he has enabled to speak. If I may add here a personal comment, I myself was fortunate enough to work closely with Williams as his colleague for several years, and made much the same social transition as himself. The necessarily astringent criticisms which follow are made in that spirit of comradeship and good faith.

If Caudwell lacked a tradition, Williams did not entirely do so: what he had to hand, essentially, was the work of *Scrutiny*. He rejected, naturally, the political consequences of that case, which he recognised and combated long before they emerged into the strident crudity of their current forms; but the *phenomenological* basis of that criticism was of peculiarly direct relevance to him. As the son of Welsh working-class parents, entering Cambridge University from an unusually close and supportive rural community, questions of class, culture, politics and education presented themselves to him in spontaneously personal terms, inseparable from the very stuff and problem of individual identity. His particular social transition made him an extraordinarily 'typical' bearer of some of the classic contradictions of the social formation: proletariat/bourgeoisie, region/ metropolis, rural/urban, and indeed the division of agricultural and industrial labour within the land, since his family context encompassed both types of work. *Scrutiny*'s insistence on community, tradition, moral value and the centrality of the 'lived' thus offered itself as the intellectual terms in which questions of personal identity could be explored and politically generalised. His early work on drama, turning on such notions as 'community of sensibility' and 'community of process' to describe the drama–audience relationship, was directly indebted to *Scrutiny*; but for exactly that reason it could not carry him very far, could not touch the specificity of what he sought. The partial 'break' occurred with *Culture and Society*, in which Williams seeks to extend and connect (symptomatic terms in his writing) what is still in many ways a Leavisian perspective to a 'socialist humanism' radically hostile to *Scrutiny*'s political case. What the work did, in effect, was to take the only viable tradition Williams had to hand – the Romantic 'radical–conservative' lineage of nineteenth-century England – and extract from it those 'radical' elements which could be ingrafted into a 'socialist humanism'. That is to say, the 'radical' elements extracted – tradition, community, organism, growth, wholeness, continuity and so on – were inter-locked with the equally corporatist, evolutionary discourse of Labourism, so that the organicism of the one language reproduced and elaborated the organicism of the other. The book thus para-doxically reproduced the nineteenth-century bourgeois exploitation of Romantic 'radical-conservative' ideology for its own ends – only this time the ends in question were socialist. And it could do so, of course, because the working-class movement is as a matter of historical fact deeply infected with the Carlylean and Ruskinian ideology in question. It was a matter of the book *rediscovering* that tradition, offering it as a richly moral and symbolic heritage to an ideologically impoverished labour movement, just as in nineteenth-century England that tradition became available as an ideological crutch to the industrial bourgeoisie. The manoeuvre was enabled, of course, by the fact that both Romantic and labourist ideologies are in partial conflict with bourgeois hegemony; but it is precisely that partiality which allows them to embrace. Neither tradition is purely antagonistic to bourgeois state-power: the first preserves it by dis-placing political analysis to a moralist and idealist critique of its worst 'human' effects, the second seeks to accommodate itself within it. What the book did, then, was to consecrate the reformism of the labour movement, raise it to new heights of moral and cultural legitimacy, by offering to it values and symbols drawn in the main from the tradition of most entrenched political reaction.

For all its eloquence and engagement, then, *Culture and Society* was in reality an idealist and academicist project. It could sustain its thesis only by systematic inattention to the reactionary character of the tradition with which it dealt – an inattention evident in the drastically partial and distorted readings of particular writers (Carlyle, Arnold and Lawrence in particular), who were wrested from their true ideological *loci* and manipulated by selective quota-tion and sentimental misconception into the cause of a 'socialist

humanism'. (When Williams wrote in another context that, of
Cobbett, Dickens, Ruskin, Morris and Lawrence, all except Ruskin
opposed moral paternalism, his judgement was simply inaccurate.)[5]
The *progressive* elements of the bourgeois ideological tradition (a
concept which Williams has consistently opposed from a 'humanist'
standpoint) were consequently passed over, with one or two lonely
exceptions. Even more fundamentally, the fact that 'culture' is itself
an *ideological* term is fatally missed. Williams's work, in the
characteristic mode of the early New Left, tended to a dangerous
conflation of productive modes, social relations, ethical, political and
aesthetic ideologies, collapsing them into the empty anthropological
abstraction of 'culture'. Such a collapsing not only abolishes any
hierarchy of actual priorities, reducing the social formation to a
'circular' Hegelian totality and striking political strategy dead at
birth, but inevitably *over-subjectivises* that formation.[6] For all structures are consequently distilled together in the textures of the 'lived':
since what they have in common is that they are all experienced, the
simultaneity of experience becomes a guarantee of the real 'simultaneity' of structures. It has been pointed out that the title *Culture
and Society* is a kind of unconscious translation of *Gemeinschaft und
Gesellschaft*; but Williams does not perceive the ideological significance of 'culture' which such a comparison graphically reveals.
Alert as he is to its political tendentiousness in the hands of a Leavis
or Eliot, he would still seem to believe it possible to *redeem* this
'neutral' category from the ideological misuses to which it has been
put. It is this which enables him to offer, as an ideologically *innocent*
definition of culture, 'the study of relations between elements in a
whole way of life'.[7] The distance from the organicist to the ecological
is shorter than he thinks. *Culture and Society* is a work which, in
the very act of 'placing' a tradition, places itself within it; its cross-

5. 'The British Left', *New Left Review* 30 (March/April 1965).
6. Williams's latest work has shown a progression from this point: he now
explicitly recognises the dangers of such a concept of 'totality', and insists on
the necessity of identifying its primary determinations. (See his 'Base and
Superstructure in Marxist Cultural Theory', *New Left Review* 82, November/
December 1973.) But the chief determination he isolates is that of 'intentions' –
the goals of a particular ruling class. The totality is, so to speak, teleological.
By formulating the issue in this way, Williams remains within the very
historicist problematic he is trying to escape.
7. 'Literature and Sociology: in memory of Lucien Goldmann', *New Left
Review* 67 (May/June 1971).

breed of labourism and literary idealism was the product of the very history it critically assessed. The 'solution' it tenders was thus, precisely, the problem.

Democracy as a gradual extension of the existing culture of the labour movement into society as a whole, opposing one class-ideology (solidarity) to another (selfish individualism): it is no wonder that the liberal intellectuals responded to *Culture and Society* with such enthusiasm. (And, let it be added, have become notably more churlish and bemused as Williams has developed.) The 'destruction and then innovation of institutions, imagined at some finite point in time' which Williams dismissed in *Communications* is countered by the classically 'centrist' stance summarised in the calculated oxymoron 'The Long Revolution' – the gradualist, and so utopian, perspective of extending 'participation'. The political gradualism was inseparable from an epistemological idealism: for if meanings and values are given on a level with material production, then the 'process' of social change is the inevitably complex and protracted affair of transforming those meanings.[8] If the 'whole social process' (conceived as a 'circular' totality) is involved, then the complexity and protractedness become intense. But more than that: it is also a matter of sustaining a complex historical continuity, absorbing fresh reality into already-evolved conventions, as in the case of art. The new work of art 'has to be fitted into our whole organisation':[9] it is art which consolidates given meanings, rather than art which ruptures and subverts them, which characteristically attracted Williams's emphasis. The idealist epistemology, organicist aesthetics and corporatist sociology of *The Long Revolution* went logically together.

The root of all three was a form of Romantic populism. Williams's political gradualism rested on a deep-seated trust in the capacity of individuals to create 'new meanings and values' *now* – meanings and values which will extend (at some *in*finite point in the future?) to socialism. The creation of new values which is in fact only *enabled* by revolutionary rupture was read back by him as a description of the present. Indeed it is not only that men and women *can*

8. It is not, naturally, that Williams ignores institutional change – it is rather that these two processes are seen as aspects of a single practice, so that in *The Long Revolution* and *Communications* he conceives of institutional change also in gradualist, experimental terms. One might say that the relation in question is conceived 'dialectically', but not 'asymmetrically'.

9. *The Long Revolution* (London, 1961), p. 35.

create such meanings now: they are doing so all the time, simply by living. This generous reverence for human capacities, turned to fine polemical effect against conservative cynic and liberal sceptic, entailed a drastic misconception of the structures of advanced capitalist formations. For Williams's belief in the *need* for a 'common culture' was continually crossed and confounded with an assertion of its present *reality*, albeit in suppressed and partial form – an assertion he cannot relinquish, for to do so would seem to him to surrender to a cynical, demeaning estimation of the very class from which he came. It is an attitude encoded in his aphorism 'culture is ordinary'. In recounting his own social transition from Wales to Cambridge, he was quick to stress the *normality* of this – that it was habitual for individuals to move out as poets, scholars, schoolteachers from the community.[10] The political polemic, directed against a class-divided educational system which makes such mobility untypical, was effectively confiscated by the populist claim. Williams often manoeuvred himself into the contradictory position of opposing a crippling hegemony whose power he had simultaneously to deny, because not to do so would have suggested that 'ordinary people' were not, after all, the true creators of 'meanings and values'. '. . . there is not a special class, or group of men, who are involved in the creation of meanings and values, either in a general sense or in specific art and belief. Such creation could not be reserved to a minority, however gifted, and [is] not, even in practice, so reserved: the meanings of a particular form of life of a people, at a particular time, seem to come from the whole of their common experience, and from its complicated general articulation.'[11] To which the simple answer is that there are indeed such special classes and groups, and their effectiveness is demonstrated by the fact that the 'meanings and values' of 'common experience' are for the most part *their* meanings and values.

Three distinct examples of this confusion in Williams's thought can be examined. The first concerns his well-known rejection of the concept of 'masses': 'There are in fact no masses; there are only ways of seeing people as masses.'[12] In thus defending 'people' against what he sees as a cynically manipulative abstraction, Williams traded

10. 'Culture is Ordinary', in *Conviction*, ed. N. Mackenzie (London, 1959).
11. *From Culture to Revolution*, p. 28.
12. *Culture and Society 1780–1950* (Harmondsworth, 1963), p. 289.

a theoretical instrument of revolutionary struggle for the short change of a liberal humanitarianism. For the massing together of individuals by industrial capitalism is a material condition of their political emancipation; and there is no doubt that, in rejecting the bourgeois definition of 'masses', Williams firmly rejected the revolutionary definition along with it. That men and women really are now unique individuals was Williams's (unexceptionable) insistence; but it was a proposition bought at the expense of perceiving the political fact that they must mass and fight to achieve their full individual humanity. One has only to adapt Williams's statement to 'There are in fact no classes; there are only ways of seeing people as classes' to expose its theoretical paucity; and indeed Williams himself came near to rewriting it thus, when he argued in *The Long Revolution* that 'We can group individuals into particular classes, nations or races, as a way of refusing them individual recognition.'[13] Classes, like masses, seemed figments of a way of seeing; we were invited to replace one way of seeing with another.

There was a parallel confusion between 'political reality' and 'essential humanity' in the opening paragraph of Williams's second novel, *Second Generation*:

'If you stand, today, in Between Towns Road, you can still see either way: west to the spires and towers of the cathedral and colleges; east to the yards and sheds of the motor works. You see different worlds, but there is no frontier between them; there is only the movement and traffic of a single city.'[14]

Is the division of material and intellectual labour real, and the 'single' city in fact divided, or is the city really one city, and the division of labour a phenomenal appearance? It is more, of course, than that, as the novel will make plain; but the emphasis on the *essential* unity of the city is revealing. There are different worlds, and yet there is only one world; there is indeed a frontier (Between Towns Road itself), yet there is no frontier at all. This is true enough of a *city*, of course, but the topographical image conveniently resolves a real contradiction. For Williams wants to insist on the *artifice* of divisions, from the standpoint of a 'general common humanity', at the same time as he urges their social reality. A similar metaphorical

13. *The Long Revolution*, p. 96.
14. *Second Generation* (London, 1964), p. 9.

device occurs in the novel's final paragraph, where the wind beats down from the Welsh mountains into England, sweeping indifferently through colleges and car-factory. The wind knows no frontiers: its movement is that of a unity, gathering the novel's disparate, mutually divided locales into a single landscape. It is on this note that the novel ends: on the *essential* oneness of what it has shown to be a fissured, fractured society.

How 'real' the border is is a consistent ambiguity in Williams's work: it is at once his most central and least clarified metaphor. In one sense the border is undeniably there, cleaving its path between Wales and Cambridge, car-factory and college, rural and urban, democratic and dominative, communal and individualist. But because the social formation is now, in principle, a single 'culture', the border is unreal, and can be crossed either way. One might image this as a 'horizontal' border shifting to one on a 'vertical' scale – dividing not one 'culture' from another, but dividing *the* culture, the 'common life' of millions, from the alien hegemonic class set above them. One might image it, alternatively, as a border which is 'real' one way and 'unreal' the other: real enough to prevent the dominant culture from penetrating and contaminating the traditional community, but unreal in the sense that it is right and proper to cross from that community into society at large. Williams's own comments on the composition of his first novel, *Border Country*, are interesting in this respect. He writes that those readers who had assumed that Harry Price, the signalman in the novel, was a portrait of his own father were really mistaken; what he had actually done was to split off his father's qualities of absorbed work into the character of Price, and project the more restless, socially mobile traits into the figure of Morgan Rosser, the dealer and politician. The reason for this division of values, he claims, was the need for a *relationship* to dramatise the full complexity of what he had seen in his father as an internal conflict.[15] It is far from my intention to suggest that Williams is misreporting his purpose; but it is clear how one effect of this division of qualities in the novel is to render Price an almost wholly admirable representative of the best values of the rural community, dissociating from him those rather less praiseworthy characteristics displayed by Rosser. The 'border' be-

15. See *The Country and the City* (London, 1973), p. 299.

tween two conflictive sets of values was internalised within the community, sure enough, but it was not carried to the (historically accurate) point of internalisation within the community's major representative. To the extent that Harry Price was thus an *idealised* figure, the 'border' operated to protect the values he incarnated from the hegemonic culture. It embodied itself as an internal limit only for Price's son, who had moved beyond it. In this sense, *Border Country* enacted that reductive binary opposition between 'common' and 'hegemonic' meanings which is symptomatic of Williams's populism.

The contradiction I am trying to define crops up in a different form in *Modern Tragedy*. In that book, Williams argued two closely connected positions in relation to the concept of tragedy. The first was that tragedy is not the property of an élite, a special and extraordinary event, a metaphysical occurrence or, necessarily, a 'world-historical' action. Tragedy is part of the common texture of life of human societies: it is not only the death of princes, but a mining disaster, a broken career, a smash on the roads. The second position which Williams adopted was that tragedy can be historically surmounted by the action of men struggling to transform intolerable conditions – that we are even now in the midst of the long tragic action of global revolution. Both cases were deeply anchored in Williams's humanism: the first as a salutary 'democratising' of an aesthetic concept jealously expropriated by patrician academics, the second as a necessary politicising of the notion. But the two cases were mutually incompatible. If one reserves the term 'tragedy' for 'world-historical' conflicts of forces, then it is indeed possible to argue that these can be historically transcended; but if one simultaneously returns the idea of tragedy to the local, contingent violations of common experience, then whether *these too* can be absolutely surmounted is surely questionable. Once more, Williams's generous 'democratic' impulse is in at least partial contradiction with his estimation of political reality.

The implication of Williams's earlier work, then, was clear: a 'common culture' already in some sense exists, but is being opposed 'by violence and fraud'.[16] Men *do* in fact create their meanings and values in common, but this common process is then blocked and

16. *From Culture to Revolution*, p. 297.

divided by the impositions of political hegemony. The proposition involved a logical slide from 'fact' to 'value' in the notion of the 'common', for to claim that individuals create their values together is not necessarily to claim that they create cooperative values. It also entailed a naively historicist conception of ideology, reducing it to a unitary world-view imposed on the social formation from above by the hegemonic class. If it were not for that, the implication ran, the gradually extending movement towards 'participation', aided by the 'actions of millions',[17] would run its course unimpeded into socialism. Socialism is merely an *extension* of bourgeois democracy. It should be added at once that Williams has now – finally – rejected this formulation, discovering through Gramsci a more complex concept of hegemony.[18]

Williams's residual populism is also at the root of his consistent over-subjectivising of the social formation. Profoundly influenced by the Lawrentian metaphysic, he has always prized a 'wholeness' of senses and intellect – an organicist metaphor which is more than once covertly transferred into an image of society. It is as though society – 'ordinary men and women' – were the sensuous body from which values and concepts are crystallised – concepts whose very validity hinges upon their direct reference back to concrete existence, their immediate locus within sensuous life. Unless reasoning springs organically from lived experience, it is likely to be suspect: this vein of commonplace English empiricism runs throughout Williams's work, inherited from *Scrutiny*, and accounting among other things for his admiration for David Hume – an unlikely candidate otherwise, one would have thought, for his approval.[19] Paradoxical though it may seem for this most intellectually serious and dedicated of critics, his work betrays a muted strain of anti-intellectualism which has played its role in his quarrel with Marxism – a mistaking of scientificity for positivism which links him not only with some of the most myopic aspects of *Scrutiny*, but also with the Romantic 'anti-scientism' of Lukács and the Frankfurt school. Writing of his admiration for the work of Lucien Goldmann, he comments revealingly: 'The fact that I learned simultaneously that [Goldmann's

17. *The Long Revolution*, p. x.
18. 'Base and Superstructure in Marxist Cultural Theory.'
19. See his essay 'David Hume: Reasoning and Experience', in *The English Mind*, ed. H. S. Davies and G. Watson (London, 1964).

work] had been denounced as heretical, that it was a return to Left Hegelianism, left-bourgeois idealism, and so on, did not, I am afraid, detain me. If you're not in a church you're not worried about heresies; the only real interest is actual theory and practice.'[20] One can almost see the approving marginal tick of the relieved liberal reader. If Williams is not in fact interested in the theoretical task of assessing Goldmann's place within the Marxist tradition, then he ought to be; the briskly pragmatic turning to the practical tasks to hand (characteristically covered by that '*actual* theory', whatever that may be) is no substitute for analysis. It is an exact repetition of the device used thirteen years before in *Culture and Society*, when Williams, examining the intricacies of an important debate in Marxist aesthetics, concludes a pact with the wry bemusement of his liberal readers by throwing up his hands in mock defeat: 'This is a quarrel which one who is not a Marxist will not attempt to resolve.'[21]

It is not fortuitous, then, that at the centre of Williams's two novels stand ex-working-class historians or sociologists (Matthew Price in *Border Country*, Peter Owen in *Second Generation*) sunk in intellectual self-doubt – a self-doubt occasioned by their 'experiential' closeness to the materials they try to analyse. There is no question as to the novels' endorsement of that self-questioning – one which counters the sociological methods of bourgeois positivism with an equally bourgeois 'phenomenology'. 'We begin to think where we live' is the symptomatic phrase with which Williams opens one of his essays,[22] and the point is valuable; but it passes over that more crucial mode of thought which necessarily places such personal living within brackets. The strength and weakness of this proposition is evident in his personally invented concept of a 'structure of feeling' – that firm but intangible organisation of values and perceptions which acts as a mediating category between the psychological 'set' of a social formation and the conventions embodied in its artefacts. What this concept designates, in effect, is ideology; but it is a mark of Williams's originality that here as elsewhere he privately re-discovers an essential category which is either objectively absent, or (as with the available definitions of ideology) theoretically inadequate.

20. 'Literature and Sociology: in memory of Lucien Goldmann.'
21. *Culture and Society*, p. 269.
22. From *Culture to Revolution*, p. 24.

The English Novel from Dickens to Lawrence puts this notion to superb use: the novel, for Williams, is one medium among many in which men seek to master and absorb new experience by discovering new forms and rhythms, grasping and reconstructing the stuff of social change in the living substance of perceptions and relationships. Yet the calculated tension between 'structure' and 'feeling' is also the mark of a limit within his own thought. For in striving to transcend the merely empiricist or phenomenological methods of, say, Hoggart's *The Uses of Literacy*, in reaching beyond a notion of feeling-*complex* to feeling-*structure*, he none the less lacks the theoretical terms which might specify the precise articulations of that structure. It is, accordingly, reduced back to the status of a mere 'pattern'. It is for this reason that the structural analysis of British capitalism attempted in the final section of *The Long Revolution* slides into impressionistic comments on speech-habits, deprived of even the most elementary method.

'We begin to think where we live': the limits of Williams's thinking have indeed been limits of his world. For the populism and reformism which marred his work were clearly enough the product of a political moment. The intellectual synthesis which Williams undertook was one forced upon him by the non-availability of a revolutionary tradition and the paucity of working-class ideology. Marooned between Stalinism and reformism, personally and theoretically divorced from a politically becalmed working class, the early New Left movement to which Williams belonged was constrained to piece together its own eclectic theory and strategy in response to an objective political 'break' (Hungary, Suez). In that process, Williams's rediscovery of the 'Culture and Society' lineage played a central role – a spiritual recuperation of the values of the labour movement which saw itself as a challenge to that movement's political inertia. Yet, as I have argued, that challenge in fact reproduced the very ideological causes of the inertia, investing them with mythological, symbolically potent status. The absence of mass working-class struggle at that time (an absence vicariously filled by the petty-bourgeois populism of the nuclear disarmament movement), and the upsurge of a literary Left-reformism to replace revolutionary theory, were structurally related moments. In Williams's work, paradigmatically, the one absence nurtured and confirmed the other. The idealist bent of his political conceptions was the effect of the divorce of the Left-reformist intellectuals from the working class; but it was also the product of the ideological character of the class itself, by which, despite that divorce, Williams's work remained contaminated. His intellectual relation to the working class was at once academicist alienation and ideological complicity – a parody of the classic relation between revolutionary intellectual and the proletariat. When Williams wrote in the *May-Day Manifesto* of a social democratic government having 'taken our values and changed them', the tone of affronted moral indignation was a precise function of the unperceived structural complicity between those values and social democracy itself. It is worth adding, too, that the collapse of the 'Manifesto' movement, as the last-ditch strategic 'intervention' (Williams's term is eloquent) of the early New Left, was almost mathematically predictable. The essentially liberal conception of socialist organisation implicit in the 'circular totality' of the New Left – 'connecting', 'cooperating', 'explaining', 'communicating', 'extending' – was politically sterile from the outset. Only the media could provide a provisional point of intersection between the literary academics and real politics. May 1968, the date of the Manifesto's publication in book-form, signalled a political moment of rather more import than this well-intentioned academic offering, before which it was inevitably thrust into oblivion.

It is a curious feature of Williams's intellectual career that, working by his own devious, eclectic and idiosyncratic route, he has consistently pre-empted important theoretical developments. His arrival at a kind of hermeneutical phenomenology by the use of J. Z. Young, of all sources, is a peculiarly bizarre instance of his almost intuitive 'prevention' of such new births. It is also a symptom of his intellectual provincialism – a term he would find particularly offensive, suggesting as it would to him a dismissive 'metropolitan' gibe. But the word is intended in an exact, and not wholly critical, sense. Williams's remarkably deep rootedness in the literary and political heritage of his own society has at once generously funded his entire enterprise, and partly closed him to intellectual evolutions elsewhere. His habit has been to look across with a certain proprietory interest to Europe, to find echoes of his own independently-produced work reflected back to him. What the French call *éducation permanente* is what he has been meaning by 'culture'; Goldmann's 'transindividual structure' is what he has intended all along by 'structure of feeling'. It is not that he has not more than once explicitly acknowledged his debt to such theories; it is rather that he gives the unmistakeable suggestion of appropriating such 'alien' elements into his native speech. It is an intellectual provincialism akin to Leavis's, but also in some way to Lukács's, with whom Leavis himself has much in common. Williams resembles Lukács not only in his theoretical idealism but in his aesthetic predilections. In the extensive literary *oeuvre* of both men, *poetry* is a significant lacuna; apart from his early *Reading and Criticism*, it makes its appearance in Williams's writing only in *The Country and the City*, where it is more than once reduced to little more than historical documentation. This striking absence is not fortuitous: for poetry is the most searching test of a Marxist or para-Marxist criticism accustomed to dealing in structural generalities and historical abstractions. If Lukács confines himself almost wholly to the novel, Williams restricts himself to the novel and drama – more overtly 'social' forms in which the relations between the aesthetic and the historical are relatively exposed. In both cases, then, a crucial methodological challenge is merely evaded. But even within the novel-form itself, Williams reflects the provincialism of a Lukács. It is not that he shares Lukács's stiff-necked Stalinist disapproval of 'modernism', as his enthusiasm for Joyce would itself attest; but in critical practice he behaves more or less as though he does. The predilections which he betrays are in this sense not quite at one with what he would theoretically claim. *The English Novel from Dickens to Lawrence* is an implicit riposte to Leavis's *The Great Tradition*, just as *Modern Tragedy* is an unavowed critique of George Steiner's *The Death of Tragedy*; yet its parallelism to Leavis's text is as notable as its antagonism. It is a powerful plea for the 'English tradition' – not, to be sure, Leavis's tradition exactly, for suppressed links are inserted (Hardy), lines of continuity consequently redrawn, and the political assumptions forcefully at odds with the Leavisian ideology. But for all that the book is a *rewriting* of the 'great tradition' from an alternative standpoint, rather than a total displacement of that critical terrain. Williams remains as ideologically bound to the moment of nineteenth-century realism – a moment supposedly paradigmatic of 'fiction' as such – as do Lukács and Leavis; it is simply that in his case the allegiance is less declared, instinctual, almost, rather than polemical. The limits of such an allegiance are glaringly obvious in

Second Generation, which attempts to recreate the 'totalising' forms of Victorian realism to render the 'whole social process' of contemporary society – which is, in effect, a *Middlemarch* or *Bleak House* of developed monopoly capitalism. Except, of course, that it is not and cannot be. The novel, despite its merits, is stilted, abstract, overcrowded and unwieldy, inviting the sardonic judgements which Brecht delivered on Lukács's nostalgic fetishism of the traditional realist form.

Something similar might be said of *Koba*, the tragic drama of Stalinism which Williams, with a courageous innovation in the techniques of critical production, published as the final section of *Modern Tragedy*. *Koba* fails as a drama because it is unable to make a decisive rupture with realist and naturalist modes. Experimental in much of its language and stagecraft, its stretches of flatly naturalist discourse and preternaturally slow-moving action none the less force it to loiter hesitantly on a brink between poetic drama and historical documentary. What seems intended as some form of historical expressionism emerges as academic closet-drama. It is, once more, as though Williams's theoretical predilections are at odds with his actual sensibility – as though the 'English realism' which is his almost by instinct is locked in combat with an intellectual and imaginative thrusting beyond its confines. It is perhaps not accidental in this respect that much of his critical work on drama has recurrently focused on the fraught moment of historical transition from naturalist to post-naturalist forms. It is as though this deadlocked or stalemated moment, as displayed in Ibsen, Chekhov, Strindberg and Eliot, is itself the trope of an internal tension within Williams's own sensibility.

Indeed the place of dramatic criticism within his work is an interesting, even intriguing one. Drama was the subject of two of his earliest books (film was another), has been a persistent concern ever since, and is now his professorial subject; a volume of dramatic criticism has regularly punctuated his production of 'social' texts. But the relations between the two bodies of work are not easy to decipher. *Drama in Performance* and *Drama from Ibsen to Eliot* stand in oblique, unsettled relation to *Culture and Society* and *The Long Revolution*: if there are obvious overlaps, it is also true that the two sets of work preserve a certain relative autonomy of one another. The interest in drama is, of course, an interest in the most 'living', sociable literary form, a point of intersection between study and society, and so of obvious attraction to a socialist critic. Yet if the dramatic criticism is distinguished by a tenacious attention to the artefact and a somewhat submerged, sideways engagement with its social history (an enquiry reserved for a chapter of *The Long Revolution*), the 'social' writing is notable on the other hand for its detailed study of social forms and concepts and what is often an illegitimately 'illustrative' use of literature. The unity of the two realms which for Williams is a theoretical given is not, in fact, really achieved: one is inevitably 'foregrounded' at the expense of the other. It is not until *Modern Tragedy* that the two lines of enquiry converge into the same book: and even there it is to some extent a matter of 'book' rather than 'text', spatial juxtaposition rather than unified discourse. The secret of this disjunction is twofold. In the first place, it exposes at the level of method an inner contradiction of 'Left-Leavisism'. The techniques of textual analysis which Williams inherits from *Scrutiny* and reproduces without question in *Reading and Criticism* are a radically inadequate medium of structural enquiry and conceptual discourse: in that, precisely, lies their ideological power. But the more generalising language of, say, *The Long Revolution* is simply disabling as a *critical* style. It is here that the lack of a language of Marxist aesthetics is most visible in Williams's work – a lack which impresses itself on his own literary style. For that style's curious blending of 'abstract' and 'concrete' qualities is a kind of linguistic disturbance which marks an attempt to heal the schism I have outlined – to speak conceptually, yet to invest those abstractions with full experiential force. What this means, in effect, is that Williams tends to speak abstractingly of literary texts and 'experientially' of social formations – an inversion of the relations between 'abstract' and 'concrete' as a Marxist aesthetics would conceive them.

The second reason for this disjunction refers us once more to the question of intellectual provincialism. For drama is in effect the only 'international' area in Williams's work – the only place where he discusses in detail authors who are other than English. Internationalism is, so to speak, exported into the drama, leaving 'social' criticism organically coupled with his native literature. His interest in what could be loosely termed 'avant-garde' art is divorced from his 'social' concerns and sealed off in a distinct sphere. It is as though, since drama is *inherently* social, it can be studied in its own right, cut loose from any precise enquiry into the social conditions of its making; it can be 'internationalised' because it carries its social guarantee within its very structures. The English literature which most preoccupies Williams, however, is not typically of this experimental kind: it is, to use his own revealing organicist metaphor, more easily 'fitted into our whole organisation'.

Williams's intuitive knack of pre-empting intellectual positions is nowhere more apparent than in his development since 1968. The work of this period can be seen as constituting a definitive phase of his production, just as the period from *Culture and Society* to *Modern Tragedy* represents a partial but significant break with the early literary-critical writings. That early phase, characterised by such works as *Reading and Criticism* and *Drama from Ibsen to Eliot*, is most aptly describable as 'Left-Leavisite': at this probationary point, Williams still has to discover the idiom which will allow him to extend 'practical criticism' and organicist social positions into fully socialist analysis. It is this task which is undertaken in the work of the 'middle' period, in which the concept of 'culture' becomes a crucial mediation between literary analysis and social enquiry, and the socialist orientation of Williams's enterprise receives increasingly explicit, if gradualist, formulation. *Modern Tragedy* preserved the gradualist ideology of Western social revolution encapsulated in *The Long Revolution*, but simultaneously marked an opening to the reality of violent insurrection in the Third World, encompassing both within the concept of a 'single tragic action'. From here onwards, in response to the crisis of social-democratic and left-reformist ideologies in the West, Williams's writing has revealed an increasing engagement with the revolutionary tradition which, however reticent and ambiguous in its attitude towards insurrectionary organisation, none the less signifies a partial, tentative surpassing of the 'middle period' gradualism. Williams is now closer to Marxism than at any stage in his career – an evolution which seems logically continuous, yet which has come about precisely at the point where the Marxist challenge to his early positions is gathering strength. *The Country and the City*, despite its angry rejection of particular Marxist attitudes to rural society, inhabits a different political world from the earlier texts. A full examination of that work, certainly one of the most brilliant and seminal he has produced,

40

is beyond the scope of this brief survey; yet one or two points can be noted in passing. If there is one sense in which the book's title is a kind of 'translation' of *Culture and Society*, there is another sense in which it is a critical interrogation of that earlier work. *Culture and Society*, like *Drama from Ibsen to Eliot*, is still haunted by an uncertain nostalgia for the 'organic' – a nostalgia which persists despite Williams's explicit recognition of its dangers.[23] 'Wholeness', 'natural growth', 'total process' are keystones of the book's entire conceptual structure. But if there is one point at which Williams is most decisive in his rejection of the 'organic' image, it is in its application to *rural* society – the patronising *Scrutiny* mythology of the lost organic England. Naturally so: for quite apart from the intellectual bankruptcy of that case, it strikes directly at the deepest roots of Williams's own formative experience, as the product of a rural proletariat about whom there was nothing 'pastoral' whatsoever. The very reality of his own formative process is denied, stolen from him, by the metropolitan 'pastoral' myth. On the contrary, Williams rightly insists, rural society is rural capitalism, permeated at every level by the forces and relations of capitalist production; it provides no alternative enclave to the dominant social mode. But for Williams to 'defend' the reality of his own childhood conditions by emphasising their integration with industrial capitalism is for him a significantly uncharacteristic move. For it forces him to break with the reductive binary opposition he otherwise employs: regional culture/dominant culture, working class/middle class, solidarity/individualism and so on. The reason for that break with the binary model is, indeed, part of the very reason which motivates it in the first place: it is to insist on the real existence of rural society, as 'community' is set against 'individualism', to underline the already-existent reality of an alternative culture. But because the bourgeois ideology of pastoral absorbs the rural by *alienating* it, positing it as an 'unreal' enclave, Williams in turn opposes bourgeois

23. 'It is perhaps true that the ideas of an 'organic' society are an essential preparation for socialist theory, and for the more general attention to a 'whole way of life', in opposition to theories which consistently reduce social to individual questions, and which support legislation of an individualist as opposed to a collectivist kind. But the theories can hardly be abstracted from actual social situations, and the "organic" theory has in fact been used in support of very different, and even opposing, causes.' (*Culture and Society*, p. 145.)

ideology by insisting on the contradictory *unity* of the agrarian and industrial. This is not at all the 'essential' unity of an 'ordinary culture' artificially disrupted by a hegemonic system; it is precisely the unity of that hegemonic mode itself, outside which nothing can escape into innocence. To defend the realities of rural society, Williams is necessarily led to a political language which transcends the populist idealism of his earlier case. The 'oppositional' culture which at times in that early work seemed the 'real' culture is now increasingly seen as 'residual'.[24]

The Country and the City is the mature consequence of that developed case – a book which Williams, one feels, had necessarily to write, recrossing the border to his homeland at a point where he knew himself finally released from the identity-crisis which besets Matthew Price in *Border Country*. If he is able to go home and stay there for a while, it is because he is surer than ever of the political route back. *The Country and the City* is to be taken together with Williams's growing rapprochement with Marxism; indeed it is the only one of his texts in which Marxist positions constitute the very terms of debate. The earlier, idealist hostility to the dominance of material over mental production is being progressively modified, although in a paradoxical way: anxious to preserve the 'primal' reality of art, yet increasingly ready to acknowledge the primacy of material production, Williams 'resolves' the dilemma by effectively collapsing art back into the material base itself.[25] His previous strategy – to collapse the base forward, as it were, into the superstructure – is merely inverted; the fact of a superstructure is hesitantly allowed, but the privileged activity of art is removed from it. What he in some sense perceives, but fails to clarify, is that in capitalist formations above all literature belongs *at once* to 'base' and 'superstructure' – figures at once within material production and ideological formation. But the articulation of these two moments cannot be studied by reducing either of them to the other. His argument turns, in fact, on a partly verbal confusion about the 'secondary'

24. See 'Base and Superstructure in Marxist Cultural Theory.'
25. 'If we have the broad sense of productive forces, we look at the whole question of the base differently, and we are then less tempted to dismiss as superstructural, and in that sense as merely secondary, certain vital productive forces, which are in the broad sense, from the beginning, basic' ('Base and Superstructure in Marxist Cultural Theory'). Those 'vital productive forces' clearly include art.

character of superstructures. For in wanting properly to dispel any *weak* connotation of 'secondary', and so to seal off the routes which lead to vulgar Marxism, he offers us instead the concept of hegemony, 'which is not merely secondary or superstructural, like the weak sense of ideology, but which is lived at such a depth, which saturates the society to such an extent . . . that it corresponds to the reality of social experience very much more clearly than any notions derived from the formula of base and superstructure'.[26] It is symptomatic of Williams's whole method that he should point to the *experiential* force of hegemony as an index of its structural primacy. Hegemony is deeply, pervasively lived, and so cannot be superstructural since the superstructural is the 'secondary': i.e., the 'weakly experienced'. It goes logically with this confusion that his concept of hegemony is itself a structurally undifferentiated one: 'a central system of practices, meanings and values' which is not distributed into its constitutive economic, political and ideological formations. Williams's rapprochement with Marxism is still, evidently, a fraught, dissentient, intellectually unclarified affair; the question which remains, and which only his future work can answer, is whether he will seek to have it on his own terms, or whether he will make a vital individual contribution to the development of a Marxist aesthetics. For no contribution could be more vital than his.

With this latest moment in Williams's work, we return to the present and to its critical dilemmas. How is the troubled passage between text and reader to be smoothed, so that literary consumption may be facilitated? The answer, naturally, is that it is not: the myth of a passage, of criticism as a midwife to the text, must itself be eradicated. But there are alternative ways of eradicating it. It is possible to object to the authoritarianism of such a concept – to the obtrusive shadow which even the most humbly self-effacing criticism will cast over the product it mediates. Criticism as the repressive father who cuts short the erotic sport of sense between text and reader, binding with the briars of its metasystem the joyfully pluralist intercourse of meanings between them. A *libertarianism* of text and reader, in short, typical of the *Tel Quel* group, which like all

26. *ibid.*

libertarianism fatally inverts itself into a mirror-image of bourgeois social relations. But there are other forms of eradication, which are not fixated in the moment of release which follows on the dethrone-ment of the ultimate donor of meaning – which accept that if God is truly dead there is no need to resurrect Nietzsche, since their reference-point is the 'taken-for-granted' post-atheism of Marx rather than the 'always-to-be-validated' atheism of his compatriot. Criticism is not a passage from text to reader: its task is not to re-double the text's self-understanding, to collude with its object in a conspiracy of eloquence. Its task is to show the text as it cannot know itself, to manifest those conditions of its making (inscribed in its very letter) about which it is necessarily silent. It is not just that the text knows some things and not others; it is rather that its very self-knowledge is the construction of a self-oblivion. To achieve such a showing, criticism must break with its ideological prehistory, situating itself outside the space of the text on the alternative terrain of scientific knowledge.

2

Categories for a Materialist Criticism

Every work is the work of many things besides an author
(Valéry)

The work of Raymond Williams, flawed as it has been by
'humanism' and idealism, represents one of the most significant
sources from which a materialist aesthetics might be derived.
Refusing that pervasive form of critical idealism which would
repress the whole material infrastructure of artistic production,
Williams has properly insisted on the reality of art as 'material
practice'. Yet it is not only that his conception of art as 'practice'
retains strong residual elements of humanism; it is also that, to date
at least, the constituent structures of that practice have received little
systematic analysis in his work. It is necessary, then, to develop a
method whereby those structures can be rigorously specified, and
their precise articulations examined.

It is possible to set out in schematic form the major constituents of
a Marxist theory of literature. They can be listed as follows:

(i)   General Mode of Production (GMP)
(ii) Literary Mode of Production (LMP)
(iii) General Ideology (GI)
(iv) Authorial Ideology (AuI)
(v)   Aesthetic Ideology (AI)
(vi) Text

The text, strictly speaking, is hardly a *constituent* of literary theory;
it is, rather, its object. But in so far as it must be examined in its
relations with the other elements set out, it can be regarded method-
ologically as a particular 'level'. The task of criticism is to analyse

the complex historical *articulations* of these structures which produce the text.

(i) *General Mode of Production* (GMP)

A mode of production may be characterised as a unity of certain forces and social relations of material production. Each social formation is characterised by a combination of such modes of production, one of which will normally be dominant. By 'General Mode of Production' I designate that dominant mode; I use the term 'general', not because economic production is ever anything other than historically specific, but to distinguish economic production from:

(ii) *Literary Mode of Production* (LMP)

A unity of certain forces and social relations of literary production in a particular social formation. In any literate society there will normally exist a number of distinct modes of literary production, one of which will normally be dominant. These distinct LMPs will be mutually articulated in varying relations of homology, conflict and contradiction: they will constitute an 'asymmetrical' totality, since the dominance of a particular LMP will force other modes into positions of subordination and partial exclusion. Structurally conflictual LMPs may thus coexist within a particular social formation: if it is possible in Western societies to produce fiction for the capitalist market, it is also possible to distribute one's handwritten poetry on the streets. Coexistent LMPs, however, need not be historically synchronous with one another. An LMP produced by an historically previous social formation may survive within and interpenetrate later modes: the co-presence of the 'patronage' system and capitalist literary production in eighteenth-century England, the persistence of 'artisanal' literary production within the capitalist LMP. A classical instance of such survivals is typically to be found in the historical mutation from 'oral' to 'written' LMPs, where the social relations and kinds of literary product appropriate to the 'oral' LMP normally persist as significant constituents of the 'written' LMP itself, both interactive with and relatively autonomous of it. In medieval England, for example, 'reading' continues to mean, almost invariably, reading aloud in public; and much of the 'written' LMP consists in committing to manuscript form products of the 'oral' mode. Conversely, the emergence of the 'written' LMP perpetuates certain more complex and extensive oral products, developing that LMP as it is itself developed by it. With the development of a 'written' LMP in sixth-century Ireland, the druidic 'oral' mode, nurtured by the powerful intellectual caste of the *filí*, continues its own separate existence independent of (although not uninfluenced by) written literary production. The Irish 'oral' LMP is thus for some considerable time peculiarly unsubordinated to the written mode, even though in passing into that mode it undergoes certain mutations as a literary product, modified in such predominantly oral traits as alliteration and repetition. The significant moment in the mutual articulation of two such distinct LMPs occurs when the acts of composition and writing become more or less simultaneous – when the 'written' LMP assumes a certain autonomy of the 'oral' rather than consigning its products to manuscript. This unity of writing and composition is exemplified by a number of early Irish texts which recreate the oral tradition – a *genre* closely associated with the scribal activities of the early monastic schools, who as 'amateur' producers synthesising native and Latin literary elements (and so producing new literary *forms*) emerge in seventh-century Ireland as a distinct LMP in conflict with the dominant LMP of the professional, legally privileged, ideologically hegemonic *filí*.

The disjunction between historically coexistent LMPs, then, may be synchronic – determined by the structural distribution of possible modes of literary production enabled by the social formation – or diachronic (determined by historical survivals). There is also the case of diachronic disjunction which arises not from survival but from 'prefigurement': LMPs which enter into contradiction with the dominant LMP by 'anticipating' the productive forms and social relations of a future social formation (the revolutionary artists' commune, 'epic theatre'[1] and so on). A particular LMP, then, may

---

1. Drama, strictly speaking, belongs to a distinct mode of production from literature, characterised by its own relatively autonomous forces and relations. Dramatic *texts* may belong to the LMP, depending upon the historical character of the theatrical mode of production; but the assimilation of drama to literature is an ideologically significant appropriation.

combine elements or structures of other past, contemporary or 'future' modes. The 'little magazine', for example, characteristically combines structures of the dominant capitalist LMP with elements of collaborative production, 'informal' distribution mechanisms and 'consumer-participation' untypical of the dominant productive mode. An LMP may constitute a complex unity in itself, as well as forming a complex contradictory unity with other LMPs; its internal complexity will be a function of its modes of articulation with those other LMPs.

Every LMP is constituted by structures of production, distribution, exchange and consumption. Production presupposes a producer or set of producers, materials, instruments and techniques of production, and the product itself. In developed social formations, an initial private stage of production may be transmuted by a subsequent social mode of production (printing and publishing) to convert the original product ('manuscript') into a new one ('book'). The forces of literary production consist in the application of labour-power organised in certain 'relations of production' (scribes, collaborative producers, printing and publishing organisations) to certain materials of production by means of certain determinate productive instruments. These forces of literary production determine and are over-determined by the modes of literary distribution, exchange and consumption. The handwritten manuscript can only be distributed and consumed on a hand-to-hand basis, within, let us say, a courtly caste; the multiply dictated work (one copied simultaneously by several scribes) is able to achieve wider social consumption; the ballads pedalled by a chapman may be consumed by an even wider audience; the 'yellowback' railway novel is available to a mass public.

Unified with these productive forces, then, are specific social relations of literary production. The tribal bard professionally authorised to produce for his king or chieftain; the 'amateur' medieval poet presenting to his patron a personally requested product for private remuneration; the peripatetic minstrel housed and fed by his peasant audience; the ecclesiastically or royally patronised producer, or the author who sells his product to an aristocratic patron for a dedication fee; the 'independent' author who sells his commodity to a bookseller-publisher or to a capitalist publishing firm; the state-patronised producer: all of these forms are familiar enough to the 'sociology of literature'. The point is to analyse the complex articulations of these various LMPs with the 'general' mode of production of a social formation.

Before considering that question, however, it is important to note that the character of an LMP is a significant constituent of the literary product itself. We are not merely concerned here with the sociological outworks of the text; we are concerned rather with how the text comes to be what it is because of the specific determinations of its mode of production. If LMPs are historically extrinsic to particular texts, they are equally internal to them: the literary text bears the impress of its historical mode of production as surely as any product secretes in its form and materials the fashion of its making. The product of an 'oral' LMP is typically more socially stylised, 'anonymous', shorn of idiosyncratic introspectiveness than the product of a private printing press; the ecclesiastically patronised work is characteristically more devout and didactic than the fiction produced for the markets of monopoly capitalism. The work which survives solely by word of mouth from region to region is constrained to deploy conventions of 'impersonality' inimical to the confessional forms of a producer whose relatively 'privatised' LMP is under severe pressure from more public modes which threaten to dislodge it. A poet whose professional function is to recount heroic, mythological tales of military victory before kings and noblemen preparing for war will perpetuate *genres* superfluous to an author whose LMP constrains him to woo a Whig aristocrat dedicated to international capitalist 'peace'. One might add, too, that every literary text in some sense internalises its social relations of production – that every text intimates by its very conventions the way it is to be consumed, encodes within itself its own ideology of how, by whom and for whom it was produced. Every text obliquely posits a putative reader, defining its producibility in terms of a certain capacity for consumption. These, however, are questions of ideology which are properly postponable to a later point; it is enough to assert for the moment that the character of an LMP is an internal constituent rather than merely an extrinsic limit of the character of the text.

(iii) *Relations of LMP and GMP*

The forces of production of the LMP are naturally provided by the GMP itself, of which the LMP is a particular substructure. In the case of literary production, the materials and instruments employed normally perform a common function within the GMP itself. This is less true of certain other modes of artistic production, many of whose materials and instruments, though of course produced by the GMP, perform no significant function within it. (Trombones and greasepaint play no world-historical part within general production.) The relations between LMP and GMP, however, are dialectical, in that new productive forces developed for purposes specific to the LMP may enter into the field of general production. The extent to which the LMP contributes to the expansion of general production is historically variable. The role of pre-printing LMPs within general production is historically negligible; in such situations, the LMP operates with a high degree of autonomy of the GMP from the viewpoint of its contribution to the development of the productive forces. With the growth of printing, however, extensive speculative book production and marketing finally integrate the dominant LMP into the GMP as a specific branch of general commodity production. (This integration, in which literature becomes merely another aspect of commodity production, is typically coupled with significant mutations within the aesthetic region of ideology, and a subordination of that region within the dominant ideological formation.) In developed capitalist social formations, then, the most significant relation of LMP to GMP is that of the LMP's function in the reproduction and expansion of the GMP.

The LMP represents a specific division of labour determined by the character and stage of development of the GMP, becoming more specialised and diverse as the GMP develops. Only with a certain stage of development of the GMP is the relatively autonomous existence of an LMP possible. Literary production and consumption presuppose certain levels of literacy, physical and mental well-being, leisure and material affluence: the material conditions for writing and reading include economic resources, shelter, lighting and privacy. The capitalist mode of production develops its dominant LMP by increasing the population, concentrating it in urban centres where it is within reach of the mechanisms of literary distribution, and permitting it limited degrees of literacy, affluence, leisure, shelter and privacy. At the same time it increasingly specialises and extends its modes of literary production and distribution to sell literary commodities on this market, and produces the material and cultural conditions essential for professional literary production within it. In such phenomena as poverty, physical and mental debility consequent on prolonged and intensive labour, illiteracy or partial literacy, lack of sufficient shelter, privacy and lighting (Charles Dickens described the window-tax as 'a tax upon knowledge'), the GMP bears upon the LMP to exclude or partially exclude certain social groups and classes from literary production and consumption – a factor which, as we shall see, is also of ideological significance.

The social relations of the LMP are in general determined by the social relations of the GMP. The literary producer stands in a certain social relation to his consumers which is mediated by his social relations to the patrons, publishers and distributors of his product. These social relations are themselves materially embodied in the character of the product itself. The *fili* of early Ireland may again provide a convenient example. Before the emergence of a 'written' LMP, the *fili* caste formed the dominant group of a *mélange* of literary entertainers, musicians, lampooners and others (generically categorised as 'bards'), controlling the ideological apparatuses of learning and literature as advisers to kings, preservers of oral literary traditions and composers of heroic, panegyric and elegiac verse. They were social functionaries occupying a legally enshrined, privileged status within the social formation, exercising extensive ideological influence over it, and handsomely remunerated by their patrons. These social relations embodied themselves in the character of their literary products: as a secular, traditionalist caste, the *fili* preserved the Gaelic despised for its 'pagan' elements by the higher, Latin-oriented clergy; the poetic *genres* they worked were the 'privileged', heroic, genealogical and mythological modes of the literature of the Gaelic aristocracy. In this case, then, a peculiarly visible homology between the social relations of LMP and GMP is to be observed: the *fili*'s function as literary producers is effectively coterminous with their function within the social relations of Irish society as a whole. By contrast, the individual class-position of a literary producer in certain other LMPs may be in contradiction with his mode of insertion into the class-structure *as an author*. A producer who is himself a member of the dominant social class may, as occasionally in Elizabethan England, be selected for literary patronage in preference to one from a subordinate social class; yet the aristocratic poet or haut-bourgeois novelist becomes, within the capitalist LMP, a petty-bourgeois producer. (This, indeed, is a contradiction which may enter into 'aesthetic ideology' itself, as in the case of bourgeois Romanticism.) The social relations of the LMP, then, while in general determined by the social relations of the GMP, are not necessarily homologous with them. In developed capitalist social formations, the dominant LMP of large-scale capitalist printing, publishing and distributing reproduces the dominant GMP, but incorporates as a crucial constituent a *subordinate* mode of production: the artisanal mode of the literary producer himself, who typically sells his product (manuscript) rather than his labour-power to the publisher in exchange for a fee.

The social classes into which the productive agents of a social formation are distributed may also exert a determination on the character of the LMPs. Coexistent LMPs may be mutually 'disjunct' because each stands in distinct and particular relation to a specific social class. Thus, a dominant courtly class may operate an LMP constituted by the 'amateur' production of texts for 'informal', 'coterie' distribution and consumption; an LMP based upon the professional producer and the capitalist mode of production, distribution, exchange and consumption (into which such 'amateur' texts may enter) may simultaneously exist to supply literary commodities to a wider, aristocratic and bourgeois readership, while a complex combination of 'oral' LMPs may persist within the most subordinate social classes. Such a schema naturally elides the degree of interdetermination which one would expect concretely to exist between such class-structured LMPs. In medieval England, for example, publicly-performed vernacular literature was consumed by all social classes, and the text produced by the 'amateur' author at the request of his patron might be gradually disseminated until a stationer would undertake simultaneous duplication of the original, privately-owned manuscript for profit. Granted such interdeterminations, however, the class-determinations of literary consumption are a significant constituent of an LMP. In developed capitalist formations, for example, the distribution of income and high price of literary products determined by the GMP produces the social relation of 'borrowing' rather than exchange between the mass of proletarian and petty-bourgeois consumers and the LMP; the purchase of books is increasingly confined to members of the dominant classes. Indeed the growth of the circulating libraries in nineteenth-century England is a classic instance of a major mutation in the dominant LMP, a radical reconstitution of the structures of production, distribution and consumption. The privileged status of the 'three-decker' (three-volume) novel within the aesthetic ideology of Victorian England is a function of the economic power within the LMP of the circulating libraries, for whom such commodities were especially profitable since three subscribers could thus read a novel simultaneously. The libraries and publishers cartelised to keep the market price of such commodities prohibitively high, hence establishing the libraries as effectively the sole structure of literary distribution and consumption. The dominant social relation of consumption in the dominant LMP of Victorian England was the three guineas subscription of a consumer to Mudie's circulating library of New Oxford Street. The libraries, moreover, reconstituted the structures of literary production: they were powerful determinants in the *selection* of producers (if an author failed to get into Mudie's advertising list, he or she was effectively finished), of the *pace* of literary production (an author would need to produce one three-decker a year to scrape a modest living), and of the literary *product* itself. The multiple complicated plots, elaborate digressions and gratuitous interludes of such works were the effect of producers ingeniously elongating their material to meet the requirements of the form. Parallel modifications were produced in the printing process itself, where margins were widened and type enlarged to achieve the prerequisite bulk. Coupled with these material and textual factors was the hegemony exercised by the libraries in the region of aesthetic ideology: what was produced and consumed was regulated by their severely censorious owners in accordance with the demands of 'general' ideology. In the Victorian circulating libraries, then, we observe at work a peculiarly close, complex conjuncture of GMP, LMP, 'general' and 'aesthetic' ideology, and text. The struggle of a producer like Thomas Hardy against elements of Victorian bourgeois ideology is intimately related to his scathing assaults on this particular LMP.

The extent to which the social relations of literary production reproduce the social relations of 'general' production, then, is historically variable and determinate. In the case of the tribal bardic system, the two sets of relations are identical: the literary social relations between chief or king, bard and listeners are themselves 'general' social relations, the bard himself is professional ideologue of the social formation. The literary social relations of the medieval era preserve elements of this structure: the medieval author is typically a cleric, part of an ideological apparatus. But his literary production is an aspect of this function rather than identical with it, a voluntary and 'amateur' mode of exercising his priesthood; literary relations assume a certain relative autonomy of 'general' ones. The same is true of the patronised medieval producer, whose literary relations to his patron and consumers is a specific articulation of the 'general' social relations which hold between them. Capitalist formations differ from all of these modes. The specificity of the articulation between 'general' and literary social relations in capitalist formations is to be found in the fact that although the literary social relations in general reproduce the social relations of the GMP, they do not necessarily reproduce these social relations as they hold between the *particular individual agents of the literary productive process*. In both tribalist and feudalist formations, the social relations in which the agents of literary production (patrons, authors, consumers, etc.) stand are determined by or effectively identical with the social relations in which these individual agents stand outside the LMP, in relation to the GMP. The individual functions within 'general' social relations fulfilled by the LMP agents in capitalism, however, are autonomous of the functions they fulfil within the social relations of literary production. An aristocratic novelist may be consumed by proletarian readers, or *vice versa*, but these 'general' social relations of the particular agents are 'cancelled' by the market relations of literary commodity production. It is this unique and peculiar feature of the capitalist LMP which differentiates it markedly from other LMPs whose social relations depend upon certain 'general' relations between the particular agents – relations which pre-exist the act of literary production. The capitalist LMP produces its own social relations between the particular agents independently of their pre-existent social functions — social relations which in general reproduce the 'general' social relations appropriate to general commodity production.

(iv) *General Ideology* (GI)

As well as giving rise at a certain historical stage to a series of LMPs, a GMP also always produces a dominant ideological formation – a formation I provisionally term 'general' to distinguish it from that specific region within it known as the aesthetic region, or, more summarily, as 'aesthetic ideology'. A dominant ideological formation is constituted by a relatively coherent set of 'discourses' of values, representations and beliefs which, realised in certain material apparatuses and related to the structures of material production, so reflect the experiential relations of individual subjects to their social conditions as to guarantee those misperceptions of the 'real' which contribute to the reproduction of the dominant social relations.

It is important to stress here that GI denotes, not some abstraction or 'ideal type' of 'ideology in general', but that particular dominated ensemble of ideologies to be found in any social formation. In speaking of the 'relations' or conjunctures between GI and aesthetic or authorial ideologies, then, one is speaking not of certain extrinsically related 'sets', but of the mode of insertion of authorial and aesthetic formations into the hegemonic ideology as a whole. I stress this point to avoid that hypostatisation of GI, AI and AuI which might follow from designating them thus for the purposes of analysis.

(v) *Relations of GI and LMP*

GI typically contains certain general elements or structures, all or some of which may at a particular historical stage bear significantly on the character of the LMP. These general structures can be distinguished in the main as the linguistic, the political, and the 'cultural'. A set of complex interdeterminations will normally hold between them, which demand historical specification.

A literary text is related to GI not only by how it deploys language but by the particular language it deploys. Language, that most innocent and spontaneous of common currencies, is in reality a terrain scarred, fissured and divided by the cataclysms of political history, strewn with the relics of imperialist, nationalist, regionalist and class combat. The linguistic is always at base the *politico-*

linguistic,[2] a sphere within which the struggles of imperial conqueror with subjugated state, nation-state with nation-state, region with nation, class with class are fought out. Literature is an agent as well as effect of such struggles, a crucial mechanism by which the language and ideology of an imperialist class establishes its hegemony, or by which a subordinated state, class or region preserves and perpetuates at the ideological level an historical identity shattered or eroded at the political. It is also a zone in which such struggles achieve stabilisation – in which the contradictory political unity of imperial and indigenous, dominant and subordinate social classes is articulated and reproduced in the contradictory unity of a 'common language' itself. The moment of consolidation of the 'nation-state' is of paradigmatic significance here – a moment in which the hegemony of a 'national' class reflects itself in the linguistic coherence essential to its integrative, centralising state apparatuses. The history of the genesis of English as a 'national' language is the history of imperialism and its aftermath – the linguistic class-division between Norman French and English, the development of Anglo-Norman French after the loss of Normandy, the mutations of Old English under Norman French influence, the gradual development from these sources of a distinctive English language legally recognised in 1362, the selection of the old East Midland dialect (embracing the political and ideological power-centres of London, Oxford and Cambridge) as the basis of the hegemonic language. Parallel interactions between the LMP and the linguistic, ideological and political structures of state power can be found by turning once more to the instance of Ireland. Towards the end of the twelfth century in Ireland there arose a cultural apparatus based upon the hereditary custody of native learning and literature by certain families within the hegemonic class – an apparatus which is shattered by the English subjugation of Ireland in the seventeenth century. Bereft of social institutions within which to perpetuate itself, indigenous literary culture passes from the possession of the extirpated native ruling class and is forced down to the level of the Gaelic-speaking peasantry,

2. I do not mean to imply that language is merely 'superstructural'. Without language, there could be no material production in the sense characteristic of the human animal. Language is first of all a physical, material reality, and as such is part of the forces of material production. The specific historical forms of this general human reality are then constituted at the social, political and ideological levels.

with resultant changes in aesthetic form and developments in dialectal and provincial literary production. The traditional LMP based on tales of the *Fíanna* recounted by peripatetic or home-based bards is also effectively destroyed by English imperialism: few such tales pass over into the alien language of the imperial class.

The interdeterminations of the linguistic and the political, and their effect on the constitution of an LMP and the character of its products, are thus of central significance to a materialist criticism. No more graphic example of this conjuncture in English literary history can be found than in John Milton's decision to write *Paradise Lost* in his native tongue. Milton's decision was a radically political act – an assertion of bourgeois Protestant nationalism over classical and aristocratic culture, or rather an assertive appropriation of those classical modes for historically progressive ends. The very forms and textures of his poem are a product of this linguistic, political and religious conjuncture within ideology. All literary production, in fact, belongs to that ideological apparatus which can be provisionally termed the 'cultural'. What is in question is not simply the process of production and consumption of literary texts, but the function of such production within the cultural ideological apparatus. That apparatus includes the specific institutions of literary production and distribution (publishing houses, bookshops, libraries and so on), but it also encompasses a range of 'secondary', supportive institutions whose function is more directly ideological, concerned with the definition and dissemination of literary 'standards' and assumptions. Among these are literary academies, societies and book-clubs, associations of literary producers, distributors and consumers, censoring bodies, and literary journals and reviews. In developed social formations, the literary substructure of the cultural apparatus interacts more or less intensively with the ideological apparatus of 'communications'; but its real power lies in its articulation with the *educational* apparatus. It is within this apparatus that the ideological function of literature – its function, that is to say, in reproducing the social relations of the mode of production – is most apparent. From the infant school to the University faculty, literature is a vital instrument for the insertion of individuals into the perceptual and symbolic forms of the dominant ideological formation, able to accomplish this function with a 'naturalness', spontaneity and experiential immediacy possible to no other ideological practice. But it is not only a question

of the ideological use of particular literary works; it is, more fundamentally, a question of the ideological significance of the cultural
and academic institutionalisation of literature as such. What is finally
at stake is not literary texts but Literature — the ideological significance of that process whereby certain historical texts are severed
from their social formations, defined as 'literary', bound and ranked
together to constitute a series of 'literary traditions' and interrogated
to yield a set of ideologically presupposed responses. The precise
ideological function of this process is historically variable. It is
determined in general by the internal structures of the educational
apparatus, which are themselves determined in the last instance by
the GMP; but it may present itself ideologically in the form of a
conservative academicism, related to GI in its literary *positivism*, or
(say) in the form of a liberal humanism which preserves a besieged
enclave of idealist values supposedly incarnate in Literature from
the invasions of a real history now moving beyond its liberal
humanist phase. In any case, it is important to emphasise that the
cultural ideological apparatus contains a dual set of literary institutions: 'primary' institutions of production such as publishing
houses, which exist both as elements of the GMP and as parts of the
ideological apparatus of 'culture', and 'secondary' institutions,
including the educational ones with which the cultural apparatus
interacts, whose relation to the GMP is the more indirect one of
contributing to its reproduction by aiding in the reproduction of its
social relations through ideology.

A discussion of the specific relations between GI and the literary
text belongs to the next chapter; but since the text is, after all, the
product of the LMP, it is worth noting here one or two incidental
points about the GI–LMP relation as it affects the literary text. The
first point is that different LMPs may, in terms of the ideological
character of their textual products, reproduce the same ideological
formation. There is no necessary homology between GI and LMP:
a serialised and directly published Victorian novel, despite belonging
to alternative modes of production, may inhabit the same ideology.
Conversely, the same LMP may reproduce mutually antagonistic
ideological formations: the fiction of Defoe and Fielding. An LMP
which reproduces the social relations of the GMP may conflict with
some of its dominant ideological modes: the Romantic dissent from
bourgeois values and relations is in part determined by the very

integration of the LMP into general commodity production. Conversely, an LMP in conflict with GMP social relations may nevertheless reproduce its dominant ideological forms.

The second point concerns that direct bearing of GI on the literary text which is censorship. Such modes of direct ideological control over the text may take the form of simple repression at the point of production, distribution or consumption, or may be effected more obliquely: licensing, politically select patronage and so on. The most efficient form of censorship is, of course, the perpetuation of mass illiteracy. The factor of literacy represents a peculiarly complex conjuncture of GMP, LMP, GI and aesthetic ideology. The degree and social distribution of literacy are determined in the last instance by the GMP, but literacy is clearly in turn a significant determinant of the LMP, affecting the size and social composition not only of readers but of producers. The degree of literacy of producers and consumers may also influence the character of the literary product – whether, for instance, it is distributed orally, as well as its length and elaborateness (for there is a limit to the memorising capacity of the non- or semi-literate producer). Illiteracy may be effected by the exclusion of certain social groups and classes from the educational apparatus for political reasons; but there is a possibility of conflict here between those reasons and competing ideological imperatives. In nineteenth-century England, for example, there were sound political reasons why the proletariat should be excluded from literacy, but sound religious reasons why it should not be. Literacy is also determined by aesthetic ideology, which in ratifying (in conjuncture with GI) certain languages (French, Latin), or certain uses of language as appropriate to literature, determines the degree of its general availability. There is a practical, as well as theoretical, literacy.

(vi) *Authorial Ideology* (AuI)

I mean by 'authorial ideology' the effect of the author's specific mode of biographical insertion into GI, a mode of insertion over-determined by a series of distinct factors: social class, sex, nationality, religion, geographical region and so on. This formation is never to be treated in isolation from GI, but must be studied in its articulation with it. Between the two formations of GI and AuI, relations of effective homology, partial disjunction and severe contradiction are possible. The producer's biographical (as opposed to 'aesthetic' or 'textual') ideology may be effectively homologous with the dominant ideology of his or her historical moment, but not necessarily because the producer lives the social conditions of *class* most appropriate for such harmonious insertion into it. The producer may in terms of (say) class-position inhabit an ideological sub-ensemble with conflictual relations to the dominant ideology, but by an overdetermination of other biographical factors (sex, religion, region) may be rendered homologous with it. The converse situation is equally possible. The degree of conjuncture or disjuncture between AuI and GI may also be 'diachronically' determined: an author may relate to his or her contemporary GI by virtue of 'belonging' to an historically previous GI, or (as with the case of the revolutionary author) to a putatively future one.[3] As GI mutates, an AuI which was at one point homologous with it may enter into conflict with it, and *vice versa*. It is not, in short, always a simple matter to specify the historical period to which a writer belongs; nor does a writer necessarily belong only to one 'history'. It is significant in this respect that the two generally acknowledged major authors of Restoration England – John Milton and John Bunyan – do not in fact 'belong' to 'Restoration ideology' at all. It is equally true, however, that their modes of ideological disinheritance from their contemporary historical moment are determined, in the last instance, by the nature of that moment itself.

AuI is not to be conflated with GI; nor is it to be identified with the 'ideology of the text'. The ideology of the text is not an 'expression' of authorial ideology: it is the product of an aesthetic working of 'general' ideology as that ideology is itself worked and 'produced' by an overdetermination of authorial-biographical factors. AuI, then, is always GI as lived, worked and represented from a particular overdetermined standpoint within it. There is no question here of 'centring' the literary text on the individual subject who produces it; but neither is it a matter of liquidating that subject into

3. There is also the case of the insertion of an author into the GI of *another* society, whether contemporaneous or not: the problem of 'cosmopolitanism'. Such insertion is always in the last instance a question of the determination of the 'native' GI.

'general' aesthetic and ideological forms. It is a question of specifying the ideological determinations of the text – determinations which include the effect of the author's mode of insertion into GI.

(vii) *Aesthetic Ideology* (AI)

I denote by this the specific aesthetic region of GI, articulated with other such regions – the ethical, religious, etc. – in relations of dominance and subordination determined in the last instance by the GMP. AI is an internally complex formation, including a number of sub-sectors, of which the *literary* is one. This literary sub-sector is itself internally complex, constituted by a number of 'levels': theories of literature, critical practices, literary traditions, *genres*, conventions, devices and discourses. AI also includes what may be termed an 'ideology of the aesthetic' – a signification of the function, meaning and value of the aesthetic itself within a particular social formation, which is in turn part of an 'ideology of culture' included within GI.

(viii) *Relations of AI, GI and LMP*

A GMP produces a GI which contributes to reproducing it; it also produces a (dominant) LMP which in general reproduces and is reproduced by the GMP, but which also reproduces and is reproduced by the GI. We may speak of the 'ideology of the LMP' to designate the mutually reproductive relation which holds between GI and LMP – a relation which produces within the LMP an ideology of producer, product and consumer, as well as of the activities of production, exchange and consumption. This ideology is itself encoded within AI; more precisely, it is the effect of a conjuncture between AI and GI. The literary producer may be viewed as the privileged servant of a social order symbolised by his royal, ecclesial or aristocratic patron, as the inspired articulator of the collective values of his community, as an 'independent' producer freely offering his private product to an amenable audience, as the prophetic or bohemian rebel dissidently marginal to 'conventional' society, as a 'worker' or 'engineer' on a fraternal footing with his readership, and so on. Literary production itself may be ideologically encoded as revelation, inspiration, labour, play, reflection, fantasy, reproduction; the literary product as process, practice, medium, symbol, object, epiphany, gesture; literary consumption as magical influence, arcane ritual, participatory dialogue, passive reception, didactic instruction, spiritual encounter. Each of these ideologies will be determined by a specific conjuncture of LMP/GI/AI, on the basis of the final determination of the GMP. There is, however, no question of a necessarily *symmetrical* relation here between the various formations involved. Each of these formations is internally complex, and a series of internally and mutually conflictual relations may hold between them. An LMP which is itself an amalgam of historically disparate elements may thus combine in contradictory unity disparate ideological elements of both GI and AI. A double-articulation GMP/GI–GI/AI/LMP is, for example, possible, whereby a GI category, when transformed by AI into an ideological component of an LMP, may then enter into conflict with the GMP social relations it exists to reproduce. The bourgeois-Romantic category of the producer as 'individual creator', for example, reproduces but also conflicts with the bourgeois conception of the human subject as nuclear individual. Or again, the Romantic and symbolist ideology of the literary product as mysteriously autotelic object at once reproduces and represses its real status as commodity. Similarly, the ideology of 'instant' or 'disposable' literary art reproduces the consumer ideologies of advanced capitalism at the same time as it conflicts with certain imperatives of deferred fulfilment integral to that ideological formation.

The forces and relations of literary production, on the basis of their determination by the GMP, produce the possibility of certain distinct literary *genres*. The novel, for example, can be produced only at a certain stage of development of an LMP; but whether this potential is historically activated is determined not by the LMP alone, but by its conjuncture with GI and AI. What forms and *genres* are actually selected for development may be dictated by what exists already – dictated, that is, by AI on the basis of GI. Conversely, the concept of and 'need for' a new form may develop relatively autonomously within aesthetic ideology, and an LMP modified or transformed to produce it. GI may occasionally impress itself directly upon the LMP to produce a particular form (say, 'socialist realism') which is then encoded and elaborated by AI; but such unilateral action is historically untypical. GI more usually appears within the LMP in its particular aesthetic articulation; literary practices are typically the product of a complex conjuncture of LMP/GI/AI, with one or another of these elements assuming dominance.

GI and AI determine not only the process of production but also the process of consumption. The literary text is a text (as opposed to 'book') because it is read; with it as with any other social product, the act of consumption is itself constitutive of its existence. Reading is an ideological decipherment of an ideological product; and the history of literary criticism is the history of the possible conjunctures between the ideologies of the text's productive and consumptive moments. Between those two ideological moments there will be relations of effective homology, conflict or contradiction, determined in part by the history of ideological receptions of the text which has intervened between them. The text is consumed within an aesthetic ideology constituted in part by a set of conjunctures between GI and AI which is the history of the text's production and consumption as constructed by the GI/AI conjuncture of the particular moment of consumption. GI may act as a dominant element within the ideology of consumption (witness the eccentric instance of the considerable increase in Trollope readers during the period of the Second World War), but more commonly operates in the high degree of relative autonomy it ascribes to the aesthetic region. As well as an ideology of particular consumption, there will also be one of general consumption within which the former operates – an ideology of *the act of reading itself*, which may be encoded as religious ceremony, socially privileged compact, moral instruction and so on. Any particular act of reading is conducted within a general set of assumptions as to the ideological signification of reading itself within a social formation – assumptions which, as part of AI, belong also to the general 'ideology of culture' of GI.

(ix) *Relations of GI, AI and AuI*

The complexity of relation between GI and AI as constitutive of the literary text is properly the subject of the next chapter. It is enough to say here that as an aesthetic product the text is a multiply articulated structure, determined only in the last instance by the moment of its contemporary GI. Its various aesthetic elements may be the product of distinct ideological formations, may belong to disparate 'histories', so that it is not necessarily identical, ideologically speaking, with itself. Nor need the 'ideology of the text' be consonant with the historical progressiveness or obsolescence of the LMP within which it is produced. An author may produce progressive texts using outmoded forms within an obsolescent or partly obsolescent LMP (William Morris), or may produce ideologically conservative texts within an historically progressive LMP (Henry Fielding). It is a question in each case of specifying the precise relations between LMP, 'ideology of LMP', GI and AI.

Authorial ideology may be an important determinant of both the type of LMP and the aesthetic ideology within which an author works. As with Alexander Pope's 'choice' of satire, elegy and the mock-heroic, a certain AuI will exclude certain modes of literary production and license others. At certain levels of production, AuI may be so subordinated to AI that the question of differential relations between them does not arise. In such a situation, to be a literary producer at all is inevitably to work within a particular set of ideological representations of the character and significance of literary production. The relations between AuI and GI may be transformed by their mediation in terms of AI: within the text itself (Balzac is the classical example), the production of GI by means of certain aesthetic forms may 'cancel' and contradict that production of GI which is authorial ideology. The methodological significance of AuI in the analysis of the text is therefore variable: it may be effectively homologous with GI/AI, or it may be 'cancelled' as a specific factor by their distinct or conjoint effects. In either of these cases, AuI as a particular 'level' effectively disappears.

(x) *Text*

The literary text is the product of a specific overdetermined conjuncture of the elements or formations set out schematically above. It is not, however, a merely passive product. The text is so constituted by this conjuncture as to actively determine its own determinants – an activity which is most apparent in its relations to ideology. It is those relations which we must now go on to examine.

3

Towards a Science of the Text

Adam Smith's contradictions are of significance because they contain problems which it is true he does not resolve, but which he reveals by contradicting himself.

(Karl Marx, *Theories of Surplus Value*)

In the previous chapter I have examined the process whereby the literary text is produced by an interaction of structures. It is now necessary to work in reverse, to take our standpoint within the text itself, and to analyse its relations to ideology and to history.

The literary text is not the 'expression' of ideology, nor is ideology the 'expression' of social class. The text, rather, is a certain *production* of ideology, for which the analogy of a dramatic production is in some ways appropriate. A dramatic production does not 'express', 'reflect' or 'reproduce' the dramatic text on which it is based; it 'produces' the text, transforming it into a unique and irreducible entity. A dramatic production is not to be judged by its fidelity to the text in the sense that a mirror-image can be judged faithfully to reflect its object; text and production are not commensurable formations to be laid out alongside one another, their distance or relation measured as one measures the distance between two physical objects. Text and production are incommensurate because they inhabit distinct real and theoretical spaces. Nor is the dramatic production to be conceived of as an 'interpenetration' of these two spaces, textual and theatrical, or as a 'realisation' or 'concretisation' of the text. The relation between text and production is not imaginable as that of an essence to an existence, soul to body: it is not simply a question of the production 'bringing the text alive', revitalising and de-reifying it, releasing it from its suspended animation so that the imprisoned life it contains becomes fluid and mobile. The production is not in this sense the soul of the text's corpse; nor is the converse relation true, that the text is the informing essence of the production. The text does not contain, *in potentia*, dramatic 'life': the life of the text is one of literary significations, not a typographical 'ghosting' of the flesh of production. The text is not the production 'in rest', nor is the production the text 'in action'; the relation between them cannot be grasped as a simple binary opposition (rest/motion, soul/body, essence/existence), as though both phenomena were moments of a single reality, distinct articulations of a concealed unity. The notion of binary opposition here is, indeed, a curious one, since it includes the possibility of a passage, a transition, from one phenomenon to another, while at the same time in Cartesian fashion rendering that passage mysteriously inexplicable – the miracle of resurrection, reanimation or realisation, of the word becoming flesh. It is only by the materialist concept of productive labour, as the definitive relation between text and production, that such a notion can be demystified, and the myth of a 'passage' eradicated. For the idea of a passage between text and production implies that they are congruent realities, adjacently situated on a single terrain; and it is no escape from this to claim, more suavely, that the passage between them is complex and difficult – that the relation is 'deflected' or 'refracted' rather than direct. One does not escape from reflectionist models by imagining a somewhat more complicated mirror. Nor is it a question of the dramatic production 'enacting' the text; the metaphor of enactment is itself a misleading one, suggesting as it does a simple miming of the pre-existent. An actor in the theatre does not 'enact'; rather, he *acts* – functions, performs, behaves. He 'produces' his role, not as a conjurer produces a playing card, but as a carpenter produces a chair. The relation between text and production is a relation of *labour*: the theatrical instruments (staging, acting skills and so on) transform the 'raw materials' of the text into a specific product, which cannot be mechanically extrapolated from an inspection of the text itself. The question of two different productions of the same dramatic text is relevant here; for two such productions can vary to the point where the question of in what precise sense we are dealing with the 'same' text becomes pertinent. Of course in a literal sense the text is in both cases identical; but the productions to which it gives rise may diverge to the point where we can speak, figuratively, of the production of a 'different' text in each case – where the *Othello* of one director is not the *Othello* of another. The character of the text will determine the nature of the production, but conversely, the production will determine the character of the text – will, by a process of selection, organisation and exclusion, define 'which' text is actually being put to work. The theatrical mode of production in no sense merely 'mediates' the text; on the contrary, its practices and conventions 'operate' the textual materials according to an internal logic of their own.

This relative autonomy of the theatrical mode of production is, in fact, historically variable. Certain theatrical modes will display in their very structure an ideology of the 'faithful representation' of the text; others will view the text as rewritable raw material, dethroning it from its privileged status as absolute arbitrator. No single, unalterable relation is in question here: certain texts will confer greater or lesser degrees of relative autonomy on theatrical practice, while certain theatrical practices will unilaterally constitute the text as licensing such autonomy. Yet what is not variable is the fact that text and production are distinct formations – different material modes of production, between which no homologous or 'reproductive' relationship can hold. They are not two aspects of the same discourse – the text, as it were, thought or silent speech and the production thought-in-action, articulate language; they constitute distinct kinds of discourse, between which no simple 'translation' is possible. For translation can occur only between two categorially comparable systems, and this is not the case here. There can be no more question of 'translating' text into production than there can be of 'translating' stone into a sculpture, or cotton into a shirt. The text–production relationship is not to be theorised as one between thought and word; it is more analogous to the relation between grammar and speech. Speech is a product, not a reproduction, of grammar; grammar is the determining structure of discourse, but the character of discourse cannot be mechanically derived from it. The analogy is obviously imperfect, since grammar is a formal, abstract corpus of rules whereas speech is 'concrete'; and the text–production relationship cannot be considered in terms of an abstract/concrete opposition, which could only be Platonic or empiricist. Indeed the whole problem arises because the text is as 'concrete' as the production itself, but in its own distinct mode. The text is not a mere set of abstract notations, a skeletal framework which 'inspires', 'cues' or 'intimates' the production, a threadbare score on which the production improvises. If this were so then the relations between text and production would be obvious – the former as the map of the real terrain of the latter, the text as the mere enabling conditions of the production, or as the 'deep structure' of its contingent speech. Such a conception abolishes the problem by effectively abolishing the materiality of the text, dwindling it to a ghostly presence, and so reverting to the essence/existence duality which belongs also to the opposing error of fetishising the text. The text's determination of the dramatic performance is considerably more rigorous than such metaphors would suggest: in the conventional way, every line, every gesture, every item of the text must be produced on stage. Directorial 'freedom', once the production is in hand, is the freedom of *producing* this text, not of producing *this* text; for once the initial decision for the text is taken, the text is ineluctable. In studying the relations between text and performance, then, we are studying a mode of determination which is precise and rigorous, yet which cannot be accounted for in terms of a 'reflection' or 'reproduction'. We are examining, in short, the conditions of a *production*.

Before we proceed to apply this analogy to the relations between literary text and ideology, it is worth pursuing briefly another potentially suggestive aspect of it. The dramatic performance is a production of the dramatic text; but the text itself is not a terminus. It exists in some complex relation to history which has yet to be determined – but in any case, if our analogy of dramatic production-literary text is correct, we may say that the dramatic text is itself a production. What is at issue here, then, is the *production of a production*. The dramatic text is the determinate product of a particular history; and in considering its relations to the dramatic performance, we are thus dealing with two complexly articulated sets of determinants. The dramatic production, as I have argued, is an operation, a *mise-en-scène*, of the text; but in so producing it, it simultaneously produces the text's internal relations to its object. The dramatic production, in other words, can never simply be the production of the text as autotelic artefact, as an exhibition of jewellery might display a necklace; it is, inevitably, a production of the text as *product* – of the text in its relations to what it speaks of. It does not simply 'give' us those relations, in the manner in which the text itself conceives them; the production does not merely 'double' the text's self-understanding but constructs an interpretation of that self-understanding, an ideology of that ideology. In doing so, it can alert us to the text's ignorance and miscomprehension, to modes of sense intimated but suppressed by the text itself. A dramatic production may, indeed, take this as its conscious end – Brecht's *Coriolanus*, for example – or, as more generally with 'epic theatre', seek those modes of theatrical production which display the product precisely as product. But it is not such conscious demystification which is in the first place at issue here. For every dramatic production fashions a relationship between itself and the text by fashioning a relationship between the text and what it speaks of. The determining basis of that relationship is, naturally, the text's own self-comprehension; for if that were thrown completely aside, discarded and abolished, there would be no play to produce. But if the production cannot absolutely transcend its text, it can at least round on it, torture and interrogate it with a critical rigour which, since it exists only in the *relation* of production to text, can be shown but not stated. The production moves now with, now athwart the ideology of its text, in a double movement constituted at once by the aesthetic logic of its ideologically determinate productive techniques and the ideological demands which determine those aesthetic devices. Some productions move almost wholly 'with' their texts, as with the naturalist performance of naturalist drama; but the apparent homology of text and performance here is merely the illusory concealment of a labour. One might imagine at the other extreme a naturalist text produced by 'epic' or expressionist techniques, and so radically 'defamiliarised' to yield up conflicts and absences unknown to itself. And one can imagine, too, a whole hierarchy of possible productions intermediate between these poles, in which the relations between mode of production, 'ideology of production' and 'ideology of text' are precisely determinable.

The parallel I am pursuing, then, may be schematised as follows:

history/ideology———→dramatic text———→dramatic production
history———→ideology———→literary text

The literary text, that is to say, produces ideology (itself a production) in a way analogous to the operations of dramatic production on dramatic text. And just as the dramatic production's relation to its text reveals the text's internal relations to its 'world' under the form of its own *constitution* of them, so the literary text's relation to ideology so constitutes that ideology as to reveal something of its relations to history.

Such a formulation instantly raises several questions, the first of which concerns the relation of the text to 'real' history. In what sense is it correct to maintain that *ideology*, rather than *history*, is the object of the text? Or, to pose the question slightly differently: In what sense, if any, do elements of the historically 'real' enter the text? Georg Lukács, in his *Studies in European Realism*, argues that Balzac's greatness lies in the fact that the 'inexorable veracity' of his art drives him to transcend his reactionary ideology and perceive the real historical issues at stake. Ideology, here, clearly signifies a 'false consciousness' which blocks true historical perception, a screen interposed between men and their history. As such, it is a simplistic notion: it fails to grasp ideology as an inherently complex formation which, by inserting individuals into history in a variety of ways, allows of multiple kinds and degrees of access to that history. It fails, in fact, to grasp the truth that some ideologies, and levels of ideology, are more false than others. Ideology is not just the bad dream of the infrastructure: in *deformatively* 'producing' the real, it nevertheless carries elements of reality within itself. But it is not enough, therefore, to modify the image of 'screen' to that of 'filter', as though ideology were a mesh through which elements of the real could slip. Any such 'interventionist' model of ideology holds out the possibility of looking behind the obstruction to observe reality; but in the capitalist mode of production, what is there to be observed is certainly not the real. The real is by necessity empirically imperceptible, concealing itself in the phenomenal categories (commodity, wage-relation, exchange-value and so on) it offers spontaneously for inspection. Ideology, rather, so produces and constructs the real as to cast the shadow of its absence over the perception of its presence. It is not merely that certain aspects of the real are illuminated and others obscured; it is rather that the presence of the real is a presence constituted by its absences, and *vice versa*. Balzac was indeed able to achieve partial insight into the movement of real history, but it is mistaken to image such insight as a transcendence of ideology into history. No such displacement of realms occurs: it is rather that

Balzac's insights are the effect of a specific conjuncture of his mode of authorial insertion into ideology, the relations of the ideological region he inhabited to real history, the character of that stage of capitalist development, and the 'truth-effect' of the particular aesthetic form (realism) he worked. It is by force of this conjuncture that he was able to be at once exceedingly deluded and extraordinarily percipient. There is no more question of Balzac's texts having 'by-passed' the ideological and established a direct relation to history than there is of Shakespeare's drama having launched its critique of bourgeois individualism from outside a highly particular ideological standpoint.

The notion of a direct, spontaneous relation between text and history, then, belongs to a naïve empiricism which is to be discarded. For what would it mean to claim that a text was *directly* related to its history? The text can no more be conceived as directly denoting a real history than the meaning of a word can be imagined as an object correlated with it. Language, among other things, certainly denotes objects; but it does not do so in some simple relationship, as though word and object stood adjacent, as two poles awaiting the electric current of interconnection. A text, naturally, may speak of real history, of Napoleon or Chartism, but even if it maintains empirical historical accuracy this is always a *fictive* treatment – an operation of historical data according to the laws of textual production. Unless real history can be read as fiction in such a case, we are dealing not with literary but with historiographical discourse. To say that the 'historical' literary work must operate as fiction is not, of course, to suppress the relevance of the particular history with which it deals, as though this might be *any* history. It is to claim that *this* particular history is being fictionalised – construed in terms of an ideological production of its agents' modes of ideological insertion into it, and so rendered as *ideology to the second power*.

It is not that the text, in allowing us access to ideology, swathes us in simple illusion. Commodities, money, wage-relations are certainly 'phenomenal forms' of capitalist production, but they are nothing if not 'real' for all that. It is not that Jane Austen's fiction presents us merely with ideological delusion; on the contrary, it also offers us a version of contemporary history which is considerably more revealing than much historiography. And this is not just the effect of Austen's aesthetic forms, which so 'distantiate' ideology as to light up the shady frontiers where it abuts, by negation, onto real history. If ideology is indeed mere illusion, then it would certainly demand some such formal, unilateral operation to embarrass it into a betrayal of truth. But if Austen's forms do this, it is because they themselves are the product of certain ideological codes which, in permitting us access to certain values, forces and relations, yield us a sort of historical knowledge. It is not, to be sure, knowledge in the strict scientific sense; but epistemology does not divide neatly down the middle between strict science and sheer illusion. If Austen's texts can be spoken of as partly veridical, it is because the capacity of their aesthetic devices to yield complex, historically significant perceptions is determined by their productive relation to an ideological conjuncture which itself 'feels' more of the historical real than, say, *Gryll Grange*. It is not, however, a question of 'degrees of knowledge', in the sense that the more 'knowledgeable' text (let us say, *Caleb Williams*) necessarily achieves the more valuable perceptions. On the contrary, the value of Austen's fiction thrives quite as much on its ignorance as on its insight: it is because there is so much the novels cannot possibly know that they know what they do, and in the *form* they do. It is true that Austen, because she does not *know*, only 'knows'; but what she 'knows' is not thereby nothing at all, cancelled to a cypher by the exclusion of the real. For without the exclusion of the real as it is known to historical materialism, there could be for Austen nothing of the ethical discourse, rhetoric of character, ritual of relationship or ceremony of convention which she presents – nothing, in short, of those elements for which we find her fiction 'valuable'. These rituals and discourses are not just the vacant spaces left by the withdrawal of the real; there is nothing 'unreal' about the fierce ideological combats they encode. It is because the ideological is 'real' (if not in the strongest sense) that it is not always essential for it to submit to a formal, quasi-scientific self-distantiation for it to hint at history. It is true that this is what happens when ideology enters fiction; but it is not always merely by virtue of this 'fiction-effect' that the ideological may be waylaid into delivering up its historical truth. For it depends on the ideological conjuncture in question, and on the character of the forms which go to work upon it. The mode of a text's insertion into an ideological sub-ensemble, the mode of that sub-ensemble's insertion into the dominated ensemble of ideologies, the ideological character of its formal devices: these articulations, determined in the last instance by the historical real, are simultaneously what determine the nature, degree and quality of textual access to itself which that historical real permits.

History, then, certainly 'enters' the text, not least the 'historical' text; but it enters it precisely *as ideology*, as a presence determined and distorted by its measurable absences. This is not to say that real history is present in the text but in disguised form, so that the task of the critic is then to wrench the mask from its face. It is rather that history is 'present' in the text in the form of a *double-absence*. The text takes as its object, not the real, but certain significations by which the real lives itself – significations which are themselves the product of its partial abolition. Within the text itself, then, ideology becomes a dominant structure, determining the character and disposition of certain 'pseudo-real' constituents. This inversion, as it were, of the real historical process, whereby in the text itself ideology seems to determine the historically real rather than *vice versa*, is itself naturally determined in the last instance by history itself. History, one might say, is the *ultimate* signifier of literature, as it is the ultimate signified. For what else in the end could be the source and object of any signifying practice but the real social formation which provides its material matrix? The problem is not that such a claim is false, but that it leaves everything exactly as it was. For the text presents itself to us less as historical than as a sportive flight from history, a reversal and resistance of history, a momentarily liberated zone in which the exigencies of the real seem to evaporate, an enclave of freedom enclosed within the realm of necessity. We know that such freedom is largely illusory – that the text is *governed*; but it is not illusory merely in the sense of being a false perception of our own. The text's illusion of freedom is part of its very nature – an effect of its peculiarly *overdetermined* relation to historical reality.

One might express this sense of freedom by saying that the literary text, in contrast with, say, historiography, appears to have no determinate object. Historiography, whatever its ideological mode, has such an object: history itself. But what is the precise object of the literary text? What does the text 'denote'? For even those empathetic, hermeneutical forms of historiography which seek to reconstruct real history out of the categories of the 'lived' – which, in short, take as their object history-as-ideology – nonetheless thereby take as their indirect object history itself. But the literary text seems rather to produce its own object, which is inseparable from its modes of fashioning it – which is an *effect* of those modes rather than a distinct entity. In so far as it presents itself as its own product, the text appears to be *self-producing*. It is possible, certainly, to draw a theoretical distinction between the text's means of production and what is produced: the former would include those aesthetic categories relatively independent of specific contents (*genres*, forms, conventions and so on), while the latter might encompass particular themes, plots, characters, 'situations'. But this distinction is clearly not of the same kind as the material and temporal distinction between a power-loom and its products. A power-loom, for one thing, is not altered by its products (I leave aside the question of the value it transfers to them) in the way that a literary convention is transformed by what it textually works. The text appears to produce itself in the sense that, within its space, producer, mode of production and product seem coterminous and indissociable. In textual analysis, propositions about the authorial producer are properly reducible to descriptions of textual operations, which are in turn merely an alternative metaphor for what is being textually operated. 'Product' and 'producer' appear thus merely figurative abstractions for that self-generative process of the production of meanings which *is* the text.

That the text is *in a certain sense* self-producing is, as I shall argue later, a valid claim. Yet the notion that the text is simply a ceaselessly self-signifying practice, without source or object, stands four square with the bourgeois mythology of individual freedom. Such freedom is not mythological because it does not, after a fashion, exist, but because it exists as the precise effect of certain determinants which enforce their own self-concealment. The text's 'freedom', similarly, is the precise effect of its ineluctable relation to history, the phenomenal form of its real necessity. A comparison with the historiographical work may clarify the point. Historiography conventionally organises its significations so as to yield an 'objective' account of the real; that it does not typically do so is because of an ideological construction of that real which is *contingent* to its character as a discourse. It is, however, intrinsic to the character of literary discourse that it does not take history as its immediate object, but works instead upon ideological forms and materials of which history is, as it were, the concealed underside. Literary and historiographical texts are thus 'ideological' in quite distinct senses. The literary text does not *take* history as its object, even when (as with 'historical' fiction) it believes itself to do so; but it does, nevertheless, *have* history as its object in the last instance, in ways apparent not to the text itself but to criticism. It is this *distantiation* of history, this absence of any particular historical 'real', which confers on literature its air of freedom; unlike the historiographical work, it seems to be liberated from the need to conform its meanings to the exigencies of the actual. But this liberation is merely the other face of an internal necessity. The text, we may say, gives us certain socially determined representations of the real cut loose from any particular real conditions to which those representations refer. It is in this sense that we are tempted to feel that it is self-referential, or conversely (the twin idealist error) refers to 'life' or the 'human condition', since if it denotes no concrete state of affairs it must denote either itself, or states of affairs in general. But it is precisely in this absence of the particular real that the text most significantly refers – refers, not to concrete situations, but to an ideological formation (and hence, obliquely, to history) which 'concrete situations' have actually produced. The text gives us such ideology without its real history alongside it, as though it were autonomous – gives us states of affairs which are imaginary, pseudo-events, since their meaning lies not in their material reality but in how they contribute to fashioning and perpetuating a particular process of signification. In this sense, as history is distantiated, becoming, so to speak, more 'abstract', the signifying process assumes greater dominance, becoming more 'concrete'. The literary work appears free – self-producing and self-determining – because it is unconstrained by the necessity to reproduce any particular 'real'; but this freedom simply conceals its more fundamental determination by the constituents of its ideological matrix. If it seems true that at the level of the text's 'pseudo-real' – its imaginary figures and events – 'anything can happen', this is by no means true of its ideological organisation; and it is precisely because *that* is not true that the free-wheeling contingency of its pseudo-real is equally illusory. The pseudo-real of the literary text is the product of the ideologically saturated demands of its modes of representation.

History, then, operates upon the text by an ideological determination which within the text itself privileges ideology as a dominant structure determining its own imaginary or 'pseudo' history. This 'pseudo' or 'textual' real is not related to the historical real as an imaginary 'transposition' of it. Rather than 'imaginatively transposing' the real, the literary work is the production of certain produced representations of the real into an imaginary object. If it distantiates history, it is not because it transmutes it to fantasy, shifting from one ontological gear to another, but because the significations it works into fiction are already representations of reality rather than reality itself. The text is a tissue of meanings, perceptions and responses which inhere in the first place in that imaginary production of the real which is ideology. The 'textual real' is related to the historical real, not as an imaginary transposition of it, but as the product of certain signifying practices whose source and referent is, in the last instance, history itself.

The literary text, accordingly, is characterised by a peculiar conjuncture of 'concrete' and 'abstract'. It resembles historiography in its density of texture, yet is analogous to philosophical discourse in the 'generality' of its object.[1] It differs from both in taking this 'abstract' object as concrete. The text strikes us with the arresting immediacy of a physical gesture which turns out to have no precise object – as though we were observing the behaviour of a man urgently gesticulating, and so *intimating* an actual state of affairs, only to realise that his gestures were in some sense mere ritual and rehearsal – learnt, studied actions which indicated nothing immediate in his environment, but revealed, rather, the *nature* of an environment which could motivate such behaviour. Our mistake was to search his environment for an object to correlate with his gesture, rather than to grasp his gesturing as a relationship to the environment itself. (As though we thought he was pointing, when in fact he was dancing.) What may seem gratuitous in such a man's behaviour, removed as it is from any 'concrete' motivation, then appears, on the contrary, as the rehearsed and calculated behaviour of an actor; it seems gratuitous, not because it is spontaneous, but precisely because it is not. The ambivalent status of the text, located, so to speak, between phenomenological historiography and philosophy, arises from its specific relation to ideology. As a production

1. One is happy to observe here a remarkable consonance of viewpoints between materialist criticism and Sir Philip Sidney's *Apology for Poetry*.

of the 'lived' it approximates to the former; as a production of the 'lived' shorn of particular real conditions, it resembles the latter. Philosophy, of course, deals with the lived not as 'spontaneous' response and perception but in terms of the general categories underlying it – categories which may or may not be ideological, or more or less entwined with ideology. In this sense it differs from literature, whose aim is to give us the lived as it were spontaneously; but literature nonetheless resembles it in so far as this 'spontaneity' is in fact phenomenal. Literature, too, as I shall argue, reveals more or less indirectly the categories of the lived; it is merely that it typically produces those categories so as to conceal them, dissolving them in the 'concrete'. (Pope's *Essay on Man* presents certain categorial propositions, but in so far as the rhetorical strategy of its form is to induce an *experience* of them, it is a literary rather than philosophical text.)

To say that the text 'concretises the abstract', however, would be an inadequate formulation. It would be more accurate to say that what I have provisionally termed the 'abstraction' of the 'textual real', its lack of identity (or purely fortuitous identity) with any particular historical real, produces, and is the product of a peculiar overdetermination of the text's significatory devices. It is in that overdetermination – in the complex concentration of its many determinants – that the text's 'concretion' inheres. (When Marx speaks in the *Grundrisse* of '*rising*' from the abstract to the concrete he abolishes a whole tradition of philosophy in a single verb.) For the literary text behaves as though it fashions its 'real' in order the more concretely (in Marx's sense) to fashion its representational modes; or, to put it conversely, as though the very rigorousness of its ideological determinations necessitated, paradoxically, a certain flexibility and provisionality of its 'textual real'. This is not, after all, to suggest that in the text anything can happen; it is rather to indicate that 'textual reals' are dissolved, displaced, condensed and conflated by the predominant demands of textual ideology, and that this provisionality is then typically *naturalised*. Such a claim should not be mistaken for the Formalist doctrine that the text selects only such 'contents' as will reinforce its form; for as I shall argue later, the forms which 'select' such content are themselves selected from that always preformed content which is ideology. An example of the dominance within the text of 'ideology' over the 'pseudo-real', of the relation of *production* between them, can be found in the so-called 'typicality' of the figures and events in the lineage of realist fiction. What is meant by the Hegelian proposition that such characters and situations appear at once as irreducibly individual and historically representative is that they are overdetermined products – that by a certain displacement and conflation of multiple 'pseudo-real' components they assume, reciprocally, an unusually intense degree of concretion, concentrating those diverse determinants within themselves.

It is true that some texts seem to approach the real more closely than others. The level of the 'textual real' in *Bleak House* is considerably more predominant than it is in, say, Burns's lyric, *My love is like a red, red rose*. The former seeks to illuminate, among other things, a highly localised history; the latter has an extremely abstract referent. Yet whereas it is obvious that Burns's poem refers us to certain modes of ideological signification rather than to a 'real' object, so that whether he had a lover at all is, of course, entirely irrelevant (and is *intimated* to be so by the poem's very form), the same is true, if not so obviously, of Dickens's novel. It is simply that Dickens deploys particular modes of signification (realism) which entail a greater foregrounding of the 'pseudo-real'; but we should not be led by this to make direct comparisons between the imaginary London of his novel and the real London. The imaginary London of *Bleak House* exists as the product of a representational process which signifies, not 'Victorian England' as such, but certain of Victorian England's ways of signifying itself. Fiction does not trade in imaginary history as a way of presenting real history; its 'history' is imaginary because it negotiates a particular ideological *experience* of real history. It is useful in this respect to think of the text not merely as the *product* of ideology, but as a *necessity* of ideology – not in an empirical sense, since ideologies without literature have certainly existed, but theoretically, in that fiction is the term we would give to the fullest self-rendering of ideology, the only logical form that such a complete rendering could assume. And this is not, of course, because fiction is 'untrue', and so a fit vehicle for 'false consciousness', but rather that in order to reconstruct a society's self-representations we would finally encounter the need to cut them loose from particular 'reals' and mobilise them in the form of situations which, because imaginary, would allow for the range, permutation, economy and flexibility denied to a mere reproduction of the routinely lived.

The literary text's lack of a real direct referent constitutes the most salient fact about it: its fictiveness. There are familiar problems here, over predominantly fictive texts with much 'factual' material, or preponderantly 'factual' texts with significant fictive elements. But it is enough for the present to say that fictiveness is the most general constituent of the literary text, and that this refers not at all to the *literal* fictiveness of the text's events and responses (for they may happen to be historically true), but to certain modes of producing such materials. A poet's biographical experience becomes 'fictive' when produced in poetic form – when a specific mode of production gives rise to a different *object*, enforces our attention not to the biographical accuracy or significance of the experience but to its function as part of a structure of representations of a more general history. (It is from this fact, among others, that the conventional notion of the 'universality' of major art doubtless arises.) The primary constituent of this aesthetic mode of production is, as I have suggested, a certain dominance (or 'excess') of the signifying practice over the signified – so that as the signified becomes more 'abstract', putative or virtual, the signifying process is correspondingly thrown into a certain relief. What might be conventionally called 'typical' literary discourse – at least what is commonly thought of as such discourse: the 'poetic' – is characterised by such a 'disturbance' of the normative relations between signifier and signified. The effect of this disturbance is so to highlight and intensify the signifying practice itself as to produce, in Formalist parlance, a 'defamiliarisation' of experience. This is not the case with every kind of literary discourse: it is not true, for example, of much realist or any naturalistic language. But 'poetic' language nonetheless reveals a relation between signifier and signified shared also, if less obviously, by the realist or naturalist text. I mean simply that a statement such as 'Thou still unravished bride of quietness' *self-evidently* belongs to literary discourse, whereas a statement such as 'After a while I went out and left the hospital and walked back to the hotel in the rain' may or may not do so, depending on its context. Both statements in fact belong to literary discourses which lack a real particular referent; it is simply that in the first case this absence inscribes itself in the very letter of the text, which proclaims its lack of a real object in its very internal disproportionment of elements, flaunts its relative autonomy of the real in the formal structures of its proposition. It is the very eloquence of the 'poetic' which alludes to a kind of silence. Realist prose, on the other hand, 'pretends' to a real particular referent in its every phrase, only to unmask that pretence in its status as a complete discourse ('novel'). The 'poetic' is in this sense its concealed truth, parading in its very microstructures the macrostructural character of the realist work.

The literary relations between signifier and signified are not, of course, given once and for all as an invariable absolute. On the contrary, they shift and mutate in response to the determinations of aesthetic ideology, as Roland Barthes demonstrates for a particular span of French literary history in *Le Degré Zéro de L'Écriture*. A text may so 'foreground' its signifiers as to radically deform, distantiate and defamiliarise its signified; or it may strictly curb such excess, in apparent humble conformity to the logic of its 'content'. This aesthetic contrast should not be misread as a political one, as though the former text were necessarily 'progressive' and the latter inevitably 'reactionary'. Defamiliarisation may revitalise an ideology for reactionary ends, and the conformist, 'transparent' text is in part to be judged in the light of that to which it 'conforms'. But the contrast is in any case misleading if it suggests that some texts *really* distantiate their object while others really conform to it. Both statements are metaphorical descriptions of alternative aesthetic effects: they do not articulate a changed general relation between text, ideology and history. No text literally 'conforms itself to its content', adequates its signifiers to some signified distinct from them; what is in question is not the relation between the text and some separable signified, but the relation between textual signification (which is both 'form' and 'content') and those more pervasive significations we name ideology. This is not a relation which can be gauged simply by the degree to which the text *overtly* foregrounds its significations, even though such a practice in particular texts may well produce, and be produced by, a peculiar relation to ideology. For, to repeat, even the 'prosaic' text reproduces – although not in its every phrase – that dominance of signifier over signified paraded by the poem. It reproduces it in its entire structure – in that internal distribution of its elements, characterised by a high degree of relative autonomy, which is possible only because it has no real particular referent.

It remains to resolve a possible ambiguity as to what precisely constitutes the literary work's 'signified'. The signified *within the text* is what I have termed its 'pseudo-real' – the imaginary situations which the text is 'about'. But this pseudo-real is not to be directly correlated with the historically real; it is, rather, an effect or aspect of the text's whole process of signification. What that whole process signifies is ideology, which is itself a signification of history. The relations in question here can be clarified by a simple diagram:

The 'disturbance' of relation between signifier and signified in 'prototypical' literary discourse is an effect of the relation between that discourse as a whole and ideology. It is because the text's materials are ideological rather than historical – because, as it were, the text exists in the 'hollow' it has scooped out between itself and history – that it lacks a real particular referent, and displays that lack in the relative autonomy of its structuration. The 'poetic' text displays it also in its disproportioning of signifier and signified, whereby the absence of a concrete historical object is proclaimed, made manifest, in the very predominance of the signifying process over the 'pseudo-real'.

We need, however, to be more precise both about the ideology which the text works, and the process of that working. To formulate the issue in this way is already to risk falsification, for the text, as I shall argue later, does not simply 'take' ideological materials which are extrinsic to it. Ideology pre-exists the text; but the *ideology of the text* defines, operates and constitutes that ideology in ways unpremeditated, so to speak, by ideology itself. The particular production of ideology which we may term the 'ideology of the text' has no pre-existence: it is identical with the text itself. What is in question here, indeed, is a double relation – not only the objectively determinable relation between text and ideology, but also (and simultaneously) that relation as 'subjectively' flaunted, concealed, intimated or mystified by the text itself. Every text implicitly manifests a relation to its pre-existent materials, suggesting (contrast Trollope and Mallarmé) how far they pre-exist it. Nor is this relation necessarily a single one: for a work may acknowledge its dependence on the pre-existent in some of its elements only to assert a pure autonomy in others.

'Pre-textual' ideology presents itself to the work in diverse forms: in 'ordinary language', accredited symbol and convention, codes of perceptual habit, other artefacts. It offers itself also in more formalised ways: in those particular aesthetic, political, ethical and other formulae which may at once permeate 'ordinary language' yet emerge from it as distinct crystallisations of meaning. That the work may establish a relatively direct relation to such formulae is not to be overlooked. It is true that ideology most typically presents itself to the text as 'life' rather than category, as the immediate stuff of experience rather than as system of concepts. But much of the literature of Christendom, neo-classicism, Stalinism allows ideology to enter the text in relatively 'pure' form, rehearsing its categories in ways which to some degree disengage them from the contingencies of the 'lived'. In such cases we can observe unusually direct relations between:

(i) 'General' ideological categories
(ii) 'General' ideological discourses
(iii) Aesthetic ideological categories
(iv) Aesthetic ideological discourses
(v) Text

In the case of Stalinism, for example, aesthetic categories ('socialist realism') bear a peculiarly direct relation to 'general ideology', producing modes of aesthetic discourse which seem merely to mime 'general' ideological modes. Even with such a work, however, there can be no question of *reducing* textual to ideological discourse. The categories of an ideology produce a series of ideological significations which form the immediate materials of the text; and those significations can be seen as a concrete 'production' of the ideological categories. The study of the text is a study of the production of such produced categories – an analysis of ideological production to the second power. In the relatively 'pure' ideological work, ideological discourses are so produced as to appear 'inverted back' into the categories which give rise to them. This is not to be understood in Hegelian fashion as the text 'universalising' its materials, discovering the general within the particular. It is not in 'raising' the particular to the general that such a work reveals its ideology, but in the very particularity of its operations upon it – in a precise set of mutations and displacements which produces the effect of a simple 'miming'.

There are other texts, however, where the materials appropriated for production are more obviously those of ideology 'at work' – as spontaneously secreted in immediate experience, and so as 'unconscious' of its categorial structure. Ideology here comes to the text intensively *worked*, ready-made for the text's transformative operations. The relation of the literary work to 'ordinary language' is relevant here, for it is in 'ordinary language' that ideology is produced, carried and naturalised, and the text's relation to it is a crucial index of its ideological character. Apart from the case of works whose 'relation' to ordinary language is one of direct negation – those, for example, written in the alien language of an imperial ruling class – every text bears some relation to the common discourse of its society. But there is a clear difference between the text which seems to reproduce it ('seems', since this too is a convention – we have to *learn* how to read such a text) and the work whose devices radically transmute such speech. Nor is it only a question of language in the strict sense: for to say that everything that happens in the text happens in terms of language is equivalent to saying that everything happens in the world because of God. Such a statement is so pervasively applicable as to cancel itself out and leave everything exactly as it was. The linguistic devices of *The Faerie Queene* or *Finnegans Wake* signal a set of mutations of ideological 'discourses' in a wider sense – perceptions, assumptions, symbolisations. Here, by the working of aesthetic ideology, a production of already-produced categories is achieved; and it can be claimed that it is in this production to the second power that the true relation of the text to ideology inheres. The text, through its formal devices, establishes a transformative relation between itself and ideology which allows us to perceive the usually concealed contours of the ideology from which it emerges.

It is this position which Louis Althusser argues, in a well-known passage in *Lenin and Philosophy*:

'*I do not rank real art among the ideologies*, although art does have a quite particular and specific relationship with ideology. . . . Art (I mean authentic art, not works of an average or mediocre level) does not quite give us a *knowledge* in the *strict sense*, it therefore does not replace knowledge (in the modern sense: scientific knowledge), but what it gives us does nevertheless maintain a certain specific *relationship* with knowledge. This relationship is not one of identity but one of difference. Let me explain. I believe that the peculiarity of art is to "make us see", "make us perceive", "make us feel" something which *alludes* to reality. . . . What art makes us *see* . . . is the ideology from which it is born, in which it bathes, from which it detaches itself as art, and to which it *alludes*. . . . Balzac and Solzhenitsyn give us a "view" of the ideology to which their work alludes and with which it is constantly fed, a view which presupposes a *retreat*, an *internal distantiation* from the very ideology from which their novels emerge. They make us "perceive" (but not know) in some sense *from the inside*, the very ideology in which they are held. . . .'[2]

This is a suggestive, radically unsatisfactory statement. To begin with, there is the notable evasion of 'real' and 'authentic' art, as ambiguous in its own way as Lucien Goldmann's concept of the 'valid' text. In both cases, an evaluative judgement is illegitimately inserted into (or snatched out of) what purports to be a scientific account of the structures of art as such. Is it *constitutive* of aesthetic 'authenticity' that the process described here occurs, or does it merely follow from works whose 'authenticity' is to be assessed by other, unexamined criteria? Is the work 'real' because it permits us to perceive the ideology in which it bathes, in which case how, precisely, is this an *aesthetic* judgement? Or is that distantiation one effect of a value which has other determinants? And how, exactly, is this distantiation achieved? Pierre Macherey elaborates the argument by suggesting that it is the effect of the form which the text bestows on ideology;[3] but to leave the matter there is merely to stand convicted of formalism. For if it is true that the text's relation to ideology is crucially effected by its forms, it is not the whole truth.

2. *Lenin and Philosophy* (London, 1971), pp. 203–4.
3. *Pour une Théorie de la Production Littéraire* (Paris, 1974), pp. 77–83.

Althusser and Macherey appear to want to *rescue* and *redeem* the text from the shame of the sheerly ideological; yet in these passages they can do so only by resorting to a nebulously figurative language ('allude', 'see', 'retreat') which lends a merely rhetorical quality to the distinction between 'internal distantiation' and received notions of art's 'transcendence' of ideology. It is as though the aesthetic must still be granted mysteriously privileged status, but now in embarrassedly oblique style. If 'real' art is not to be ranked among the ideologies, does it then form a distinct region within the social formation, additional to the Althusserian categories of the economic, political, ideological and scientific? That indeed would seem a considerable – one might think, excessive – privilege to confer on it. The fact is that Macherey in particular is forced into his quasi-formalist position by the logic of his view of ideology itself. For if ideology is spoken of as 'illusion' (Macherey's term), then it would indeed only be by virtue of some formal *mise-en-scène* that it could approximate to the status of a knowledge. But if ideology is not knowledge, it is not pure fantasy either. The text establishes a relationship with ideology by means of its forms, but does so on the basis of the *character* of the ideology it works. It is the character of that ideology, *in conjunction with* the transmutative operations of the literary forms it produces or enables, which determines the degree to which the text achieves significant or nugatory perceptions. Engels does not attribute Balzac's valid perceptions, nor Lenin Tolstoy's, nor Trotsky Mayakovsky's, merely to the inherently realising, revelatory function of form. The process of the text is the process whereby ideology produces the forms which produce it, thus determining in general both the instruments and devices which work it, and the nature of the work-process itself. It is true that in producing ideology the text grants it a form, but that form is not merely arbitrary, as Macherey's discussion of the text 'giving ideology a form' might suggest. For the form which is given is determined in the last instance by the 'form' of the problematic which the text operates. This is not, to be sure, a *rigorous* determination, for the same ideology may be produced by a variety of literary forms; but it will, none the less, enable a series of possible forms and disable others. The 'materials' worked by the text already offer themselves to it in a certain 'form', as more or less coherently ranked and organised significations which partly constitute what Fredric

Jameson has called the 'logic' of the text's content.[4] It is not, naturally, as though form vanquished the inchoateness of ideology – a proposition parallel to the bourgeois critical assumption that art orders the 'chaos' of experience. Ideology is a relatively coherent formation, which thus broadly determines those structural definitions and distributions of meaning we term literary form; but the forms of the text are not, on the other hand, mere epiphenomena of an ideological 'content'. The form of the ideological content – the categorial structure of the ideological problematic – has a *generally* determining effect on the form of the text, not least in the determination of *genre*. But the form of the text itself is not, of course, identical with its *genre*: it is, rather, a unique production of it.

If the literary work can be seen as an ideological production to the second power, it is possible to see how that double-production may, as it were, partly cancel itself out, invert itself back into an analogue of knowledge. For in producing ideological representations, the text reveals in peculiarly intense, compacted and coherent form the categories from which those representations are produced. 'Reveals' is perhaps a misleading term here, for not every text displays its ideological categories on its surface: the visibility of those categories depends on the text's precise modes of working them, as well as on the nature of the categories themselves. Indeed in most literary works it is an effect of the productive modes to conceal and 'naturalise' ideological categories, dissolving them into the spontaneity of the 'lived'. In this sense, what ideology does to history the literary work raises to the second power, producing as 'natural' the significations by which history naturalises itself; but the work simultaneously reveals (to criticism, if not to the casually inspecting glance) how that naturalness is the effect of a particular production. If the text displays itself as 'natural', it manifests itself equally as constructed artifice; and it is in this duality that its relation to ideology can be discerned.

It is essential, then, to examine in conjuncture two mutually constitutive formations: the nature of the ideology worked by the text and the aesthetic modes of that working. For a text may operate an ideology which contains elements of the real and simultaneously 'dissolve' those elements, in whole or part, by the manner of its

4. See his *Marxism and Form* (Princeton, 1971), pp. 327–40.

working. Conversely, a notably 'impoverished' ideology may be transmuted by aesthetic forms into something approximating to knowledge. More complex situations are also possible. One might say, for example, that a poem like *The Waste Land* emerges from a potentially more 'productive' problematic, in terms of the range and complexity of the questions it is able to pose, than, say, Georgian poetry, but that this potential is 'blocked' or repressed by the peculiar effect of its mythological forms. But it could also be claimed that those forms inhere in the problematic itself, and that it is the poem's dislocatory, experimental devices which transmute that problematic into perceptions normally beyond its scope. Ideology and mode of aesthetic production are both typically complex formations, between whose elements multiple particular relations of homology and contradiction are possible.

A further weakness of Althusser's formulation is what might be called its consumer-centredness. It is as if the *reader* were the final guarantor of the validity of the text – as if it were 'our' (whose?) 'seeing' and 'feeling' the ideology in which the work 'bathes' (ominously gestural terms) which ensures its 'authenticity'. True, it is the work itself which produces such an effect; but because the mechanisms of this process are left unexamined, the focus shifts to the 'reader's response'. The liberal humanist problematic is preserved in different form: it is just that it is now ideology, rather than reality, which is revealed to us in a privileged moment of insight. It is surely necessary here to return to the productive process of the text itself. I have suggested that the relatively 'pure' ideological text so produces ideological discourses as to 'invert them back' into the categories which give rise to them. But other relations between text and ideology are clearly possible: there is no question of a fixed, historically immutable relationship here. Other texts so produce ideological discourses as to display variable degrees of internal conflict and disorder – a disorder produced by those displacements and mutations of ideology enforced upon the text by the necessity to arrive, in accordance with the laws of its aesthetic production, at a 'solution' to its problems. In such a text, the relative coherence of ideological categories is revealed under the form of a concealment – revealed by the very *incoherence* of the text, by the significant disarray into which it is thrown in its efforts to operate its materials in the interests of a 'solution'.

It is important not to take the term 'solution' too literally here. I do not mean by 'solution' simply the determinate answer to an articulate question, which is palpably not the case with much modernist and post-modernist literature. In a less literal sense of the terms, every text can be seen as a 'problem' to which a 'solution' is to be found; and the process of the text is the process of problem-solving. Every text, that is to say, proposes an initial situation which then undergoes some mutation; in every text, something *happens*. This is most obvious in narrative, the simplest structure of which is a–b–c, where b intervenes to mutate a into c; but it is true also of non-narrative works, true even of the tersest Imagist poem. By 'problem', I mean the initial given elements of the text, of which something is to be *made*; and it is only in certain texts (narrative in particular) that this making is formally figured as diachronic. The initial given elements of the text need not be *temporally* initial; and even if they are, this is merely the formal or generic index of a problem-solving which is essentially 'synchronic'. The narrative-structure of *Tom Jones* mutates Tom's initial situation at Paradise Hall into a series of episodes which are then 'resolved' by the novel's final settlement. But this diachronic axis is no more than the index of a 'synchronic' resolution of certain persistent ideological conflicts (liberty/authority, fraternity/hierarchy, charity/prudence and so on) which in adjacent texts of the time – Pope's *Moral Essays*, for example – assume such directly 'synchronic' form. This is not to argue that the diachronic axis is merely contingent, a purely phenomenal level of the text; on the contrary, it is ideologically significant that at a certain conjuncture the 'problem' must be 'chronologised', put in train. But 'problem' and 'solution' are always given together, as alternative descriptions of the work's modes of operation on its ideology. It is not, to repeat, that the text necessarily provides a definite answer to a specific question; but the nature of a 'non-solution' is as significant as the nature of a 'solution'. No text lacks a resolution in the sense of merely stopping: if it is to be a 'finished' text – and strictly speaking there are no others, for that the text is complete as we have it is part of its definition – its 'non-solution' must signify. It is still *this* 'non-solution' rather than that which is at issue – a 'non-solution' determined by the way in which the 'problem' has been posed. In this sense, every text is the answer to its own question, proposing to itself only such problems as it can resolve, or leave unresolved without radically interrogating the terms of its problematic. Problem and solution are synchronic in the sense that the text so works upon its materials as to cast them from the outset into 'resolvable' (or *acceptably* unresolvable) form in the very act of trying to resolve them. It is therefore important to read the text, as it were, backwards – to examine the nature of its 'problems' in the light of its 'solutions'. Given the initial elements of the work, we can already construct from them a typology of ideologically permissible 'solutions'; and this is one of the senses in which it can be said that the work 'determines itself'. Within a certain conjuncture of 'general' and 'aesthetic' ideology, only certain permutations of textual elements will be possible: having posited *a*, the text may then posit either *b* or *c* but not *x*. It is, indeed, in the dual character of the text which results from this – in its combination of suspense and internal logic, openness and closure, free-play and fixity, the provisional and the determinate, that the characteristic experience of *reading* lies.

It is important to grasp here the closeness of relation between the 'ideological' and the 'aesthetic'. The text does not merely 'take' ideological conflicts in order to 'resolve' them aesthetically, for the character of those conflicts is itself overdetermined by the textual modes in which they are produced. The text's mode of resolving a particular ideological conflict may then produce textual conflicts elsewhere – at other levels of the text, for example – which need in turn to be 'processed'. But here the work is 'processing' ideological conflict under the form of resolving specifically *aesthetic* problems, so that the problem-solving process of the text is never merely a matter of its reference outwards to certain pre-existent ideological cruxes. It is, rather, a matter of the 'ideological' presenting itself in the form of the 'aesthetic' and *vice versa* – of an 'aesthetic' solution to ideological conflict producing in its turn an aesthetic problem which demands ideological resolution, and so on. It is not simply that ideology furnishes the 'materials' for the text's formal aesthetic operations; the textual process is, rather, a complex mutual articulation of the two, whereby aesthetic modes so define and determine ideological problems as to be able to continue to reproduce themselves, but only within the limits and subject to the problems which their own overdetermination of the ideological sets. This is one sense in which the processes of conflict and resolution are synchronic rather than diachronic. Every phrase, every image of the text, in so far as it is both in general determined by and exerts a determination on the whole, in so far as it is always both product and producer, destination and departure, is at once an 'answer' and a 'question', mobilising new possibilities of conflict in the very moment of taking the weight of a provisional 'solution'. We may say, then, that the text in this sense 'produces itself' – but produces itself in constant relation to the ideology which permits it such relative autonomy, so that this ceaseless elaboration and recovery of its own lines of meaning is simultaneously the production of a determining ideology. One might say, too, that the text's *relation to itself* is problematical because it is simultaneously a relation to certain ideological problems. The text is thus never at one with itself, for if it were it would have absolutely nothing to say. It is, rather, a process of *becoming* at one with itself – an attempt to overcome the problem of itself, a problem produced by the fact that the text itself is the production, rather than reflection, of an ideological 'solution'.

It may be useful to refer once more at this point to the work of Pierre Macherey. Macherey claims that literary works are internally dissonant, and that this dissonance arises from their peculiar relation to ideology. The distance which separates the work from ideology embodies itself in the internal distance which, so to speak, separates the work from itself, forces it into a ceaseless difference and division of meanings. In putting ideology to work, the text necessarily illuminates the absences, and begins to 'make speak' the silences, of that ideology. The literary text, far from constituting some unified plenitude of meaning, bears inscribed within it the marks of certain determinate absences which twist its various significations into conflict and contradiction. These absences – the '*not-said*' of the work – are precisely what bind it to its ideological problematic: ideology is present in the text in the form of its eloquent silences. The task of criticism, then, is not to situate itself within the same space as the text, allowing it to speak or completing what it necessarily leaves unsaid. On the contrary, its function is to install itself in the very incompleteness of the work in order to *theorise* it – to explain the ideological necessity of those '*not-saids*' which constitute the very principle of its identity. Its object is the *unconsciousness* of the work – that of which it is not, and cannot be, aware. What the text 'says' is not just this or that meaning, but precisely their difference and separation: it articulates the space which both divides and binds together the text's multiple senses. It is criticism's task to demonstrate how the text is thus 'hollowed' by its relation to ideology – how, in putting that ideology to work, it is driven up against those gaps and limits which are the product of ideology's relation to history. An ideology exists because there are certain things which must not be spoken of. In so putting ideology to work, the text begins to illuminate the absences which are the foundation of its articulate discourse. And in doing this, it helps to 'liberate' us from the ideology of which that discourse is the product.

It is worth noting here that these formulations of Macherey suggest the possibility of an encounter between Marxist criticism and the great scientist who has so often figured within such criticism merely as an eloquent silence: Freud. In his *The Interpretation of Dreams* and elsewhere, Freud argues that the analyst of dreams must penetrate the manifest content of the dream to uncover its latent content. But this is not a simple hermeneutical exercise, since the analyst's task is not only to lay bare the meaning of a distorted text, but to expose *the meaning of the text-distortion itself*. Psychoanalysis, that is to say, must reconstruct what Freud calls the '*dream-work*' – the actual process of production of the dream. The 'truth' of the dream lies precisely in its distortion. The analyst must indeed strip off what Freud terms the 'uppermost dream layer', which is the result of a secondary elaboration of the dream by consciousness after the dreamer awakes; but this is simply preparatory to tackling the 'depth' layer of the dream, the symbols which express a latent content in disguised form.

Freud's 'uppermost dream layer' exists to systematise the dream, fill in its gaps and smooth over its contradictions, produce from it a relatively coherent text. But beneath this lies the real, incomplete, self-divided, mutilated text of the dream itself, which resists interpretation – a resistance manifest in the patient's hesitating and circuitous associating, his forgetting of portions of his text. This pressure of resistance, Freud believes, is at the very root of the genesis of the dream, responsible for the 'gaps, obscurities and confusions which may interrupt the continuity of even the finest of dreams'. The dream, as distorted and mutilated text, is a conflict and compromise between unconscious material seeking expression, and the intervention of an ideological censor. The typical consequence of this is that the unconscious is able to say what it wanted, but not in the way it wanted to say it – only in softened, distorted, perhaps unrecognisable form. This dissonance is especially apparent in the dream's gaps: 'the breaks in the text', Freud remarks, 'are places where an interpretation has prevailed which is ego-alien even though a product of the ego.'

Freud's 'uppermost dream layer' corresponds, perhaps, to what Macherey terms 'normative' criticism: that criticism which *refuses* the text as it is, 'corrects' it against a rounded, ideal construction of what it 'might' be, rejects the determinate nature of its partial, conflictual presence. Grasping the text as a mere fictive rehearsal of an ideal object which 'precedes' it, an ideal present within the text as an abiding truth or essence from which it deviates, the typical gesture of 'normative' criticism is to inscribe a 'Could do better' in the work's margin. The 'normative' critical illusion, as such, is merely a displacement of the empiricist fallacy which simply 'receives' the work as a spontaneous given: it is just that 'normative' criticism intervenes to treat and modify the text so that it can be better consumed. The uppermost dream layer, then, is analogous to the literary text as defined by 'normative' criticism, and as defined, as it were, by itself – the text as it would 'want' to appear, as spontaneous, complete and so as ideological. The 'real' dream-text, by contrast, corresponds to the literary text as defined by scientific criticism, and so as 'unconscious' of itself, constituted by that *relation* to ideology which it cannot speak of directly but can only manifest in its mutilations. Both Freud and Macherey explain the text's lacunae and hiatuses by referring the discourse in question to the conditions of its production: indeed Macherey himself draws this parallel, when he comments that Freud situates the meaning of the dream *elsewhere*, outside of itself, in the structure of which it is the product. In the case of both dream and literary text, that structure is not 'microcosmically' present within the discourse, but is precisely what ruptures that discourse into asymmetry; ideology appears 'in' the text as a mode of disorder. The task of both criticism and dream-analysis, then, is to articulate that of which the discourse speaks-without-saying-it – or, more precisely, to examine the distortion-mechanisms which produce that ruptured discourse, to reconstruct the work-process whereby the text suffers an internal displacement by virtue of its relations to its conditions of possibility.

Freud's 'uppermost dream layer' may be taken, perhaps, to correspond to what could be termed the 'phenomenal' text – that self-coherent plenitude of sense which 'spontaneously' offers itself to the inspecting glance as continuously 'readable' discourse. It is this phenomenal presence of the text which, within bourgeois ideology, plays its part in constituting the reader as equivalently self-coherent 'subject', centred in the privileged space of an entirely appropriable meaning. But 'athwart' that phenomenal presence may be constructed the 'real' text, the discourse which the 'phenomenal' text exists to conceal by its constant suturing. The critic is not, of course, a *therapist* of the text: his task is not to cure or complete it, but to explain why it is as it is. Nevertheless, the analogy between criticism and the analysis of dreams is a suggestive one, not least because of the resemblances between text and dream as modes of discourse. The problematical relation between them and their conditions of production results in both cases in an inherently *ambiguous* discourse, such that the terms in which Freud characterises the devices of dream suggest 'literariness' – dream as a degrammaticised language with shifting semantic emphases, operating through 'loosely related compressions', blendings and condensations of its materials which may entail the suspension of elementary logical rules. It is an ambiguity appropriate to the displacement and ellision of meaning, and it is therefore an equally appropriate mode for the literary text. I have argued already that the text's high degree of relative autonomy of the real produces its typical *concretion*, its peculiarly overdetermined concentration of meanings; but this concentration also gives rise to the prototypically ambiguous, polysemic nature of literary language. Because literary discourse has no real particular referent, its significations remain multiple and partly 'open' in a way which enables those displacements and ellisions of meaning occasioned by its relation to ideology.

Macherey's conception of the text–ideology relation is a fertile, suggestive one; but it is also, it must be said, partial. The central concept of *absence* behaves in his work as a theoretical nexus between Marxist and structuralist elements of thought: it allows him, in short, to preserve a high degree of autonomy of the artefact while simultaneously relating it to history. It is, in other words, an absolutely necessary concept if an essentially formalist theory of literary language is to cohabit with historical materialism – if the Russian literary debates of the 1920s are to be transcended at a stroke. But there is not only something curiously Hegelian about conceiving of the work's identity as wholly constituted by what it is not; it is also that an essentially *negative* conception of the text's relation to history, while doubtless posing a salutary countercheck to those heavily 'positive' models employed by some neo-Hegelian and 'vulgar' Marxist theory, runs the danger of its own kind of dogmatism. For it is not invariably true that a text is thrown into grievous internal disarray by its relation to ideology, or that such a relation consists simply in the text's forcing ideology up against the history it denies. We have seen already that there are texts which establish a less 'fraught' relation to ideology, without thereby merely 'reproducing' it. Pope's *Essay on Man* is a highly 'produced' version of an ideology which is not thereby thrown into conflict with itself – where the *acceptable* contradictions ('paradoxes') inherent in the ideology can be negotiated without notable self-mutilation. There are other texts which in working, displacing and transmuting ideological components in the name of a 'solution' display a set of dissonances which do not, however, twist them into severe self-contradiction. In such texts, the ideological discourses selected are often more 'innocent' of direct ideological determination, more impure and ambiguous from this viewpoint, and so, in needing to be produced more rigorously, betray in this act a certain index of recalcitrance to the mode of production. It is as if the ideological categories at issue here do not 'spontaneously' determine their appropriate discourses, but rather 'present' to the aesthetic operation a number of alternatives and indeterminacies – indeterminacies of which they must be 'shorn', but which to a greater or lesser degree may remain clustered around them in the final product. Some of Pope's poetry is again exemplary here: for part of the particular 'aesthetic effect' of that work is the constant dramatic visibility of the mechanisms of aesthetic transmutation, a visibility which is in the same act concealed and 'naturalised'. The text, that is to say, parades an illusion of limited 'freedom' in its materials, as though their specific weight and allusiveness might allow them to escape from submission to aesthetic processing, only to demonstrate that such submission is after all inexorable. Words and phrases gesture to their places in 'pre-textual' discourses only to yield up the inevitability of their textual locus, and so of their place in its specific ideological formation. Or, once again, there are texts where, as Macherey argues, the *mis-en-scène* of ideology produces severe self-divisions of meaning – a work like *The Prelude*, for example, in which an organicist evolutionary ideology is ruptured by starkly epiphanic 'spots of time', recalcitrant material which refuses to be absorbed. Here the 'official' ideology of the text is in contradiction with its modes of producing it, what is said at odds with what is shown. In so far as *The Prelude* draws back from the tragic brink to which its isolated epiphanies allude, its 'official' ideology might be said to triumph; but the reverse might be said of one or two of the 'Lucy' poems, where certain obscure pressures of feeling force their way through to throw the 'official' ideology into radical question. There are, in other words, conflicting ways in which ideology presses the text into disorder; and even here we must discriminate between disorder of *meaning* (or levels of meaning) and disorder of *form*. *The Prelude* is *formally* fissured by its ideological contradictions, unable to rise to the seamless impersonal epic it would wish itself to be: its generic uncertainty, unevenness of texture, haltings and recoveries of narrative and shifts of standpoint are at odds with the consoling evolutionism of its outlook, indices of its lack of unity with itself. But the ideological conflicts of some of the 'Lucy' poems, by contrast, are illuminated precisely by the unruffled intactness of their form.

To argue for differential relations between text and ideology is not to argue for eclecticism. It is to claim that those relations are historically mutable – as mutable as 'general' and 'aesthetic' ideologies themselves – and therefore demand specific historical definition. Indeed such variability can be traced in the career of a single author: I have in mind Thomas Hardy. *Under The Greenwood Tree* produces a 'pastoral' ideology and in doing so displays its limits, dramatising forms of social mobility, disruption and dissolution which such an ideology cannot encompass. But these elements are not permitted radically to subvert the pastoral form, which, as the novel's partly self-ironic subtitle suggests ('A Rural Painting of the Dutch School'), preserves itself by a certain distantiation of what it is unable to absorb. *Far from the Madding Crowd* is a more overtly ironic title, appropriate for a novel which brings more intensively realist techniques to bear on 'pastoral' ideology, throws it into radical self-question yet uncertainly endorses it in its final refusal of tragedy. The formal dissonances of *The Return of the Native* and *The Mayor of Casterbridge*, typically 'impure' Hardyesque compounds of pastoral, mythology, 'classical' tragedy and fictional realism, are the product of a definitive ideological transcendence of pastoral which is still to find its complete formal consummation – as in *The Wood-landers* and *Tess of the D'Urbervilles* – in a fully elaborated realism. No sooner does Hardy consummate such a relation, however, than he begins in *Jude the Obscure* to force it into self-contradiction by pressing beyond it into fictional modes which highlight the limits of realism itself. The dramatic internal dislocations and contradictions of *Jude the Obscure* are indeed the effect of its forcing the ideology it operates to an extreme limit; but before Hardy reaches this point, his fiction demonstrates a series of alternative relations between text and ideology.

Macherey insists that the contradictions of the text are not to be grasped as the reflection of real historical contradictions. On the contrary: textual contradictions result precisely from the *absence* of such a reflection – from the contortive effect on the work of the ideology which interposes itself between the work and history. But if the text's internal conflicts are not the reflection of historical contradictions, neither are they the reflection of ideological ones. For strictly speaking there can be no contradiction *within* ideology, since its function is precisely to eradicate it. There can be contra-diction only between ideology and what it occludes – history itself. Textual dissonances, then, are the effect of the work's *production* of ideology. The text *puts* the ideology into contradiction, discloses the limits and absences which mark its relation to history, and in doing so puts itself into question, producing a lack and disorder within itself. But there is a danger here of lapsing into too expansionist and 'totalitarian' a conception of ideology. For it is not as though ideology is always and everywhere a seamless imaginary whole – always and everywhere 'at its best'. Ideology, seen from within, has no outside; in this sense one does not transgress its outer limits as one crosses a geographical boundary. The threshold of ideology is also an internal limit: ideological space is curved like space itself, and history lies beyond it as only God could lie beyond the universe. It is not possible to effect a 'passage' from the heart of ideology beyond its boundaries, for from that vantage-point there are no boundaries to be transgressed; ideology curves back upon itself, creating outside of itself a void which cannot be explored because it is, precisely, nothing. If it is impossible to cross its frontiers from within, it is because those frontiers – since nothing lies beyond them – have no existence. To travel indefinitely along any one track of ideological meaning is not to encounter an ultimate threshold of articulation but to describe an arc which returns one inexorably to one's starting-point. In discovering its demarcations, ideology discovers its self-dissolution; it cannot survive the 'culture shock' consequent on its stumbling into alien territory adjacent to itself. In discovering such territory, ideology finds its *homeland*, and can return to it only to die. It cannot survive the traumatic recognition of its own repressed parentage – the truth that it is not after all self-reproductive but was historically brought to birth, the scandal that, before it ever was, history existed. Such a recognition may be forced upon ideology by the unwelcome discovery of a rival sibling – an antagonistic ideology which reveals to it the secret of its own birth. That secret may be spoken directly; but it may also be that ideology, in discerning the moment when its rival emerged from the womb of history, is thereby constrained to acknowledge itself as an offspring of the same parent. It is not, in other words, simply by virtue of ideology being forced up against the wall of history by the literary text that it is terrorised into handing over its secrets. Its contradictions may be forced from it by its historically determined encounter with another ideology, or ideological sub-ensemble; indeed it is possible to claim that it is in such historical conjunctures that the moment of genesis of much major literature is to be found. It is true that Shakespearean drama does not merely 'reproduce' a conflict of historical ideologies; but neither does it merely press a particular ideology to the point where it betrays its significant silences. Rather, it produces, from a specific standpoint within it, the severe contradictions of an ideological formation characterised by a peculiarly high degree of 'dissolution' – dissolution produced by a conflict of antagonistic ideologies appropriate to a particular stage of class-struggle.

The guarantor of a scientific criticism is the science of ideological formations. It is only on the basis of such a science that such a criticism could possibly be established – only by the assurance of a knowledge of ideology that we can claim a knowledge of literary texts. This is not to say that scientific criticism is merely an 'application' of historical materialism to literature. Criticism is a specific element of the theory of superstructures, which studies the particular

laws of its proper object; its task is not to study the laws of ideological formations, but the laws of the production of ideological
discourses as literature.

If literary texts were reducible to their ideological formations,
then criticism would indeed be no more than a specific application
of the science of those formations. The more notorious forms of such
reductionism have largely disappeared from Marxist criticism; but
there have arisen more sophisticated, and so more tempting versions
of the method to take their place. To conceive of the literary work
as an enigmatic 'message' whose 'code' is to be deciphered is one
such contemporary version, resting, as Pierre Macherey has argued,
on an essentially Platonic notion of the artefact. If the text is an
encoded message then it operates merely as an intermediary, as the
simulacrum of a concealed structure; and certain kinds of structuralist analysis, in elaborating a 'copy' of that structure, hence become
the simulacrum of a simulacrum. The writer's production is merely
the *appearance* of a production, since its true object lies behind or
within it; to criticise, therefore, is to reduce the 'externality' of the
text to the structure secreted in its 'interior'.

But the text is not the phenomenon of an ideological essence, the
microstructure of a macrostructure; the ideology to which the text
belongs does not figure within it as its 'deep structure'. The problematic of Lucien Goldmann's 'genetic structuralism' presses such an
error to an exemplary extreme: for here the most 'valid' work is
that which most 'purely' transposes to the plane of 'imaginary
creation' the structure of the 'world view' of a social group or class.
The text, in Goldmann's hands, is rudely robbed of its materiality,
reduced to no more than the microcosm of a mental structure. Not
only is it untrue, *pace* Goldmann, that historically disparate works
may 'express' the same 'world view'; it is not necessarily true by
any means that the works of the same author will belong to the same
ideology. And even texts which do belong to the same ideology will
not 'give' it in the same way – indeed may give it in such divergent
ways that we can properly speak of the 'ideology of the text', as a
uniquely constituted world of representations. Such a world, far
from reflecting ideology in miniature, actively extends and elaborates
it, becoming a constitutive element of its self-reproduction. In this
sense, to speak of the 'relation' between text and ideology is itself to
risk posing the issue too extrinsically. For it is less a question of two

externally related phenomena than of a 'relationship of difference' established by the text *within* ideology – a relationship which, *precisely because* it produces in the text a high degree of relative autonomy, enables it to become an inherent constituent of ideological reproduction. One might even risk saying that the text is the process whereby ideology enters into a mode of relation with itself peculiarly enabling of its self-reproduction. Such a formulation can easily be misunderstood in Hegelian terms – the text as a point where the spirit of ideology enters upon material incarnation only to reappropriate itself, literature as a mere passage or transaction within ideology itself. It is to avoid such a misconception that we need to speak of a relation of production between text and ideology; but it is equally important not to grasp that relation as merely external. An analogy may perhaps be found in the relation of ideology itself to the capitalist mode of production. Ideology is not merely a 'set of representations' externally related to that mode of production: on the contrary, it has its base in those very economic forms which cannot but conceal the truth of capitalist production in their phenomenal presence. The relation between ideology and mode of production, then, is an *internal* one; but at the same time ideology, by virtue of an 'internal distantiation', constitutes itself as a relatively autonomous formation. In a parallel way, the literary text is constituted as a relatively autonomous formation on the basis of the internal bonds which leash it to ideology.

This complex relation of text to ideology, whereby the text is neither an epiphenomenon of ideology nor a wholly autonomous element, is relevant to the question of the text's 'structure'. The text can be spoken of as having a structure, even if it is a structure constituted not by symmetry but by rupture and decentrement. For this itself, in so far as the distances and conflicts between its diverse elements are determinate rather than opaque, constitutes a structure of a specific kind. Yet this structure is not to be seen as a microcosm or cryptogram of ideology; ideology is not the 'truth' of the text, any more than the dramatic text is the 'truth' of the dramatic performance. The 'truth' of the text is not an essence but a practice – the practice of its relation to ideology, and in terms of that to history. On the basis of this practice, the text constitutes itself as a structure: it destructures ideology in order to reconstitute it on its own relatively autonomous terms, in order to process and recast it in aesthetic production, at the same time as it is itself destructured to variable degrees by the effect of ideology upon it. In this destructuring practice, the text encounters ideology as a relatively structured formation which presses upon its own particular valencies and relations, confronts it with a 'concrete logic' which forms the outer perimeter of the text's own self-production. The text works, now with, now against the variable pressure of these valencies, finding itself able to admit one ideological element in relatively unprocessed form but finding therefore the need to displace or recast another, struggling against its recalcitrance and producing, in that struggle, new problems for itself. In this way the text disorders ideology to produce an internal order which may then occasion fresh disorder both in itself and in the ideology. This complex movement cannot be imaged as the 'structure of the text' transposing or reproducing the 'structure of the ideology': it can only be grasped as a ceaseless reciprocal *operation* of text on ideology and ideology on text, a mutual structuring and destructuring in which the text constantly overdetermines its own determinations. The structure of the text is then the *product* of this process, not the reflection of its ideological environs. The 'logic of the text' is not a discourse which doubles the 'logic of ideology'; it is, rather, a logic constructed '*athwart*' that more encompassing logic.

Yet if textual structure does not reproduce ideological structure, it is important on the other hand to avoid falling into a fresh empiricism of the literary object. There is, as I have argued, a particular 'ideology of the text', reducible to neither 'general' nor 'authorial' ideologies, which in any two texts would be the same only if those texts were verbally identical. In this sense it is appropriate to speak of every author, and each text of every author, as yielding a 'different' ideology. The ideology of Wycherley is not that of Etheredge, nor is the ideology of *The Country Wife* that of *The Plain Dealer*. Yet there is nothing to be gained in the end by arguing that there are as many ideologies as there are texts – a claim as vacuous as the proposition that there are as many ideologies as there are individual subjects in class-society. We may recircle at this point to the analogy of text and dramatic performance with which we began. It is true, figuratively speaking, that two different productions of *Othello* yield different texts; but the critical analysis of those productions is possible only if they are placed in relation to the one determinate Shakespearean text. Similarly, it is not a *reduction* of the works of Wycherley and Etheredge to situate them on the same ideological terrain: it is only by doing so that their differences, and so their unique identities, can be established. An empiricism of the literary text entails, inevitably, a nominalism of ideology.

The relation between text and ideology, then, can be generally summarised as follows. Ideology presents itself to the text as a set of significations which are already articulated in a certain *form* or series of forms, displaying certain general structural relations. Ideology also presents to the text a determinate series of specific modes and mechanisms of aesthetic production – an ideologically determined set of possible modes of aesthetically producing ideological significations. These specific modes are themselves generally determined by the structural forms 'naturally' assumed by ideology: they stand in determinate relations of degrees of conflict or homology with the general forms of perception and representation inherent in the structure of the ideological significations themselves. They may be historically and ideologically 'given together' with those general forms, as a particular mode of narrative is given together with a general ideological form of representing 'individual progress', or they may be historically and ideologically non-synchronous with such general representational forms. Since the text is generally a complex unity of such modes of aesthetic production, it may therefore incorporate a set of differential, mutually conflictual relations to the general forms given to it by the structure of its significations. It may not, in this sense, be historically identical with itself. These aesthetic modes of production, on the basis of the determination of the general representional forms of the ideology, then 'produce' a set of ideological significations which are themselves the product of certain general ideological categories – categories which articulate such significations in a certain form. In producing such significations, the productive forms at once 'pre-constitute' them – that is to say, partly determine *which* significations are to be produced – and so operate on those selected as to displace, recast and mutate them according to the relatively autonomous laws of its own aesthetic modes, on the basis of those modes' ideological determination and of the specific form and character of the ideological significations put to work. This process of displacement and mutation, whereby the 'aesthetic' produces the 'ideological' on the basis of an ideological determination overdetermined by the aesthetic itself, reveals itself to criticism as a complex series of transactions between text and ideology – transactions which figure in the text as a process of more or less visible conflicts produced, resolved and thereby reproduced. It is in this process that something of the general structure of that process of the production of social significations which is ideology is laid bare. In yielding up to criticism the ideologically determined conventionality of its modes of constructing sense, the text at the same time obliquely illuminates the relation of that ideology to real history.

Literature, one might argue, is the most revealing mode of experiential access to ideology that we possess. It is in literature, above all, that we observe in a peculiarly complex, coherent, intensive and immediate fashion the workings of ideology in the textures of lived experience of class-societies. It is a mode of access more immediate than that of science, and more coherent than that normally available in daily living itself. Literature presents itself in this sense as 'midway' between the distancing rigour of scientific knowledge and the vivid but loose contingencies of the 'lived' itself. Unlike science, literature appropriates the real as it is given in ideological forms, but does so in a way which produces an illusion of the spontaneously, unmediatedly real. It is thus more removed from the real than science, yet appears closer to it. Like science, literature appropriates its object by the deployment of certain categories and protocols – in its case, *genre*, symbol, convention and so on. As with science, these categories are themselves the elaborated product of perception and representation; but in the case of literature that elaboration is not carried to the point of producing *concepts* – rather to the point of certain forms which, while performing an *analogous* function to that of conceptual categories in science, tend simultaneously to conceal and naturalise themselves, standing in apparently intimate, spontaneous relation to the 'materials' they produce. That relation is itself ideologically variable; but it is a prototypical effect of literature to partly 'dissolve' its modes of production into the 'concrete life' which is their product. Like private property, the literary text thus appears as a 'natural' object, typically denying the determinants of its productive process. The function of criticism is to refuse the spontaneous presence of the work – to deny that 'naturalness' in order to make its real determinants appear.

4

Ideology and Literary Form

I have tried in the preceding chapters to examine the critical situation in which this study intervenes, to outline a systematic conceptual topography of the field of study, and to provide a detailed analysis of the relations between text and ideology. I want now to study those relations as they manifest themselves in a particular sector of English literary history from Matthew Arnold to D. H. Lawrence.

Bourgeois ideology in nineteenth-century England confronted a severe problem. Nurtured in the sparse soil of Utilitarianism, it was unable to produce a set of potently affective mythologies which might permeate the texture of lived experience of English society. It needed, therefore, to have constant resort to the Romantic humanist heritage – to that nebulous compound of Burkean conservatism and German idealism, transmitted by the later Coleridge to Carlyle, Disraeli, Arnold and Ruskin, which has become known as the 'Culture and Society' tradition. It was a tradition which offered an idealist critique of bourgeois social relations, coupled with a consecration of the rights of capital. The peculiar complexity of English nineteenth-century ideology, founded on a complex conjuncture of bourgeois and aristocratic classes within the dominant bloc, lies in part in this contradictory unity between what Antonio Gramsci refers to as 'organic' and 'traditional' elements.[1] An impoverished

1. For Gramsci, 'organic' intellectuals are those who come into existence on the basis of an emergent social class, but who then confront – and need to vanquish and assimilate – those 'traditional' intellectual categories which survive from previous social conditions. Gramsci argues, significantly enough for the English tradition, that 'The popularised traditional type of intellectual is represented by the literary man, the philosopher, the artist' *Selections from the Prison Notebooks*, p. 9). It is important to distinguish Gramsci's use of the term 'organic' from the meaning I assign to it in this essay.

empiricism, unable to rise to the level of an ideology proper, is driven to exploit the fertile symbolic resources of Romantic human- ism, drawing on its metaphysical sanctions and quasi-feudalist social models to ratify bourgeois property relations. The 'Culture and Society' tradition is the literary record of this ideological conjuncture; John Stuart Mill, mechanistically harnessing Coleridge to Bentham in the late eighteen-thirties, provides one of its more palpable instances.[2]

Gramsci, indeed, has commented directly on this ideological formation in nineteenth-century England. 'There is a very extensive category of organic intellectuals – those, that is, who come into existence on the same industrial terrain as the economic group – but in the higher sphere we find that the old land-owning class preserves its position of virtual monopoly. It loses its economic supremacy and is assimilated as "traditional intellectuals" and as directive (*dirigente*) group by the new group in power. The old land-owning aristocracy is joined to the industrialists by a kind of suture which is precisely that which in other countries unites the traditional intellectuals with the new dominant classes.'[3]

One aspect of this assimilation can be seen in bourgeois ideology's growing dependence on 'organicist' concepts of society.[4] As Victorian capitalism assumes increasingly corporate forms, it turns to the social and aesthetic organicism of the Romantic humanist tradition, discovering in art models of totality and affectivity relevant to its ideological requirements. During the second half of the century, the initially poetic notion of 'organic form' becomes progressively extended to the dominant literary mode of the time, fiction. A serious aesthetics of fiction consequently develops, to discover its major ideologue at the end of the century in Henry James.[5] This essay will

2. See F. R. Leavis (ed.), *Mill on Bentham and Coleridge* (London, 1950). Eric Hobsbawm has noted the ideological limitations of 'pure' Utilitarianism – how its demystification of 'natural rights' could seriously weaken the force of 'metaphysical' sanctions in the defence of property, substituting for them the considerably less powerful, politically more volatile category of 'utility'. (*The Age of Revolution: Europe 1789–1848*, London, 1964, p. 236.)

3. *Selections from the Prison Notebooks*, ed. Quintin Hoare and Geoffrey Nowell Smith (London, 1971), p. 18.

4. I use 'organic' and 'organicism' to signify social and aesthetic forma- tions with the supposedly spontaneous unity of natural life-forms, and more generally to denote symmetrically integrated systems characterised by the harmonious interdependence of their component elements.

survey, in skeletal and schematic form, some relations between a sector of the major literature of the last century and the ideological formations in which it is set; it will do so by taking the concept of 'organic form' as one crucial nexus between history and literary production.[6]

1. Matthew Arnold

The assimilation of 'traditional' to 'organic' intellectuals of which Gramsci speaks is the key to the historic significance of that powerful Victorian poet, critic and ideologue, Matthew Arnold. Arnold, apostle of Culture and scourge of bourgeois philistinism, has always exercised a potent influence on modern liberals and even on socialists; did he not claim, after all, that Culture 'seeks to do away with classes', that 'the men of culture are the true apostles of equality'?[7] Yet Arnold's project is not, need one say, the revolutionary abolition of class-society. Quite the reverse: it is to effect a radical realignment of class-forces within the ruling bloc of Victorian England, so as more effectively to incorporate the proletariat. The thrust of Arnold's social criticism is to convert a visionless, sectarian bourgeoisie, pragmatically sunk in its own material interests, into a truly *hegemonic* class – a class with cultural resources adequate to the predominance it has come to hold in history. For Arnold, the

5. The notion of fiction as organic form is not, however, a merely 'super-structural' matter. By the time of James, changes in the material mode of literary production meant a shift from the densely populated 'three-decker' novel, with its diffuse, multiple plots, to the more 'organic' single volume. We have here, indeed, a singularly complex instance of the conjuncture between the capitalist mode of production in general, the literary mode of production, 'aesthetic' ideology, and the demands of the dominant ideology.

6. I must apologise for the somewhat heterogeneous quality of the materials examined in this chapter, embracing as they do social criticism, fiction and poetry, as well as writers whose relation to English society may well seem highly tangential. Yet that tangentiality, as I hope will become apparent, is part of my point; and the unity of the materials studied here lies primarily in the *theme* of organicism. It is this thematic coherence which at one or two points dictates a reversal of literary chronology – as, for example, with James and Conrad, where James seems to me to extend organicist notions in new directions.

7. *Culture and Anarchy*, ed. Ian Gregor (Indianapolis and New York, 1971), p. 56.

aristocracy is rapidly losing political hegemony, but its historical successor, the bourgeoisie, is disastrously unprepared to assume it.[8] He insists, accordingly, on the need for the middle class to attain to more corporate, cultivated forms, and to do so by enshrining itself in a civilising state educational system. What Antonio Gramsci demands for the modern proletariat – that it should achieve 'moral and intellectual leadership' as well as material power – Matthew Arnold seeks for the Victorian bourgeoisie. The proletariat, Gramsci argues in *The Modern Prince*, 'alongside the problem of the conquest of political power and of economic power must, just as it has thought about organising itself for politics and for economics, think also about organising itself for culture'.[9] Arnold's own programme could hardly be more deftly formulated.

It is this ideological necessity which underlies Arnold's apparently altruistic efforts to 'Hellenise' his stiff-necked fellow-bourgeois. State-established schools, by linking the middle class to 'the best culture of their nation', will confer on them 'a greatness and a noble spirit, which the tone of these classes is not of itself at present adequate to impart'.[10] Such an enterprise, Arnold claims, 'would really augment their self-respect and moral force; it would truly fuse them with the class above, and tend to bring about for them the equality which they are entitled to desire.'[11] The bourgeoisie is bereft of that pervasive spiritual predominance which has ratified aristocratic rule; unless it can rapidly achieve such cultural supremacy, installing itself as a truly national class at the 'intellectual centre' of society, it will fail in its historical mission of politically incorporating the class it exploits:

'It is of itself a serious calamity for a nation that its tone of feeling

8. Arnold is in fact significantly inconsistent about which class actually exercises political hegemony in England. His usual position – the result of an inability to distinguish real hegemony from the administration of the state apparatus – is that the aristocracy are still the dominant class. Indeed as late as 1879 he is writing that 'The middle classes cannot assume rule as they are at present – it is impossible' ('Ecce, Convertimur ad Gentes', *Matthew Arnold: English Literature and Irish Politics*, ed. R. H. Super (Ann Arbor, 1973), p. 17). In *Friendship's Garland*, on the other hand, he remarks that the aristocracy administer and the middle class govern.

9. *Selections from the Prison Notebooks.*

10. *The Popular Education of France*, in *Democratic Education*, ed. R. H. Super (Ann Arbor, 1962), p. 22.

11. *ibid.*, p. 23.

106

and grandeur of spirit should be lowered or dulled. But the calamity appears far more serious still when we consider that the middle classes, remaining as they are now, with their narrow, harsh, un-intelligent, and unattractive spirit and culture, will almost certainly fail to mould or assimilate the masses below them, whose sympathies are at the present moment actually wider and more liberal than theirs. They arrive, these masses, eager to enter into possession of the world, to gain a more vivid sense of their own life and activity. In this their irrepressible development, their natural educators and initiators are those immediately above them, the middle classes. If these classes cannot win their sympathy or give them their direction, society is in danger of falling into anarchy.'[12]

The bourgeoisie, then, must appropriate the civilised aesthetic heri-tage of a failing aristocracy in order to equip itself with an ideology (Culture) capable of penetrating the masses. In a 'cultured, liberal-ised, ennobled, transformed middle class', the proletariat will have 'a point towards which it may with joy direct its aspirations'.[13]

Arnold's notion of class hegemony, it should be noted at once, is theoretically invalid. It is, indeed, a classic illustration of that historicist error which grasps ideology as the 'world view' of a 'class-subject', a spiritual vision imposed by that class on society as a whole.[14] Yet Arnold's argument as a whole marks a significant mutation in nineteenth-century liberalism. As Victorian capitalism is driven to transcend its earlier individualist phase and organise itself into more corporate forms, so the classical liberalism which finds a late, defeated expression in John Stuart Mill's *On Liberty* (1859) suffers a parallel transformation. Arnold believes that 'all tendencies of human nature are in themselves vital and profitable';[15] but it is now imperative to harmonise them within a cohesive, con-flict-free order – within, in a word, Culture. Spiritual *laissez-faire* is historically obsolete; it must yield to a faith in 'the nation in its collective and corporate character, entrusted with stringent powers for the general advantage, and controlling individual wills in the

12. *ibid.*, p. 26.
13. *ibid.*, pp. 322, 324.
14. For a criticism of this conception of ideology, see Nicos Poulantzas, *Political Power and Social Classes* (London, 1973), pp. 195–224.
15. *The Study of Celtic Literature*, in *Lectures and Essays in Criticism*, ed. R. H. Super (Ann Arbor, 1962), p. 348.

name of an interest wider than that of individuals'.[16] A bourgeoisie sunk in individualist dogmatism must now consider whether state action, 'which was once dangerous, may [not] become, not only without danger in itself, but the means of helping us against dangers from another quarter'.[17]

The corporate state, then, is the social locus of Culture – of that symmetrical totality of impulses which is the organic form of a civilisation. Yet if Arnold is in this sense in advance of his age, a 'Liberal of the future'[18] bearing the new needs of the bourgeois state, he can be so precisely because he is in another sense reactionary. If his critique of bourgeois pragmatism stems from the sensed need for a more richly elaborated ideology, it springs also from a traditionalist conception of culture as 'an inward condition of the mind and spirit . . . at variance with the mechanical and material civilisation in esteem with us'.[19] The 'progressive' Inspector of Schools, and the patrician Professor of Poetry, both stand in conflict with conventional bourgeois liberalism; they meet in the aestheticised sociology of *Culture and Anarchy*.

Arnold's concern for the aesthetic meanings of Culture is both productive and disabling for the ideological ends he serves. Productive, in that art offers a prototype of how human subjects are spontaneously, subconsciously *affected*, and thus is relevant to the problem of ideology in general. Disabling, in that the consequence of such an intuitive aesthetics is a politically catastrophic vagueness. Arnold correctly perceives that ideologies establish themselves chiefly through image and representation rather than through systems of doctrine: Culture, in contrast with 'Jacobinism', is eternally dissatisfied with 'the men of a system, of disciples, of a school; with men like Comte, or the late Mr. Buckle, or Mr. Mill'.[20] Indeed it is precisely divisive rationalist debate over 'doctrines' which threatens to destroy those instinctual pieties and spiritual allegiances which ideology must

16. *Culture and Anarchy*, p. 60.
17. *Democratic Education*, p. 4.
18. His own description of himself in 'The Future of Liberalism', *English Literature and Irish Politics*, p. 138.
19. *Culture and Anarchy*, p. 38. Arnold's description of the English class-structure – Barbarians, Philistines, Populace – itself rests on an essentially aristocratic notion of 'rank'; he has no concept of social class as an inherently *relational* reality.
20. *Culture and Anarchy*, p. 54.

nurture. Doctrine, then, must yield to poetry, literature must oust dogma:

'The future of poetry is immense, because in poetry, where it is worthy of its highest destinies, our race, as time goes on, will find an ever surer and surer stay. There is not a creed which is not shaken, not an accredited dogma which is not shown to be questionable, not a received tradition which does not threaten to dissolve. . . . More and more mankind will discover that we have to turn to poetry to interpret life for us, to console us, to sustain us. Without poetry, our science will appear incomplete; and most of what now passes for religion and philosophy will be replaced by poetry. . . . The day will come when we shall wonder at ourselves for having trusted to them, for having taken them seriously; and the more we perceive their hollowness, the more we shall prize "the breath and finer spirit of knowledge" offered to us by poetry.'[21]

'Poetry', that is to say, is the final resort of a society in dire ideological crisis, replacing criticism with consolation, the analytic with the affective, the subversive with the sustaining. As such, it comes to denote less a particular literary practice than the mode of operation of ideology in general. Yet Poetry, like Culture, is thereby emptied of content in direct proportion to its all-pervasiveness, as Frederic Harrison perceived in his devastating parody of *Culture and Anarchy*:

'There is harmony, but no system; instinct, but no logic; eternal growth, and no maturity; everlasting movement, and nothing acquiesced in; perpetual opening of all questions, and answering of none; infinite possibilities of everything; the becoming all things, the being nothing.'[22]

It is a theoretical nullity obvious enough in Arnold's 'touchstones' concept of criticism, in which an entirely intuitive response to some ghostly resonance supposedly common to a handful of poetic images ripped from their aesthetic and historical contexts is solemnly elevated into an absolute measure of literary evaluation.

Culture and Anarchy opposed the claims of 'Hellenism' to 'Hebraism', liberal cultivation to moral commitment, in a drive to

21. 'The Study of Poetry', *English Literature and Irish Politics*, pp. 161–2.
22. 'Culture: A Dialogue', *Fortnightly Review*, November 1867.

deepen the spiritual hegemony of the middle class. Yet in doing so it risked liberalising out of existence the very 'absolute' moral values which in practice sustained bourgeois hegemony. In the 'theological' works which follow *Culture and Anarchy*, then, Arnold needs to counterbalance Hellenism with the Hebraistic virtues of duty, obedience and submission – virtues whereby a dangerously rationalistic working class may be ideologically integrated into political society. Many of the masses, Arnold complains in *God and the Bible*, have espoused a sort of revolutionary deism, based on the supposed 'rights of man' and hostile to all traditional culture. The essential corrective is Christianity: man in Christ knows duties rather than rights, surrendering himself to the 'sweet reasonableness' of a corporate order of divine law. Yet if the masses are to be reclaimed from 'Jacobinism', much unacceptable religious doctrine will need to be poeticised away. The proletariat have turned from the Bible, Arnold remarks in *Literature and Dogma*, because of the spurious theological categories in which it is tricked out. A wholesale demythologisation is therefore crucial: the scriptures must be stripped to a suggestive poetic structure for shoring up a conservative social morality. A Hellenised religion must become the handmaiden of a Hebraistic ethics.

One of the more discreditable facts about Matthew Arnold was his refusal to support an authentic demythologiser of his own day, Bishop John William Colenso. Arnold criticised Colenso, as Lionel Trilling has pointed out, because he believed that 'the factory operatives whom Colenso had in mind could not possibly be edified – that is, their spirits could not be raised, their moral sense heightened nor their religious faith strengthened – by this work'.[23] Colenso's scriptural questionings are ideologically damaging: 'The great mass of the human race have to be softened and humanised through their heart and imagination, before any soil can be found in them where knowledge may strike living roots . . . only when [ideas] reach them in this manner do they adjust themselves to their practice without convulsing it.'[24] Colenso, in short, is unpoetical and so politically dangerous: his rationalist critique of the Bible checks that dissolution of dogma to image which alone can infiltrate proletarian sensibilities,

23. *Matthew Arnold* (New York, 1949), p. 211.
24. 'The Bishop and the Philosopher', *Macmillan's Magazine*, January 1863.

assuring rather than disrupting, soothing rather than subverting. If Culture is too elusive and élitist an instrument for this pressing task, then religion – traditionally one of the most potent and pervasive modes of ideological control – must be refurbished and transformed for this end. Arnold's anxieties over Colenso recall his fears, recorded in the Preface to his *Poems* of 1853, about the spiritually undermining effects of his own earlier poetry. He rejects *Empedocles on Etna* from that volume because it seems calculated to depress rather than to elevate the reader; true poetry must dispense 'disinterested objectivity' rather than gloom and neurosis, appealing to 'those elementary feelings which subsist permanently in the race, and which are independent of time'.[25] 'Moral grandeur' must combat 'spiritual discomfort': poetry must become the ideological resolution of real contradictions.

2. George Eliot

To turn from Matthew Arnold to George Eliot is to see in peculiarly complex form some of the ideological conflicts which Arnold's idea of Culture is intended to resolve. Eliot's literary career, from her translation of Strauss's *Das Leben Jesu* (1846) to *Daniel Deronda* (1876), is almost exactly coterminous with the period of Victorian prosperity which follows the severe depression and fierce class-struggles of the eighteen-thirties and forties. During this period productive output increased spectacularly, Britain's volume of world trade grew rapidly, and money-wages probably rose by at least a third between 1850 and 1870. A familiar political consequence of this prosperity was a partial though marked incorporation of the working class. From the mid-century onwards, until the resurgence of proletarian militancy in the depressed eighties, corporatism becomes a prominent characteristic of wide areas of the working-class movement.[26] Having defeated the first wave of working-class militancy,

25. *On The Classical Tradition*, ed. R. H. Super (Ann Arbor, 1960), p. 4.
26. The forms of that increasing corporatism from the mid-century onwards are familiar: the large-scale expansion of industrial units and the advent of the 'high farming' period of extensive organised agriculture, the growth of capitalist partnerships and joint-stock enterprises, the railway amalgamations, the gradual emergence of an increasingly centralised state bureaucracy in such spheres as education and public health. Corresponding to these developments

the industrial bourgeoisie had begun by 1850 to consolidate its victory. Sections of the working class advanced economically, only to become at each stage politically incorporated. On the eve of the second Reform Bill, R. H. Hutton argued in *Essays in Reform* (1867) that the trade unions had taught the workers the value of cooperation, sacrifice and solidarity, and that this principle might be usefully integrated into society as a whole. Through the unions, the working class had come to appreciate the value of true government and to distrust 'mere scattered energies'. This 'class-patriotism' must at all costs be channelled to national account; the spirit of trade unionism must be grafted 'into the richer growth of our national politics'.[27]

The ideological matrix of George Eliot's fiction is set by the increasingly corporate character of Victorian capitalism and its political apparatus. Eliot's work attempts to resolve a structural conflict between two forms of mid-Victorian ideology: between a progressively muted Romantic individualism, concerned with the untrammelled evolution of the 'free spirit', and certain 'higher', corporate ideological modes. These higher modes (essentially, Feuerbachian humanism and scientific rationalism) seek to identify the immutable social laws to which Romantic individualism, if it is to avoid both ethical anarchy and social disruption, must conform. In principle, it is possible for Romantic individualism to do so without betraying its own values. For if it is true on the one hand that scientific rationalism, in judiciously curbing the disruptive tendencies of Benthamite egoism, also obstructs Romantic self-expression, it is also true that it reveals certain historically progressive laws with which the developing individual may imaginatively unite. Moreover, the Religion of Humanity imbues scientific law with Romantic humanist spirit, discovering that law inscribed in the very passions and pieties of men. Unlike the obsessively abstract, systemic

are the corporatist forms assumed by bourgeois ideology (Positivism, Christian socialism, neo-feudalism, neo-Hegelianism and so on), and by wide sections of the working-class movement: conciliatory trade unionism, cooperative and friendly societies, saving banks etc.

27. There is an untypically close correlation between this transition in the class-struggle and a particular literary development: the distance which separates the ideology of Mrs Gaskell's *Mary Barton* (1848) from her *North and South* (1855). It is a distance in which the very moment of historical mutation is disclosed.

symbology of Comtism, it can offer itself as a totalising doctrine
without detriment to the 'personal' – to a lived relation with immediate experience. The Religion of Humanity protects Romantic values
against an aggressive rationalism; but by rooting those values in the
human collective, it defends them equally against an unbridled
individualism. By virtue of this ideological conjuncture, the
Romantic individualist may submit to the social totality without
sacrifice to personal self-fulfilment.

In principle, that is; in practice, a potentially tragic collision
between 'corporate' and 'individualist' ideologies is consistently
defused and repressed by the forms of Eliot's fiction. As the daughter
of a farm-agent, the social locus of corporate value for Eliot is rural
society; it is here, most obviously in *Adam Bede* and *Silas Marner*,
that the cluster of traditionalist practices and 'organic' affiliations
imputed to the English provincial countryside is 'selected' by the
national ideology as paradigmatic, at a point where that ideology
demands precisely such images of social incorporation. Rural society
in *Adam Bede*, as John Goode has commented,[28] is chosen as a
literary subject not for its cloistered idiosyncratic charm but as a
simplifying model of the whole social formation – a formation whose
determining laws may be focused there in purer, more diagram-
matic form. The function of the framing, externalising forms of
Eliot's rural novels – pastoral, myth, moral fable – is to allow for
such 'transparency', but in doing so to recast the historical contradictions at the heart of Eliot's fiction into ideologically resolvable
terms.

It is not, naturally, that the organicist modes of Eliot's novels are
the 'expression' of her authorial ideology. As a literary producer,
George Eliot delineates a 'space' constituted by the insertion of
'pastoral', religious and Romantic ideological sub-ensembles into an
ideological formation dominated by liberalism, scientific rationalism
and empiricism. This conjuncture is overdetermined in her case by
elements of sexual ideology, which both reinforce the drive to individual emancipation and ratify the 'feminine' values (compassion,
tolerance, passive resignation) called upon to forestall it. There is no
question of reducing the metropolitan rationalist intellectual George
Eliot to the 'subject' of a provincial, petty-bourgeois 'class-ideology'.

28. *Critical Essays on George Eliot*, ed. Barbara Hardy (London, 1970),
p. 20.

The phrase 'George Eliot' signifies nothing more than the insertion of certain specific ideological determinations – Evangelical Christianity, rural organicism, incipient feminism, petty-bourgeois moralism – into a hegemonic ideological formation which is partly supported, partly embarrassed by their presence. This contradictory unity of ideological structures provides the productive matrix of her fiction; yet the ideology of her texts is not, of course, reducible to it. For Eliot's literary production must be situated, not only at the level of 'general' ideology, but also at the relatively autonomous level of the mutation of literary forms. For each of her texts displays a complex amalgam of fictional devices appropriate to distinct generic modes: 'pastoral', historical realism, fable, mythopoeic and didactic discourse, even (with *Daniel Deronda*) elements of utopian fantasy. None of these discourses can be placed in any simple expressive relation to ideological forms; on the contrary, it is the mutual articulation of these discourses within the text which *produces* those ideological forms as literary signification. Two examples of this process will have to suffice. The biographical mode of *The Mill on the Floss* encompasses at least two distinct forms of literary discourse: a kind of descriptive 'pastoral' (the Dodsons, Maggie's early life at the mill), and the complex psychological drama of Maggie's subjective development. It is the interplay of these mutually conflictual modes which produces the ideological contention between 'tradition' and 'progress' inscribed in the figures of Tom and Maggie Tulliver. But it is a contention which the novel's 'pastoral' devices simultaneously resolve. For just as the text's synthetic closure simplifies Tom to a type of eternal childhood, so the image of the river – symbol of moral drifting and wayward desire – naturalises and thus deforms the values of liberal individualism, figuring them as a mindless yielding to natural appetite rather than as positive growth. An opposition between 'natural' and 'cultural' discourses is transformed into a polarity between two modes of 'natural' signification: Nature as positive (pastoral), and Nature as negative (appetitive). Again, it is not difficult to see how in *Middlemarch* the realist form itself determines a certain 'ideology of the text'. In the earlier 'pastoral' novels, Eliot's realism is partly signified by her apologetic engagement with socially obscure destinies; yet that engagement does not necessarily extend to a fully 'internal' mode of characterisation. Once it does so, however, the novel-form is instantly decentred: since every destiny is significant, each is consequently relativised. Realism, as Eliot conceives of it, involves the tactful unravelling of interlaced processes, the equable distribution of authorial sympathies, the holding of competing values in precarious equipoise. The 'general' ideological correlative of this textual ideology is, naturally, liberal reformism; no other ideological effect could conceivably be produced by such an assemblage of fictional devices.

That Eliot's fiction recasts historical contradictions into ideologically resolvable form is evident enough in the case of *Adam Bede*. Adam himself, with his Carlylean gospel of work and stiff-necked moralism, is an 'organic' type – a petty-bourgeois pragmatist who 'had no theories about setting the world to rights', and who thus functions as a reliable agent of the ruling class. Yet these 'organic' values are forbidden by the novel's form from entering into significant deadlock with any 'authentic' liberal individualism. Such individualism figures in the text only in the debased and trivialised form of a hedonistic egoism (the anarchic sexual appetite of Arthur Donnithorne and Hetty Sorrel), which the stable structures of rural society can expel or absorb without notable self-disruption. Hetty has unwittingly ruptured the class-collaboration between squire and artisan, turning Adam against Arthur; but once she is, so to speak, deported from the novel, that organic allegiance can be gradually reaffirmed. Moreover, the morally intransigent Adam has been humanised by his trials to the point where he is now spiritually prepared to wed the 'higher' working-class girl, Dinah Morris, whose Evangelical fervour for duteous self-sacrifice matches his own doggedly anti-intellectual conformism. Adam is thus allowed to advance into more richly individualised consciousness (he ends up owning a timber-yard) without damage to his mythological status as organic type, an admirable amalgam of naturalised culture and cultivated nature.

In choosing rural petty-bourgeois life as a 'paradigmatic' region, Eliot betrays towards it an ambiguous attitude which reveals, in turn, her problematic relationship to her readership. She extends the conventions of literary realism to a sensitive treatment of socially obscure figures; but while she insists on the latent significance of the apparently peripheral lives she presents, she also apologises, with a blend of genial patronage and tentative irony, for choosing such an unenlightened enclave as the subject-matter of serious fiction.

That hesitancy of tone focuses an ideological conflict. It exposes the contradiction between a rationalist critique of rural philistinism (one coupled with a Romantic individualist striving beyond those stifling limits), and a deep-seated imperative to celebrate the value of such bigoted, inert traditionalism, as the humble yet nourishing soil which feeds the flower of higher individual achievement. *Adam Bede* tries for a partial solution of this dilemma by romantically idealising the common life in the figures of Adam and Dinah, fusing the intense with the ordinary. In *The Mill on the Floss*, however, such a synthesis calls for a considerably more obtrusive manipulation of literary devices.

The rural society of the *Mill* – one of struggling tenant farmers becoming enmortgaged and forced to ruin by the pressures of urban banking and agricultural industry – is less easily idealised than the society of *Adam Bede*. As urban capital penetrates into the country-side, those conflicts in rural society suggested yet suppressed in *Adam Bede* erupt to provide one of the *Mill*'s central images – the financial collapse of Dorlcote Mill itself. Moreover, if Hetty Sorrel can be effectively externalised as a socially disruptive egoist, Maggie Tulliver of the *Mill* is a bearer of authentic liberal values who is by no means so easily dislodged. Whereas *Adam Bede* divided moral fervour and restless individualism between Dinah and Hetty, Maggie Tulliver combines both; and this forestalls the simple resolution available to the earlier novel. Allured by a liberal individualism which decisively breaks with the stagnant oppressiveness of the rural petty bourgeoisie, Maggie must none the less refuse that ethic in the name of a commitment to the traditionalist social milieu of her childhood. In this way, nostalgia for an idealised upbringing at the mill becomes translated into a defence of clannish, claustrophobic *mores* against the Romantic spontaneity of the self, treacherously entwined as it is with appetitive egoism. The claustrophobia, and the snare of self-sacrifice, are clearly registered by the novel; yet one reason why they cannot be decisively rejected is because the only alternative commitment which the book allows Maggie is Stephen Guest. Guest cannot represent a true fulfilment for her: his personal flaws are subtly related to his class position, as an overbred product of the predatory capitalism which is ousting the old rural world of her father. In grasping this connection, the novel at once shows a complex historical sense beyond the range of *Adam Bede*, and conveniently renders Maggie's return to St Oggs more palatable. In a parallel way, the career of Tom Tulliver strikingly renders the contradictions of rural society: Tom strives to help his ruined father by prospering within the very urban capitalism which has brought about the mill's collapse. Yet it is not this historically complex and self-divided Tom with whom Maggie finally unites. The novel's transparently engineered conclusion – Maggie's self-sacrificial drowning with her brother – suppresses ideological conflict by the magical stratagem of a literary device. Maggie's death is at once guilty expiation and affirmative self-fulfilment; in uniting with her brother, object of romantic love and bigoted type of organic community, she achieves and abnegates herself in the same act, endorsing the imperatives of 'organic' morality while attaining to a fulfilling individual transcendence of them.

That the nostalgic organicism of Eliot's historically backdated rural fiction is determined in the last instance by the exigencies of the present is evident enough in *Felix Holt, The Radical*, written about the first Reform Bill on the eve of the second. Felix is essentially an urban version of Adam Bede, a petty-bourgeois craftsman no more representative of the proletariat in whose name he speaks than his pre-industrial predecessor. His 'radicalism', accordingly, consists in a reformist trust in moral education and a positivist suspicion of political change – a combination heroically opposed by the text to an unsavoury alliance of opportunist Radical politics with the insensate irrationality of the masses. Felix's *Address to Working Men*, with its call for a conversion of class interests into class duties, its apologia for cultural privilege and fear of mass action, merely projects the novel's sustaining ideology of 'organic' change into more crudely explicit terms. In this sense, *Felix Holt* highlights the ideological impotence of those 'pastoral' images which persist within Eliot's realist fictional mode. It is a self-contradictory work because it insists (as its self-consciously assertive title would suggest) on 'centring' such an image – Felix himself – in an urban context which can only enforce its effective displacement, transplanting a marooned, moralising Adam Bede to the town. The novel's 'official' project is in conflict with what it reveals: Felix's 'progressive' political critique is no more than the idealist protest of traditionalist values against the political itself. What the book wishes to assert of its protagonist – that he is more radical than the Radicals – simply cannot be reconciled with what it shows of him, as a doughty defender of landed property. The solution to this contradiction lies in the 'personalisation' of Felix himself, as a forcefully charismatic hero compensating in physical presence for what he politically lacks.

If Felix is in this sense a 'false' centre, the novel has a real but displaced centre in Mrs Transome. Both characters are historically obsolete; Mrs Transome is presented as a pathetically outdated feudalist whose pieties are ridden over roughshod by her Radical son. Yet if the novel mourns in her the death of traditional society, that mourning must be refracted in the case of the equally obsolescent Holt to a 'progressive' position. The Mrs Transome scenes are nothing less than the aesthetic betrayal of this ideological contradiction at the novel's heart – the unabsorbed region of bleakness, nostalgia and frustration with which nothing can be politically done, which is thereby forced to the work's ideological margins, but which protests by its sheer artistry against such relegation. Mrs Transome is an implicit refutation of Felix and contemporary history, even as Felix himself is fundamentally a refusal of that world; there is thus a double displacement at work in the text. *Felix Holt* betrays in its formal structure – in the disjunction between its political region and its Mrs Transome episodes – a self-division which fails to achieve thematic articulation. The artistic power of the Mrs Transome scenes suggests the residual presence of an ineradicable 'personal' disillusionment which refuses to be totalised and absorbed by the novel's official progressivist ideology. Liberalism, raised by the quasi-positivist Holt to more corporate and 'scientific' forms, at the same time disengages itself from such potentially tyrannic totalities to defend the 'personal' values they threaten. The structural dislocations of the text are produced by that ideological dissonance; but that dissonance is equally the product of the interplay between the three distinct 'texts' which struggle for dominance within the novel as a whole. For *Felix Holt* is a contradictory amalgam of organicist myth (Felix), psychological drama (Mrs Transome) and political fiction; its discourse is the product of a series of slippages or mutations from each of these traditional forms to the other. It is in the hiatuses produced by these partial, ineffective transformations of mode that the ideology of the text inheres.

Eliot's fiction, indeed, displays from the outset a conflict between ideological totalities which outstrip classical liberalism, and a fear of the disruptive effect of such totalities on the 'personal' values bred by that liberal lineage. (It is a conflict revealed in her ambiguous fellow-travelling relations with the English Positivists, whom she supported but could not bring herself to join.) Fiction is organic totality, but *phenomenological* totality; its creation of seamless, symmetrical wholes must be achieved without damage to the integrity of immediate experience.[29] That problem is thematically evident in *Romola*, where Savonarola's 'passionate sense of the infinite', his seductively corporate vision, is entwined with a moral despotism which violates liberal sanctities. Yet those sanctities are in themselves insufficient: 'tender fellow-feeling for the nearest has its danger too, and is apt to be timid and sceptical towards the larger aims without which life cannot rise to religion'.[30] In Arnold's terms, it is a conflict between a dangerously decentred Hellenism and an oppressively sectarian Hebraism.

Liberal-minded working men like Felix Holt seem to propose one answer to that problem, blending 'culture' with moral discipline; yet after *Felix Holt* Eliot did not repeat the doomed experiment of centring such 'pastoral' figures within urban landscapes. The Bede–Holt character in *Middlemarch* is Caleb Garth, stock type of rural organicism, but decidedly muted and marginal within the novel's structure. As such figures decline in ideological impact, value shifts to an alternative oppositional standpoint: in the case of *Middlemarch*, to the cosmopolitan artist Will Ladislaw. If the traditionalist craftsman forms a pocket of spiritual resistance within bourgeois society, the cosmopolitan artist inhabits such a dissentient space outside it. He is, however, no complete compensation for the outmoded organicist type: if Ladislaw has the edge over Garth in liberal culture it is because he lacks his social rootedness. It is only with Daniel Deronda, who combines synoptic vision with settled allegiance, that this ideological dilemma can be finally dissolved.

This is not to say, however, that Garth's values do not finally triumph in *Middlemarch*. They do, but in the 'higher' mode of a

29. It is significant that Eliot's well-known dictum that art, although the highest form of teaching, should never lapse from the 'picture' to the 'diagram' occurs in a letter to Frederic Harrison in which she refuses his suggestion that she should produce a full-blooded positivist novel (George Eliot, *Letters*, ed. Gordon S. Haight (London, 1956), vol. 4, p. 300).

30. *Romola* (London, 1883), vol. 2, pp. 332–3.

wide-eyed liberal disillusionment which, with the collapse of more ambitious commitments, is compelled to find solace in the humble reformist tasks nearest to hand. The irony of *Middlemarch* is that it is a triumph of aesthetic totalisation deeply suspicious of ideological totalities. Each of the novel's four central characters represents such an historically typical totalisation: Casaubon idealism, Lydgate scientific rationalism, Bulstrode Evangelical Christianity, Dorothea Brooke Romantic self-achievement through a unifying principle of action. Each of these totalities crumbles, ensnared in the quotidian; and that ensnarement can be read in two ways. It is in part a salutary empiricist check to the tyranny of theoreticism; but it also signifies the bleak victory of an entrenched provincial consciousness over rationalist or Romantic drives to transcend it. That stalemate, the novel's title suggests, springs from a transitional phase of rural society at the time of the first Reform Bill; yet there is no doubt that the novel's judiciously muted disillusion, its 'end-of-ideologies' ambience, belongs to its post-second Reform Bill present. The problem which *Middlemarch* objectively poses, and fails to resolve, is how ideology is to be conceptually elaborate yet emotionally affective – how it is to nurture 'irrational' personal pieties while cohering them into a structure which surpasses mere empiricism and Romantic spontaneity. What is needed, according to Ladislaw, is 'a soul in which knowledge passes instantaneously into feeling, and feeling flashes back as a new organ of knowledge' – a question to which we have seen Matthew Arnold address himself. Confronted with the aggressive modes of working-class consciousness caricatured in *Felix Holt*, the cautious empiricism of the bourgeois liberal tradition must be reaffirmed; yet that empiricism is in itself an ideologically inadequate response to the historical moment of post-Reform Bill England, with its demand for a more intensively incorporating ideology.

This dilemma is figured in *Middlemarch* in one of its key images: that of the *web* as image of the social formation. The web is a *derivative* organic image, a mid-point between the animal imagery of *Adam Bede* and some more developed theoretical concept of *structure*. The complexity of the web, its subtle interlacing of relatively autonomous strands, its predatory overtones, the possibilities of local complication it permits, accommodate forms of conflict excluded by the more thoroughgoing organicist imagery of *Adam*

Bede. But at the same time the web's symmetry, its 'spatial' de-historicising of the social process, its exclusion of levels of contradiction, preserve the essential unity of the organic mode. The web's complex fragility impels a prudent political conservatism: the more delicately interlaced its strands, the more the disruptive consequences of action can multiply, and so the more circumspect one must be in launching ambitiously totalising projects. Yet conversely, if action at any point in the web will vibrate through its filaments to affect the whole formation, a semi-mystical relationship to the totality is nevertheless preserved. Here, as in the novel's closing trope of the river, which in diffusing its force to tributaries intensifies its total impact, natural imagery is exploited to signify how a fulfilling relation to the social totality can be achieved, not by ideological abstraction, but by pragmatic, apparently peripheral work. And if *Middlemarch*'s natural metaphors perform this function, so does its aesthetic imagery. As Ladislaw remarks to Dorothea: 'It is no use to try and take care of all the world; that is being taken care of when you feel delight – in art or in anything else.' The problem of totality within the novel is effectively displaced to the question of aesthetic form itself, which gives structure to its materials without violating their empirical richness. The novel, in other words, formally answers the problem it thematically poses. Only the novelist can be the centred subject of her own decentred fiction, the privileged consciousness which at once supervenes on the whole as its source, and enters into empathetic relation with each part.

Middlemarch, one might say, is an historical novel in form with little substantive historical content. The Reform Bill, the railways, cholera, machine-breaking: these 'real' historical forces do no more than impinge on the novel's margins. The mediation between the text and the 'real' history to which it alludes is notably dense; and the effect of this is to transplant the novel from the 'historical' to the 'ethical'. *Middlemarch* works in terms of egoism and sympathy, 'head' and 'heart', self-fulfilment and self-surrender; and this predominance of the ethical at once points to an historical impasse and provides the means of ideologically overcoming it. History in the novel is officially in a state of transition; yet to read the text is to conclude that 'suspension' is the more appropriate term. What is officially offered as an ambivalent, intermediate era leading eventually to the 'growing good of the world' is in fact more of an historical vacuum; the benighted, traditionalist-minded Middle-march seems little more responsive to historical development than does the Hayslope of *Adam Bede*. There is, then, a discrepancy between what the novel claims and what it shows: in aesthetically 'producing' the melioristic ideology intimated by its title, it betrays a considerably less sanguine view of historical progress. It reveals, in fact, an image of the early eighteen-thirties which belongs to the jaundiced viewpoint of where they actually led to – the early eighteen-seventies, where Will Ladislaw's pioneering reformist zeal 'has been much checked'. *Middlemarch* projects back onto the past its sense of contemporary stalemate; and since the upshot of this is a radical distrust of 'real' history, that history is effectively displaced into ethical, and so 'timeless', terms. Yet such displacement thereby provides Eliot with an ideological solution: for what cannot be resolved in 'historical' terms can be accommodated by a moralising of the issues at stake. This, indeed, is a mystification inherent in the very forms of realist fiction, which by casting objective social rela-tions into interpersonal terms, constantly hold open the possibility of reducing the one to the other.[31] In *Middlemarch*, such an ethical reduction of history is achieved in the 'solution' of self-sacrifice, to which, in their various ways, Dorothea, Lydgate and (in a sense) Bulstrode struggle through. The suffering abnegation of the ego offers itself as the answer to the riddle of history.

Yet such a solution is ideologically insufficient, as Will Ladislaw's presence in the novel would suggest. For Ladislaw, while consenting to the course of social evolution, also retains an individualist verve which challenges such mature resignation. As a politically reforming artist, he suggests that empirical labour and Romantic self-affirma-tion need not be incompatible; in Mr Brooke's words, he is 'a sort of Burke with a leaven of Shelley'. The novel's difficulty in 'realising' him springs from its incapacity to see how this desirable ideological conjuncture, yoking prudent gradualism to visionary Romanticism, can be achieved in the historical conditions it des-cribes. At this point, therefore, a different kind of history becomes necessary. What cannot be effectively achieved in Ladislaw can be re-attempted on more propitious terms in that later amalgam of Romantic prophet and reformist politician, Daniel Deronda.

31. A point made by Francis Mulhern in 'Ideology and Literary Form – a comment', *New Left Review* 91, May/June 1975.

122

What is demanded, in fact, is a 'totalising' vision which binds the individual to the laws of a social formation, preserves the 'personal' pieties violated by such visions in *Romola* and *Middlemarch*, and romantically liberates the self. The answer to this problem is *Daniel Deronda*. In that novel, Eliot finds a magical solution to her ideological dilemma in Deronda's Jewishness, which provides him with a fulfilling romantic identity while incorporating him into the complex totality of a corporate historical culture. Deronda's early liberalism is fruitlessly Hellenistic, a decentred spreading of sympathies which erodes his capacity for principled action: 'a too reflective and diffuse sympathy was in danger of paralysing in him that indignation against wrong and selectness of fellowship which are the conditions of moral force'. Hebraism provides the essential corrective – a faith which involves 'the blending of a complete personal love in one current with a larger duty' through an obedient 'submission of the soul to the Highest'. Such submission, however, leaves the 'personal' values of liberalism intact: Deronda's vision is of 'a mind consciously, energetically moving with the larger march of human destinies, but not the less full of conscience and tender heart for the footsteps that tread near and need a leaning-place (*sic*)'.

The problem, in other words, can be 'solved' only by the invention of a *displaced* totality outside the sterile detotalisation of post-Reform Bill England – a totality which is then, as it were, instantly exported, as Deronda leaves to discover his destiny in the Middle East. The difficulty then is to bring this factitious totality into regenerative relation with bourgeois England – a difficulty 'solved' by Deronda's redemptive influence on the broken, dispirited victim of that society, Gwendolen Harleth. But in attempting this solution the novel splits into self-contradiction – splits, indeed, down the middle. For Daniel can only fulfil his destiny by withdrawing from Gwendolen to the Middle East, abandoning her to a nebulous Arnoldian trust in some ideal goodness. The formal dislocations of *Daniel Deronda* are the product of its attempt to overcome the ideological contradictions from which it emerges; it is in the silence between its 'Gwendolen' and 'Daniel' episodes that the truth of those contradictions speaks most eloquently.

Middlemarch's relative obliquity to 'real' history is in part a consequence of Eliot's belief (compounded of positivism and idealism) in the power of ideas to shape social existence. Yet what the novel manifests is precisely the fatal disjunction between notion and fact, rendering the one emptily utopian and the other banally empirical. If Deronda's visions are to assume historical flesh, the possibility of such contradiction must be eradicated. The novel therefore presses Eliot's trust in the determining force of ideas to a mystical extreme: dreams, desires, shadowy impulses are now grasped as proleptic symbols of what is actually to be. Such dreams effectively conspire in creating the future: Daniel muses that Mordecai's nature may be one of those in which 'a wise estimate of consequences is fused in the fire of the passionate belief which determines the consequences it believes in'. History becomes the phenomenal expression of spiritual forces at work within it; and there can thus be no essential contradiction between what the imagination seizes as true and what historically transpires. The novel, in other words, is driven to the desperate recourse of adopting a mystical epistemology to resolve its problems, and so is effectively forced beyond the bounds of realism. The whole implausible structure of coincidence and hidden kinship which props up the narrative suggests a significant transmutation of the realism of *Middlemarch*, where such devices are sparingly used.

In this sense, *Daniel Deronda* marks one major terminus of nine-teenth-century realism – a realism now buckling under ideological pressures it is unable to withstand. But it is not merely a question of the 'aesthetic' being rudely invaded by the 'ideological'. For *Daniel Deronda* also signifies a crisis-point in the relatively autonomous evolution of realist forms – a point at which the problematic *fictionality* of those stolidly self-confident forms is becoming incorporated as a level of signification within the text itself. The novel's notable preoccupation with art is in one sense a displaced desire for the organicist ideal: art liberates the individual subject but exacts submission to an impersonal order, incarnates an ideal excellence but demands much humble labour, elicits an ascetic Hebraism but calls forth a devotion akin to sexual love. Yet it also signifies the text's constant oblique meditation on its own fictive status – on that circular movement whereby 'real' events within the fiction are themselves is some sense 'fictions' which prefigure a 'reality' of illusory proportions. That there could be no Mordecai outside the limits of fictional discourse (as there could indeed be a Bulstrode) is the true index of the novel's ideological dilemma – a dilemma which is nothing less than the crisis of realist signification itself. *Daniel Deronda* is itself a proleptic sign of a desired social reality; but since that social reality is a fictional construct, unable to project itself beyond the bounds of aesthetic discourse, the text can in the end only signify itself. What it discloses, in that process of self-signification, is an absence which must necessarily evade its aesthetic constructions – the suppressed blankness of the abandoned Gwendolen Harleth, sign of the 'real' ideological paucity to which the novel is a mythological riposte.

Eliot's fiction, then, represents an attempt to integrate liberal ideology, in both its Romantic and empiricist forms, with certain pre-industrial, idealist or positivist organic models. It is an enterprise determined in the last instance by the increasingly corporate character of nineteenth-century capitalism during the period of her literary production. Yet this is not to argue for a simple homology between literary and historical systems, or for a reductively diachronic reading of Eliot's *oeuvre*. It is not a question of Eliot's work evolving from pre-industrial 'pastoral' to fully-fledged realism in response to some linear development of bourgeois ideology. On the contrary, it is a question of grasping at once the ideological synchronies and formal discontinuities of her texts – of theorising the set of disjunctures whereby distinct literary discourses produce a corporatist ideology which is present from the outset. The *differences* of Eliot's fiction are the effect of a continual repermutation of the literary forms into which it is inserted – a repermutation which in each of her texts 'privileges' a particular, dominant discourse which 'places' and deforms the others. Within this synchronic practice a significant development can be discerned: one from an essentially *metaphorical* closure of ideological conflict (social history as analogous to natural evolution) towards an essentially *metonymic* resolution of such issues ('personal' values, visions and relations as the solution to social ills).[32] The naturalising, moralising and mythifying devices of the novels effect such closures, but in the act of doing so lay bare the imprint of the ideological struggles which beset the texts. It is in the irregular transmutation of one fictional code into another, the series of formal displacements whereby turbulent

32. For this general distinction in fiction, see Francis Mulhern, *art. cit.*

issues are marginalised yet remain querulously present, that Eliot's organic closures betray their *constructing* functions. What threatens to subvert them is not a suppressed 'outside', but the absences and dislocations they internally produce.

As Victorian capitalism moves into its imperialist stage, the true historical basis of the 'idyllic' rural organicism of *Adam Bede* becomes progressively exposed. *Impressions of Theophrastus Such* (1879) places its plea for 'corporate existence' in the context of nationalist rhetoric and a warning of the dangers involved in undergoing 'a premature fusion with immigrants of alien blood'. 'The pride which identifies us with a great historic body', Eliot writes, 'is a humanising, elevating habit of mind, inspiring sacrifices of individual comfort, gain, or other selfish ambition, for the sake of that ideal whole; and no man swayed by such a sentiment can become completely abject.' The corporate society which in *Daniel Deronda* remained a goal to be realised, and so an idealist critique of contemporary England, has now become an effusive celebration of the *status quo*. The voice of liberal humanism has become the voice of jingoist reaction.

3. *Charles Dickens*

The major fiction of Victorian society was the product of the petty bourgeoisie. The Brontës, Dickens, Eliot, Hardy: it is with them, rather than with Thackeray, Trollope, Disraeli, Bulwer Lytton, that the finest achievements of nineteenth-century realism are to be found. Ambiguously placed within the social formation, the petty bourgeoisie was able on the whole to encompass a richer, more significant range of experience than those writers securely lodged within a single class. But it was also able to find epitomised in its own condition some of the most typical contradictions of bourgeois society as a whole. Indeed, 'conventional' bourgeois experience in England proved remarkably unpropitious for the production of major fiction.[33] Only writers with an ambivalent class-relation to

33. This is one reason for the structural dissonances of some of Dickens's early fiction. Novels like *Nicholas Nickleby* and *Martin Chuzzlewit* present a blankly absent centre in the figure of the conventional, bourgeois-minded protagonist; the true life of the novels is to be found in the nooks and peripheries, swirling around this absent centre.

the society could, it seemed, be open to the contradictions from which major literary art was produced. (This is true, earlier in the century, of Jane Austen, in whose work the situation of the minor gentry offers a peculiarly privileged focus for examining the conflicts and alliances between aristocracy and bourgeoisie.) As the petty-bourgeois realist tradition declines towards the end of the century into naturalism (Gissing, Wells, Bennett), its fraught, problematic relation to the society is, so to speak, confiscated by the *émigré* writers – James and Conrad, and later Eliot and Pound. A similarly ambiguous relationship occurs in twentieth-century Irish society, to produce the major art of Yeats and Joyce.

This is not to argue, however, that major nineteenth-century realism was the product of the 'class-ideology' of the petty bourgeoisie. For there is, strictly speaking, no such ideological sub-formation: 'petty-bourgeois ideology' exists as a strikingly pure and contradictory unity of elements drawn from the ideological realms of both dominant and dominated classes in the social formation. What is in question with all of these texts is the peculiarly complex, over-determined character of their mode of insertion into the hegemonic ideological forms – a complexity which is in part the product of literary 'realism' itself. For realism, as we have seen in the case of George Eliot, produces in one of its currents a 'democratic' ideology – one progressively responsive to suppressed social experience and humbly quotidian destinies. Yet its aesthetic ideology of 'type' and 'totality' (and we should be in no doubt as to the *ideological* character of such notions) insists on the integration of these elements into a unitary 'world view'. The ideology of the realist text resides not in this dominant 'world view', but in the formal mutations and displacements which signify its attempts to subordinate other modes of discourse. In the case of the earlier Charles Dickens, for example, each text is a veritable traffic-jam of competing fictional modes – Gothic, Romance, moral fable, 'social problem' novel, popular theatre, 'short story', journalism, episodic 'entertainment' – which permits 'realism' no privileged status. The later 'realism' of Dickens is thus of a notably impure kind – a question, often enough, of 'totalising' forms englobing non-realist 'contents', of dispersed, conflictual discourses which ceaselessly offer to displace the securely 'over-viewing' eye of classical realism. If Dickens's movement towards such realism produces a 'totalising' ideology, it is one constantly deconstructed from within by the 'scattering' effect of quite contrary literary devices. In the end, Dickens's novels present symbols of contradictory unity (Chancery Court, Circumlocution Office) which are the very principles of the novel's own construction. Only these symbolic discourses can finally provide an 'over-view'; but precisely because their coherence is nothing less than one of systematic contradiction, such an over-view is merely the absent space within which disparate rhetorics are articulated.

The fact that Charles Dickens was an urban rather than rural petty bourgeois marks a significant distinction between his fiction and that of George Eliot. Of all the major English writers of the past century and a half, Dickens is perhaps the least contaminated by organicist ideologies. With him, the Romantic humanist critique of industrial capitalism remains strikingly 'spontaneous', with none of the elaborate ideological realisation it receives in the work of Carlyle or D. H. Lawrence. Dickens treats the most available contemporary forms of organicism – Young England, medievalism, the cult of Nature, the Oxford movement – with the contempt of an *urban* petty-bourgeois writer, one for whom there is no satisfactory withdrawal into the mystifications of pastoral. The retreat to Nature in Dickens is for the most part a negative gesture, associated with death and regression to childhood, social disengagement rather than social paradigm. If Nature for George Eliot suggests the socially structured world of rural England, it is for Dickens a locus of sentimental moralism rather than of sociological law. Little Nell is a symbol of natural value expelled from the predatory city, but it is the archetypally urban Quilp who engages his author's imagination. The spontaneous, empiricist character of Dickens's Romantic humanism, evident in the 'Christmas spirit' and the vulgar vitalism of *Hard Times*, emerges as a significant aesthetic and ideological weakness. Yet in the mature work that very weakness productively deprives him of a ready-fashioned organicist ideology, *à la Daniel Deronda*, by which to mediate and 'resolve' the conflicts in question. In a transitional work like *Dombey and Son*, the absence of such an ideology results in a text twisted and self-divided by the very contradictions it vulnerably reproduces. The famous railways scene, for example, exhilaratedly affirms bourgeois industrial progress at the same time as it protests gloomily against it on behalf of the petty bourgeoisie it dooms to obsolescence. Yet although that protest is partly couched in natural imagery, Dickens has no organicist ideology like Eliot by which to aesthetically integrate his conflicting symbols, no ideological resources by which to secure a reconciliation of 'tradition' and 'progress'. The contradictions remain visibly inscribed in the text, to enrich and enliven its dramatically irregular development.

A central symbol of Dickens's Romantic humanism is childhood innocence, which the novels bring into a series of complex structural relations with adult experience. Since the child is isolated, victimised and unable to totalise his perceptually fragmented world, the positive value he incarnates figures effectively as a negation. Such negativity clearly reflects the theoretical limitations of Dickens's moralistic critique of bourgeois society: the child's passivity is a dramatic index of his oppression, but also removes him from the world into a realm of untaintable goodness. On the other hand, the child's very blankness brings into dramatic focus the social forces which dominate him; he becomes, in a Brechtian metaphor, the empty stage on which these historically typical forces contend. Oliver Twist is such a negative centre, whose effective absence from his own narrative allows him passively to focus the socially significant; yet his nullity is also determined by the novel's ideological inability to show him as social *product*. To do that, indeed, would be to undercut the very unhinging of Oliver from history which finally ensures his fabular triumph. The novel argues at once that Oliver is and is not the product of bourgeois oppression, just as the 'real' world of bourgeois social relations into which he is magically rescued is endorsed against the 'unreal' underworld of poverty and crime, while simultaneously being shown up by that underworld as illusory.

Dickens's fiction thus reveals a contradiction between the social reality mediated by childhood innocence, and the transcendental moral values which that innocence embodies. It is a contradiction intrinsic to petty-bourgeois consciousness, which needs to embrace conventional bourgeois ethics in an undermining awareness of the harsh social realities they suppress. One effect of this is a set of formal dissonances in the novels themselves. *Pickwick Papers*, for example, cannot really be a *novel* in the traditional sense, since Pickwick's complacent innocence renders him incapable of any significantly interconnected experience beyond the merely episodic. The book consequently needs a supplementary centre in Sam Weller, who, though officially subordinate (Pickwick's servant), is in fact the master. In a double displacement of the text's bourgeois blandness, the unpalatable experience it expels from its official narrative erupts elsewhere, in the grotesquely violent, death-obsessed tales by which that narrative is regularly interrupted. In a somewhat parallel way, Quilp in *The Old Curiosity Shop* symbolises the smouldering, anarchic vengeance which the novel wreaks on its own decorous, sentimental story-line.[34]

Dickens's fiction, like Eliot's, deploys literary devices to 'resolve' ideological conflict; but his novels are more remarkable than Eliot's for the clarity with which those conflicts inscribe themselves in the fissures and hiatuses of the texts, in their mixed structures and disjunct meanings. It is not that Eliot's work does not also reveal such formal dislocations, as I have suggested; it is rather that Eliot's writing, sustained by an aesthetic as well as social ideology of organic form, strives for such organic closure more consciously and consistently than does Dickens's. His novels, by contrast, offer their self-contradictory forms and internal inconsistencies as part of their historical meaning. Dickens's mature work certainly achieves aesthetic integration, but it is of a significantly different kind from Eliot's. Whereas Eliot's organicist ideology provides a structure for social totalisation, Dickens is forced in his later fiction to use as aesthetically unifying images the very social institutions (the Chancery Court of *Bleak House*, the Circumlocution Office of *Little Dorrit*) which are the object of his criticism. It is, ironically, these very systems of conflict, division and contradiction which provide Dickens with a principle of symbolic coherence. In this sense, the aesthetic unity of his mature work is founded, not on a mythology of 'organic community', but on exactly the opposite: on the historical self-divisions of bourgeois society. It is not that the early Dickens's perception of character as idiosyncratic and non-relational yields to a vision of social unity; it is rather that such non-relationship is now shown to be *systemic* – the function of decentred structures like Chancery, finance capitalism and the Circumlocution Office, elusive centres which seem all-pervasive yet everywhere

34. A point made by John Carey in *The Violent Effigy: a study of Dickens' imagination* (London, 1974), p. 26.

absent.[35] Characters in later Dickens remain individually graphic and grotesque, but are now increasingly grasped as the bearers of these structures, which act as the true protagonists of the later fiction.

What Eliot's writing attempts to resolve *synchronically* – a conflict between two phases of bourgeois ideology, determined by certain mutations in the historical nature of English capitalism – Dickens's fiction moves through *diachronically*. The anarchic, decentred, fragmentary forms of the early novels correspond in general to an earlier, less organised phase of industrial capitalism; the unified structures of the mature fiction allude to a more intensively coordinated capitalism, with its complex networks of finance capitalism (Merdle in *Little Dorrit*), its progressively centralised state bureaucracy (the Circumlocution Office) and its increasingly monolithic ideological apparatuses (the educational system of *Hard Times*, the juridical structures of *Bleak House*).[36] (The railways of *Dombey and Son* mark a transitional stage in this development – a visibly unifying network which none the less, in the entrepreneurial 'spontaneity' of their creation and the heterogeneous quality of experience to which they give rise, recall the arbitrary, explosive energies of the early novels.) Yet this diachronic movement is not one from 'individualism' to 'community'. It is a movement from the novel of the absent centre (innocent child, blankly conventional adult) around which certain contradictions knot themselves, to the novel of the decentred totality – a novel which mimes, in its integrated symbolism, a set of conflicts and non-relations now grasped as systemic.

4. *Joseph Conrad*

It would be a predictable error to trace the development of organicism in nineteenth-century literature from George Eliot to that later

35. These complex totalities may be contrasted with the monistic industrial system presented by the sealed and static *Hard Times*, with its crude binary opposition between that system and 'life'. *Hard Times* can be seen in this sense as a false, premature over-totalisation.

36. It is not, naturally, a question of simple homology between literary and historical systems, as this formulation might seem to suggest. What is at issue, rather, is the difference between an earlier 'impure' articulation of discourses ideologically overdetermined by a relatively unsystematic Romantic humanism, and the *relatively* more coherent codes of the later fiction, overdetermined by the increasing predominance of corporatist ideological elements.

petty-bourgeois novelist of rural life, Thomas Hardy. Yet though
Hardy inherits an ideology of organic social evolution (he writes,
echoing Eliot, of the human race as 'one great network or tissue ...
like a spider's web'[37]), his fiction is essentially preoccupied with
those structural conflicts and tragic contradictions in rural society
which Eliot's novels evade. I have argued in the previous chapter
that Hardy's movement towards a fully-developed critical realism
was laborious and uneven; it is the peculiar *impurity* of his literary
forms (pastoral, melodrama, social realism, naturalism, myth, fable,
classical tragedy) which is most striking. Ambiguously placed within
both his own declining rural enclave and the social formation at
large, exploring 'Wessex' with realist internality yet viewing it also
through the immobilising perspectives of myth, Hardy's situation as
a literary producer was ridden with contradictions. They are contradictions inseparable from his fraught productive relation to the
metropolitan audience whose spokesmen rejected his first, abrasively
radical work. His use of pastoral and mythological forms occasionally reflects an anxious pact with that readership's flat patronage of
the 'bucolic'; but he also deploys the 'universalising' frames of fable,
ballad and classical tragedy to confer major status on fictional material
liable to be dismissed as of merely provincial import. The formal
problem of how to reconcile these conflicting literary modes – is
Alec D'Urberville bourgeois *arriviste*, pantomime devil, melo-
dramatic villain, symbol of Satanic evil? – is the product of Hardy's
unusually complex mode of insertion into the dominant ideological
formation and its span of possible literary forms. Yet by the time of
Jude the Obscure, 'reconciliation' has been effectively abandoned:
that novel is less an offering to its audience than a calculated assault
on them. What have been read as its 'crudities' are less the consequences of some artistic incapacity than of an astonishing raw
boldness on Hardy's part, a defiant flouting of 'verisimilitude' which
mounts theatrical gesture upon gesture in a driving back of the
bounds of realism. It is not fortuitous that the book's epigraph is
'The letter killeth': crammed with lengthy quotations from other
texts, thematically obsessed with the violence of literary culture,
laced with typological devices, *Jude* contrasts the murderous inertia
of the *letter* with that alternative image of artistic production which

is material craftsmanship. The models, forms, moulds and productive practices over which the text broods are themselves images of its own construction – of that montage of 'seemings' ('*productions* of this pen', in Hardy's revealing phrase) whose 'permanency' or 'consistency' is beside the point. Within the radical *provisionality* of Hardy's productive practice is inscribed a second, more fundamental provisionality – the desired un-closure of social forms themselves (epitomised in sexuality), forms which in their received shape the novel 'explodes' in the act of 'exploding' the letter of its own text. Throughout the novel, hallowed manuscripts – the Nicean creed, the Book of Job – are violently transformed by Jude into angry oral assaults on an unresponsive audience – assaults through which the novel mimes its own displaced position within the literary social relations of its time. Hardy claimed that the bigoted public response to *Jude* cured him of novel-writing for ever; but whether a producer of Hardy's status stops writing merely on account of bad reviews is surely questionable. The truth is that after *Jude* there was nowhere for Hardy to go; having 'exploded' the organic forms of fiction, he was forced to disembark.

The organicist tradition in the *fin-de-siècle*, then passes not to the rural Englishman Hardy, but to the Polish *émigré* Conrad. With the entry into the English literary arena of Joseph Conrad, Polish exile and merchant seaman, we witness the emergence of a peculiarly *overdetermined* instance of the conflict between Romantic individualism and social organicism which I have traced in the work of George Eliot. Conrad's conservative patriot father became a nationalist rebel against the Russian domination of Poland – an exiled and imprisoned pan-Slavic mystic, from whom Conrad inherited a belief in his subjugated fatherland as a corporate body ('an organic living thing'[38]) with a messianic sense of its historical destiny. Yet this Romantic idealist heritage was in conflict with the pragmatic conservative realism which Conrad imbibed from his mother's family, the landowning Bobrowskis, who advocated a cautious constitutionalism and a stern renunciation of the Romantic ego. The Polish nobility to which Conrad belonged were divided: the aristocracy was effectively incorporated into the Russian ruling class, leaving landed gentry like the Bobrowskis and Conrad's own

38. Joseph Conrad. *Notes on Life and Letters* (London, 1921), p. 157.

family to devise ways of throwing off the imperial yoke. Aspiring to national independence, but deprived of their social hegemony by Russian imperialism, they were hesitant in embracing the one 'extreme' means – revolution – by which this could be achieved. Poland for Conrad thus came to symbolise an ideal fusion of national corporateness and liberal enlightenment; it was a 'spontaneous unity', yet, with its 'almost exaggerated respect for individual rights', allied itself with European liberalism against Slav 'fanaticism'.[39]

Conrad's self-imposed exile from Poland, as seaman and artist, flamboyantly affirms his freedom from an intolerably claustrophobic imperialism. Yet at thē same time both art and the merchant service recreate the organic unity which had been brutally splintered in Poland. The ship is an organic community which, with its hierarchical structure of stable functions, curtails subversive individualism and the anarchic imagination. But, like Poland, it also represents a form of collective isolation threatened by alien forces, and so – especially for an officer socially removed from the crew – pitches the individual into lonely, testing confrontation with his own problematic identity. Art, similarly, symbolises the supreme autonomy of a personal imagination free from repressive rules; but it is also an organic whole which demands the abnegation of the individual ego. English society itself offered Conrad an ideal resolution of the conflicting ideological imperatives he inherited from his Polish context; it became a welcome enclave for the conservative *émigré* in flight from European political turbulence.[40] Its tolerant, pragmatic individualism united with the organic, Romantic nationalist heritage of the merchant service to provide Conrad with precisely the ideological conjuncture he sought. England, Conrad believes, is 'the only barrier to the pressure of infernal doctrines born in continental backslums';[41] its settled, hierarchic traditionalism is a bastion against that 'fraternity [which] tends to weaken the national sentiment, the preservation of which is my concern'.[42] Conrad's entry into English letters, then, is far from the

39. Joseph Conrad. *A Personal Record* (London, 1921), p. xii.
40. See Perry Anderson, 'Components of the National Culture', *New Left Review* 50, July/August 1968, for an analysis of the conservative 'white emigration' into England crucially relevant to Conrad, Henry James and T. S. Eliot. See also my own *Exiles and Emigrés* (London, 1970).
41. *Life and Letters*, ed. G. J. Aubry (New York, 1927), p. 84.
42. Ibid., p. 269.

inruption of an 'alien' ideology into English history, the intrusion into the native social formation of a 'class-subject' produced by foreign forces. His expatriate status is relevant only as one among several possible modes of contradictory unity with the dominant native ideology. 'Expatriatism' is not a 'totalisation' of Conrad's individual position as 'subject' within either Polish or English society; it is, rather, a set of objective ideological relations occupied by the historical subject Joseph Conrad, one determined in the last instance by the internal articulations of the native ideology.

As Avron Fleishmann has argued,[43] Conrad directly inherits the organicist tradition of nineteenth-century Romantic humanism. His positive values, incarnate above all in the virile solidarity of the ship's crew, are the reactionary Carlylean imperatives of work, duty, fidelity and stoical submission – values which bind men spontaneously to the social whole. Yet his fiction, with its recurrent motif of the divided self, is also shot through with a guilty, lawless Romantic individualism which struggles to subject itself to communal discipline. Conrad's social organicism, in other words, is united with an extreme, sometimes solipsistic individualism – a metaphysical scepticism as to the objective nature of social values, a distrust of ideals as the irrational reflexes of egoism and illusion, a view of human societies as essentially 'criminal' organisations of selfish interests, a deep-rooted subjectivism which sees the world as desperately enigmatic, a sense of history as cyclical or absurd.

This ideological conjuncture in Conrad's texts is determined in the last instance by the imperialist character of the English capitalism he served; and it is overdetermined by his Polish experience, with its conflict of organicist idealism and political disillusionment. Nineteenth-century imperialism demanded the production of a corporate, messianic, idealist ideology; but it demanded this at precisely the point where mid-Victorian faith in progress was being eroded into pessimism, subjectivism and irrationalism by (in the last instance) the very economic depression which catalysed the intensified exploitation of the Empire. Imperialism threw into embarrassing exposure the discrepancy between its Romantic ideals and sordid material practice; it also bred an awareness of cultural relativism at precisely the point where the absolute cultural hege-

43. *Conrad's Politics* (Baltimore, 1967), Chapter III.

mony of the imperialist nations needed to be affirmed. The fatal disjuncture between fact and value, ideal and reality, matter and spirit, Nature and consciousness which pervades Conrad's work is a product of these contradictions.

Conrad's contemptuous rejection of humanitarianism springs in part from a recognition of the imperialist exploitation it rationalises. Yet while denouncing crudely unidealistic forms of imperialism, he is ideologically constrained to discover in the British variant a saving 'idea' – a Romantic commitment to the welding of politically amorphous tribal societies into truly 'organic' units. His onslaught upon nakedly exploitative Belgian or American imperialism is at root that of the traditionalist English conservative radically distrustful of bourgeois 'materialism' and 'commercialism'. It is only when such activity is graced by an organic ideal, as in the merchant service, that the contradiction between his own Romantic nationalism, and the brutal realities of colonialism, can be 'resolved'. Conrad neither believes in the cultural superiority of the colonialist nations, nor rejects imperialism outright. The 'message' of *Heart of Darkness* is that Western civilisation is at base as barbarous as African society – a viewpoint which disturbs imperialist assumptions to the precise degree that it reinforces them.

This conflict between organic solidarity and sceptical individualism is mediated in Conrad's aesthetic. He writes of the artist as snatching 'a passing phase of life' and showing its vibration, colour and form in an effort to evoke 'the latent feeling of fellowship with all creation – and the subtle but invincible conviction of solidarity that knits together the loneliness of innumerable hearts. . . .'[44] The ideological function of art is to affirm human solidarity against disintegrative individualism; yet to characterise its materials as vibrant and ephemeral ironically underscores the individualist impressionism which is to be ideologically overcome. For Conrad, art consists in a scrupulous refinement of recalcitrant language into concrete image and expressive nuance; for him, as for Henry James, the novel constitutes a cunningly fashioned organic unity, which in turn implies a redefinition of the writer as fastidious Flaubertian *worker* of his text. (Writing, he once commented, is a form of *action*.) Yet in redefining the writer as a worker, *fin-de-siècle* aestheticism severs

44. Preface to *The Nigger of the Narcissus* (London, 1921), p. viii.

him at the same moment from a social context. The author is a worker, but his product no longer has an assured audience. The confident mid-Victorian pact between producer and consumer has partly collapsed – a collapse reflected in the increasingly problematic status of the writer's productive means, language itself. The author must intensively 'work' his text precisely because he can no longer rely on 'ordinary language' as a nexus with his consumers, trapped as he is within an ideology which views human communication itself as no more than transiently consoling illusion. Indeed, Dickens is perhaps the last historical point at which sheer verbal exuberance has not come to signify writing-as-object – *écriture*, in Roland Barthes's sense of the term.[45] Conrad's calculated linguistic colourfulness offers a significant contrast. The text must be subtly structured into complex unity, but it is what it fails to articulate which matters most – the restlessly allusive suggestions which leave its meanings multiple, ambiguous and unachieved, the merely 'adjectival' hints of meaning which F. R. Leavis correctly identifies in *Heart of Darkness*.[46] The work, that is to say, is at once organically closed and verbally open-ended; images must be clearly etched, but 'Every image floats uncertainly in a sea of doubt . . . in an unexplored universe of incertitudes.'[47] Conrad proceeds in this letter to Edward Garnett, to question the very reality of the *reader*, coupling the formal question of how to write with the problem of his own precarious status as literary producer. What Conrad does, in effect, is to combine a Romantic aesthetic with a 'productive' one. The end of art is to penetrate the phenomenal world to reveal its elusive essence; yet this task, which as it stands is a mere commonplace of idealist aesthetics, requires a crippling amount of sweated labour. Fiction struggles constantly to deny its own artifice, to present itself as 'natural' and translucent; yet this effort must always be self-defeating. The artist, like Marlow, constantly betrays the truth in his attempt to convey it more precisely.

It is, indeed, with the discovery of Marlow as a narrative device

45. See *Writing Degree Zero* (London, 1967). This contradiction comes to a head in 'modernism', where (as with Joyce) a scrupulously precise refinement of meaning paradoxically transforms the work into a self-regarding linguistic object radically closed to its audience, defying them in the act of apparently communicating more exactly.

46. *The Great Tradition* (Harmondsworth, 1962), p. 198.

47. *Letters from Conrad*, ed. Edward Garnett (London, 1927), p. 153.

that Conrad is able to 'solve' the question of how to write. For the ploy of the narrator allows the epistemological problem of how to communicate the real to be incorporated into the formal structures of the text itself. Writing a story, discovering a form, becomes for Conrad paradigmatic of the epistemological difficulties which beset him; to construct a narrative is to construct a moral order. But that order is condemned to be as precarious and provisional as the act of writing itself – a fragile and perilous enterprise, ceaselessly constructed and deconstructed as that adventure into the unknown which is narrative unfolds its course. In working his fiction, then, the writer is shaping a vacuum, sculpting a void. Work for Conrad is a self-sacrificial sharing in the social totality, but like Kurtz's labours in *Heart of Darkness* merely exposes one's estrangement from the eternally elusive Nature which is to be reduced to order. Aesthetic form must vanquish the inchoate, as imperialism strives to subdue the 'disorganisation' of tribal society to 'rational' structure; yet such ordering always contains its own negation.

Each of Conrad's novels, indeed, is alive with such a subversive negation of its organic unity. Ideological dissonances emerge in his fiction not, as with Dickens, in an exploitation of open-ended, internally discrepant forms, but in the calculative organisation of interlacing patterns around a central absence. At the centre of each of Conrad's works is a resonant silence: the unfathomable enigma of Kurtz, Jim and Nostromo, the dark, brooding passivity of James Wait in *The Nigger of the Narcissus*, the stolid opacity of McWhirr in *Typhoon*, the eternal crypticness of the 'Russian soul' in *Under Western Eyes*, the unseen bomb-explosion and mystical silence of the idiot Stevie in *The Secret Agent*, Heyst's nonexistent treasure in *Victory*.[48] These absences are determinate – they demarcate the gaps

48. It is perhaps worth interpolating that the most striking Victorian example of the absent-centred work is *In Memoriam*. The absent centre around which the poem broods and hovers is the blank left by the death of Arthur Hallam, which fragments the poem formally into a series of brief meditations. But that absence is an ideologically determinate one, since the poem is not primarily about Hallam's death, but about the whole spectrum of ideological anxieties and insecurities (science, rationalism, loss of faith, fear of revolution) which that blankness brings into blurred focus. Hallam is the empty space congregated with these almost inarticulate anxieties. The melancholy of the poem (c.f. Freud: melancholy is grief without an object) reflects the fact that it is ideologically prohibited from knowing precisely why

and limits of the Conradian ideology, represent the 'hollows' scooped out by a collision or exclusion of meanings.

The elusiveness of Lord Jim, for example – one produced by the novel's densely-layered narrative technique – is essentially that of the cypher to which Jim is reduced by the mutual cancellation of two contradictory perspectives on him. He can be seen at once as Romantic colonialist, strenuously shaping his own destiny, and as the inexorably determined plaything of a mechanistic cosmos. A similar mutual cancellation inheres in the formal structure of *Under Western Eyes*, where the heroic but 'fanatical' Russian soul, and the humane but humdrum empiricism of the English narrator, put each other continually into question in a spiral of overlapping ironies. The sturdy silence of McWhirr embodies the ineffable values of the organicist tradition, values of dogged fidelity and unreflective heroism which can be shown but not said. The brooding passivity of James Wait, conversely, signifies an anarchic dissolution of social order too metaphysically deep-seated to be articulable. The heart of darkness in the story of that title is imperialism itself, which, since it can be figured only as farcical fantasy and metaphysical evil, must necessarily remain obscure; but it is also the African societies which imperialism plunders, societies which appear, in imperialist fashion, as baffling enigmas. The bomb-explosion in *The Secret Agent*, like Jim's jump from his ship, cannot be directly presented: it suggests a kind of cataclysmic transformation, an unpredictable 'leap' in an organically evolving Nature, which the novel's conservative ideology can accommodate only as impenetrable mystery. The absent centre of *Nostromo* is in part Nostromo himself, but also the silver of which he is the agent – the inert, opaque matter around which the human action frenetically swirls. As the determining structure of which the novel's characters are the bearers (the true protagonist of the book, as Conrad commented), the silver is the unifying principle of the entire action; but since that action has for Conrad no coherent historical intelligibility, it is a principle which must of necessity be dramatically absent. It is precisely in these absent centres, which 'hollow' rather than scatter and fragment the

---

it is sad; it is a classic document of bourgeois ideological insecurity which can only obliquely know itself as such, displacing its anxieties to the personal figure of Hallam.

organic forms of Conrad's fiction, that the relations of that fiction to its ideological context is laid bare.

'It is evident', Conrad wrote to Garnett, 'that my fate is to be descriptive, and descriptive only. There are things I *must* leave alone.'[49] This, precisely, is Conrad's major problem of form, determined by – and determining – the ideological matrix in which his writing is set. For it is not a matter of Conrad's forms 'expressing' an ideology; it is rather a question of the ideological contradictions which his literary forms inevitably produce. The characteristic Conradian work is an exotic tale of *action*, richly and concretely rendered, on whose margins play a set of sceptical questions about the very reality of action itself. The tale or yarn 'foregrounds' action as solid and unproblematic; it assumes the unimpeachable realities of history, character, the objective world. Yet these assumptions are simultaneously thrown into radical doubt by the penumbra of spectral meanings which surround the narrative, crossing and blurring its contours. If the narrative is reduced to a yarn, those crucial meanings dissolve; if the meanings are directly probed, it is the narrative which evaporates. What unifies dramatic action and 'metaphysical' intimation is mood: the exoticism of the one matches the esotericism of the other. In working the *genre* of the adventure story, then, Conrad 'produces' his own ideology in a determinate form. The adventure story gives rise to a simple, solid specificity of action, which is in turn confronted with its corrosive negation – haunted like the ship *Narcissus* or *The Secret Sharer* with the ghost it must exorcise if the narrative is to survive. Such survival is for Conrad ideologically as well as artistically essential: faith, work and duty must not be allowed to yield to scepticism if the supreme fiction of social order is to be sustained. It is for this reason that Conrad the pessimist insists that the artist's task is not to convey moral nihilism, but to cherish undying hope.[50] Yet that hope can never be anything other than ambiguous. The naturalistic form of *The Secret Agent* thickens and reifies the material world to a point where its revolutionary destruction seems naturally unthinkable; yet this very thickening lends men and objects an air of grotesque mystery which merges with the book's fear of the anarchic unknown.

49. *Letters to Garnett*, p. 94.
50 *Notes on Life and Letters*.

If such 'metaphysical materialism' is needed to confirm the naturalness of the given, it also banishes that realm of subjectivity which is an equally necessary protest against bourgeois positivism. Within a dispassionately deadlocked world, then, violent change (Winnie), motion (Verloc), spiritual vision (Stevie) must insist on thrusting themselves into the text, if only in mysterious ways. Stevie's silence is that of the 'mystical' which can be shown but not stated; the text *speaks* its contradictions, rather than speaks of them. Its discourse is circled by the abyss on whose brink the nihilist Professor is continually poised – the Professor, who, wired up for instant self-consignment to eternity, is thus a graphic image of the text itself. For *The Secret Agent* is able to reveal the truth of itself only by that ceaseless process of 'self-detonation' which is irony. Only by the revolutionary act of negating its every proposition and reconstructing itself *ex nihilo* could it articulate the real; yet this, it knows, is impossible, for it is doomed to work with discourses riddled with ideological contradiction – or, as the novel itself would say, condemned to the eternal inauthenticity of language. But the work cannot allow itself to disappear down the abyss of the unspeakable, allowing its propositions to be retrospectively cancelled, leaving itself with absolutely nothing to say. If it resembles the Wittgenstein of the *Tractatus Logico-Philosophicus* in its commitment to the transcendent, it must also mime the Wittgenstein of *Philosophical Investigations* in its consecration of that vast, stalemated 'game' which is society. Value, identified with a despised humanitarianism of which anarchist dreams are an even more degenerate extension, is thus forced beyond the frontiers of the world, exiled beyond articulation. Yet precisely because of this, everything seems to be left exactly as it was; and this provides the text with a kind of resolution, or, better, with the illusion of one. The world, as with the *Tractatus*, just is 'everything that is the case'; and in this sense there is no need for a resolution *because there is nothing, it seems, to resolve*. Stalemated games are in one way unachieved, in another way complete; the world goes on, and this is at once the question, and the answer, of the text. The need for value, and the recognition of its utter vacuity: it is here that the deepest contradiction of Conrad's enterprise, one integral to the imperialist ideology he shared, stands revealed.

5. Henry James

With Conrad, organic living is possible only in historically untypical conditions: the ship's crew, the idealised Polish or tribal community. With James we have moved a step further: organic living can now only be a matter of that organic *consciousness* supremely epitomised by art,[51] contemplatively totalising a world without inherent structure. The business of the artist is 'always to *make* a sense – and to make it most in proportion as the immediate aspects (of experience) are loose and confused.[52] James's work thus represents a desperate, devoted attempt to salvage organic significance wholly in the sealed realm of consciousness – to vanquish, by the power of such 'beautiful', multiple yet harmoniously unifying awareness, certain real conflicts and divisions. In the form of the struggle for material acquisition, those conflicts generate the wealth which makes such privileged consciousness possible in the first place. But the bearer of such contemplative consciousness is thereby absent from concrete history, displaced from what he totalises; to 'know' (a crucial Jamesian term) is both supreme transcendence and impotent negativity. A consciousness like that of Ralph Touchett in *The Portrait of a Lady*, Dr Sloper in *Washington Square*, Vanderbank in *The Awkward Age* or the anonymous narrator of *The Sacred Fount* sensitively encompasses the social reality it confronts, yet precisely because of its indolent detachment from the world emerges as privatised and peripheral; it isn't fortuitous that the bearer of such consciousness in *What Maisie Knew* should be a child. Because totalisation necessarily involves such remoteness from the real, it is constantly in danger of destructive falsification, riding roughshod over the empirical (like *The Sacred Fount* narrator or the governess in *The Turn of the Screw*) in its hunt for the single, secret principle which will transform experience into the cohesive intelligibility of an artefact.

51. 'To see it always as a whole is our wise, our virtuous effort, the very condition, as we keep in mind, of superior art... The question of the whereabouts of the unity of a group of subject data to be wrought together into a thing of art, the question in other words of the point at which the various implications of interest, no matter how many, *must* converge and interfuse, becomes always, by my sense of the affair, quite the first to be answered. (*Notes on Novelists* (London, 1914), p. 100).

52. *The American Scene* (London, 1907), p. 273.

Yet the sterile negativity of knowing is also convertible to a kind of virtue. Privileged spirits like Isabel Archer in *The Portrait of a Lady* and Milly Theale in *The Wings of the Dove*, by their fine refusal to win anything for themselves, their heroic renunciation of self-interest, triumph spiritually over the possessive individualism of others. They triumph over those less abundantly provided with the material wealth which provides such transcendental gestures with their basis. That basis, as John Goode has pointed out, is in the late James the immense fortunes of the US corporations, which enable their beneficiaries 'to have so much money that (they) no longer have to think about it'.[53] This, indeed, is the historical secret of the 'negativity' of the Jamesian spirit: negativity is the abyss which opens up between consciousness itself and the suppressed, supportive economic base of which it is finely oblivious – an abyss inscribed within consciousness itself as a blank freedom from financial constraint. It is in the darkness of this abyss that the true historical determinants of James's fiction are most clearly illuminated. In characters like Milly Theale, however, or Maggie Verver in *The Golden Bowl*, this patrician release from the possessive individualism which saturates James's world can be converted into a 'positive' negation: it is by silent self-sacrifice and suffering passivity that these characters go to work on their environments, redeeming its twisted acquisitive relationships precisely by their saintly refusal to materially intervene, transforming non-possessiveness into a mode of spiritually possessing others.

Yet such magical 'corporate' consciousness, generated by the pervasive, transformative power of enormous corporation wealth, is radically ambiguous. If it can be seen on the one hand as a sublime transcendence of historically 'lower' forms of bourgeois individualism, it can also be read as a mystifying sublimation of such modes – a dominative individualism raised to the spiritual region of exquisitely 'disinterested' awareness. This is the ideological basis of the structural ambiguity of James's fiction – of the 'double reading' continually possible of the *Turn of the Screw* governess, Fleda Vetch

53. *The Air of Reality: new essays on Henry James*, ed. John Goode (London, 1972), p. 255. The period which intervened between James's visit to the USA in 1883 and his return twenty years later was the epoch of that immense expansion of American capitalism which saw the rise of the corporations, tycoons and robber barons and the creation of a new, wholly wealth-based 'aristocracy'.

in *The Spoils of Poynton*, Masie Farange in *What Masie Knew*, Mrs Brookenham in *The Awkward Age*, Milly Theale and Maggie Verver, all of whom can be viewed as types of civilised consciousness or as subtly possessive individualists.

The contradictions of James's spiritual aristocrats, parasitic on a bourgeois material base which must be ceaselessly suppressed, are overdetermined by the contradictory form of James's own mode of insertion into bourgeois society. His grandfather was a prosperous businessman who bequeathed to his numerous descendants a fortune large enough for complete independence of 'commerce' – an independence graphically caricatured in the Swendenborgian philosophising career of James's own father, with his idealist aversion to American 'materialism' and his desire to furnish his sons with enough financial resources to allow them to remain freely uncommitted. James was consequently dislocated from the significant history which surrounded him; he speaks of his family's 'common disconnectedness' in a society where 'business alone was respectable',[54] and in the Preface to *The Reverberator* confesses his incapacity to deal artistically with the 'mystery' of commerce. His status as internal emigré in the United States, intensified by his New Yorker family's situation as 'outsiders' in Boston, is then reproduced in his literal expatriate relation to England. James flees from the 'invented', inorganic, traditionless 'huge looseness' of America to the 'high civilisation' of England, whose 'manners, customs, usages, habits, forms'[55] provide the mature soil to nourish his art; his relation to English society is therefore both parasitic (he speaks of his desire to 'feed on English life') and spectatorial. Like his conservative emigré colleague Joseph Conrad, James combines an intense ideological commitment to his adopted mother-country with an ironically contemplative dissociation from its history. Writing to Grace Norton in 1885, he declares that he can imagine 'no spectacle more touching, thrilling and dramatic than to see this precarious, artificial Empire struggling with forces which might prove too much for it'; if only England will maintain her fight against Irish nationalism rather than collapse and surrender, 'the drama may be worth watching' from the 'good near standpoint' he has.[56] (But, he adds coyly, he

54. *Autobiography*, ed. F. W. Dupec (London, 1956), p. 278.
55. *Letters of Henry James*, ed. Percy Lubbock (London, 1920), vol. I, p. 72.
56. *ibid*., p. 113.

didn't mean to be so 'beastly political'.) One year later, he writes to his brother to express his annoyance at having 'lost the spectacle' of the Piccadilly demonstration of the unemployed; if only he had been at home he would have had an excellent view from his balcony.

Like Conrad, James's expatriatism represents an objective set of ideological relations rather than an 'expression' of some 'class' or 'national' situation. The historical *fact* of expatriatism is, ideologically, an *effect* of the overdetermination of an individual's mode of insertion into the native ideology by those ideological factors which within his mother-country have constituted him as a subject. Like Conrad also, James's fiction is irreducible to a simple 'reflection' of this ideological conjuncture. For James is (like Conrad) no more than a particular name for (among other historical issues) an aspect of the crisis of nineteenth-century realism – a crisis in which the problem of literary signification itself becomes a determinant structure of literary production. The question of 'knowledge' is certainly relevant to James's historical status as expatriate; but this status is no more than a specific overdetermination of a question raised by the very ideology of 'realism' itself. For realism, not least in its liberal humanist variant, presupposes a privileged epistemological standpoint from which precise moral judgement may be effected, a fine transparent intelligence outside which there is nothing, which can be transfixed by no critical gaze from beyond the limits of its discourse. Yet it is precisely the exasperating *difficulty* of such precise judgement which this discourse takes within the text as the object of its scrutiny; and since this is so, it is inevitably constrained to glance sideways at the spurious supports of its own omniscience. How to do so without dissolving those supports to nothing is the formal problem which the later James is increasingly forced to confront – how to curve back literary discourse upon itself without collapsing it into sheer tautology. The flailing, devious syntax of the later novels struggles to preserve a coherence of textual consciousness threatened at every moment with engulfment by what it signifies. Privileged consciousness must be preserved, but must also appropriate its own shadowy limits, obliquely provoking possible readings beyond its apparent knowledge, positing a reader who will construct rather than consume its meanings. Yet all this must go on, as it were, behind the back of the classical realist form: that form, and the ideological values it both produces and secretes, must not be 'exploded' by devices which would call the stability of the spectatorial ego into explicit question. For beneath that form lies an ideology of the subject, and beneath that a social formation – regions into which not even the finest critical intelligence may be permitted to penetrate.

Yet the English social formation provided in the end no redemptive organic enclave for James. Professional house-party guest of the ruling class though he was for some twenty years, he found English life grossly materialistic and thought the condition of the upper class as rotten and collapsible as that of the French aristocracy before the revolution.[57] Organic consciousness could find no locus but art itself, which alone could circumscribe the sprawling, tangled infinity of empirical relationships with its delicately delineating forms.[58] James's later work represents the astonishing enterprise of rescuing and redeeming inorganic material existence by ceaselessly absorbing its raw contingencies into the transmutative structures of consciousness, deploying to this end the complex interlacings of a syntax constantly threatened with dissolution by the heterogeneous materials it just succeeds in subduing. 'All the value of (Strether's) total episode (in *The Ambassadors*)', he writes, 'has precisely been that 'knowing' was the effect of it.'[59] 'Knowing' – consciousness itself – is the supreme non-commodity, and so for James the supreme value; yet in a society where the commodity reigns unchallenged it is also absence, failure, negation. In 'knowing', the world is appropriated and lost in the same act. This, finally, was the contradiction which even Henry James was unable to transcend.

6. *T. S. Eliot*

Henry James's successor as a conservative American expatriate was T. S. Eliot, son of an 'aristocratic' St Louis family. The social and intellectual hegemony of the Eliots had been traumatically under-

57. *Letters*, vol. I, p. 122.
58. 'Really, universally, relations stop nowhere, and the exquisite problem of the artist is eternally to draw, by a geometry of his own, the circle within which they shall happily *appear* to do so.' (*The Art of the Novel*), ed. R. P. Blackmur (New York, 1962), p. 5. The equivalent in the content of James's fiction to the *circle* of form is the *square*: 'squaring' persons, situations and relationships, drawing them by the diplomatic negotiations of consciousness into harmonious unity, is a recurrent Jamesian metaphor.
59. *The Notebooks of Henry James*, ed. F. O. Matthiessen and K. B. Murdock (New York, 1947), p. 409.

mined in the early years of this century by revelations of the corrupt, boss-ridden system of St Louis – a corruption in which the Eliots were apparently implicated.[60] Spiritually disinherited like James by industrial capitalist America, able later to discover in America the 'blood', breeding and 'organic' regionalism he valued only in such phenomena as the right-wing neo-agrarian movement in Virginia, Eliot came to Europe with the historic mission of redefining the organic unity of its cultural traditions, and reinserting a culturally provincial England into that totality. He was, indeed, to become himself the focal-point of the organic consciousness of the 'European mind', that rich, unruptured entity mystically inherent in its complex simultaneity in every artist nourished by it. English literary culture, still in the grip of ideologically exhausted forms of liberal humanism and late Romanticism, was to be radically reconstructed into a classicism which would eradicate the last vestiges of 'Whiggism' (protestantism, liberalism, Romanticism, humanism). It would do so in the name of a higher, corporate ideological formation, defined by the surrender of 'personality' to order, reason, authority and tradition.

The wholesale demolition and salvage job which it was Eliot's historical task to carry out in the aesthetic region of English ideology was one for which he was historically peculiarly well-equipped, as an expatriate with a privileged, panoramic vantage-point on that area. He was sufficiently internal to it as a New Englander to judge 'authoritatively', yet as a 'European' American sufficiently external to identify its parochial limitations. Eliot's own description of his function is characteristically sham-casual: 'From time to time, every hundred years or so, it is desirable that a critic shall appear to review the past of our literature, and set the poets and the poem in a new order. This task is not one of revolution but of readjustment'.[61] It seems a modest description of what Graham Martin has rightly termed 'the most ambitious feat of cultural imperialism the century seems likely to produce';[62] but the bland unalarmist, evolutionary

60. See Gabriel Pearson, 'Eliot: an American Use of Symbolism', in *Eliot in Perspective*, ed. Graham Martin (London, 1970), p. 98. My turning here from fiction to poetry itself reflects an historically significant shift; as we shall see, poetry for Eliot is itself a peculiarly resourceful and appropriate *ideological* medium, as it is in different ways for Yeats.

61. *The Use of Poetry and the Use of Criticism* (London, 1933), p. 108.

62. *Eliot in Persepective*, p. 22.

stress of Eliot's formulation is central to his project. Confronted with world imperialist crisis, severe economic depression and intensifying working-class militancy, English society in the early years of Eliot's career as poet and critic stood in urgent ideological need of precisely the values his literary classicism encapsulated. Yet the ideological potency of that classicism rested in its refusal of static, rationalist forms for an empiricist, historicist mould — rested, indeed, in the production of a classicism contradictorily united with the evolutionary organicism of the Romantic tradition. Eliot's 'Tradition' is a labile, self-transformative organism extended in space and time, constantly reorganised by the present; but this radical historical relativism is then endowed with the status of absolute classical authority. What Eliot does, in fact, is to adopt the aesthetics of a late phase of Romanticism (symbolism), with its view of the individual artefact as organic, impersonal and autonomous, and then project this doctrine into an authoritarian cultural ideology.[63]

By framing his classicist doctrine in the organicist terms of the Romantic tradition, Eliot is able to combine an idealist totality with the sensuous empiricism which is its other aspect. If the aesthetic region of ideology is to be effectively refashioned, poetic language must clutch and penetrate the turbulent, fragmentary character of contemporary experience, sinking its tentacular roots into the primordial structures of the collective unconsciousness. As such, poetry offers a paradigm of ideological affectivity in general: Eliot's ideal of the organic society is one in which a finely conscious élite transmits its values through rhythm, habit and resonance to the largely unconscious masses, infiltrating the nervous system rather than engaging the mind.[64] Hence the radical anti-intellectualism of the scholarly, esoteric Eliot: the nervous distrust of abstract ideas, the insistence on the poetic transmutation of thought into sense-experience, the imagist emphasis on the hard, precise image as 'containing' its concept, yoked to the symbolist preoccupation with poetry as music.

There is, however, a latent contradiction between Eliot's concern

63. In a somewhat parallel way, the doctrine of the 'objective correlative' pivots on an arbitrary projection of subjective experience into formulae which are then merely *asserted* to be the 'objective', consistently identifiable codes for that experience.

64. See *The Idea of a Christian Society* (London, 1939) and *Notes towards the Definition of Culture* (1948). It is symptomatic of Eliot's political acumen that the regressive social utopianism of the former volume should be offered to the world on the very eve of the Second World War.

for art as organic order and his insistence on the sensuously mimetic properties of poetic language. The Olympian pontificator of *Tradition and the Individual Talent*, with his values of order and impersonality, is also the poet of *The Love-Song of J. Alfred Prufrock*, with its restlessly subjective universe of doomed emotions and discrete objects. Eliot attempts to surmount this contradiction in his recourse to the Metaphysical poets: for Donne represents the last *strained* and *tortuous* historical moment of organic coherence between mind and blood, senses and intellect, before the cataclysmic Fall into the secularist disintegration of the seventeenth century – the defeat of royalism, the puritan emigration (including the Eliots from Somerset), the demise of the catholicity of the Church of England, the rise of scientific rationalism, the linguistic disaster of Milton, the accelerating decline to the Romantic cult of the errant ego. Donne creates organic wholes from experience while enacting its actual fragmentation; and this, presumably, is also the intention of *The Waste Land*. Yet the 'form' of that poem is in contradiction with its 'content': *The Waste Land*'s fragmentary content listlessly mimes the experience of cultural disintegration, while its totalising mythological forms silently allude to a transcendence of such collapse. The poem is opaque both because of its verbal complicity in that collapse, and in the esoteric allusions which attempt to construct an ideal order across it.

It is possible to trace in this aesthetic dissonance something of Eliot's own ambiguous relationship to the crisis of European bourgeois society which *The Waste Land* records. Indeed, the question of where Eliot stands in relation to the poem becomes the question of where he stands in relation to his adopted society. As an 'aristocratic' American expatriate preoccupied in the first place with a vision of organic cultural unity, Eliot's idealism partly dissevers him from the historical reality of the crisis he confronts. Yet the cosmopolitan *avant-garde* poet of the early work is also the industrious servant of Lloyd's bank, necessarily supporting the economic system which practically ensures, even while it 'spiritually' threatens, the conditions of élitist culture. It is in the blank space between the 'form' and 'content' of *The Waste Land*, between its cosmic detachment and guilty collusion, that the ideology which produces it is most visibly inscribed.

Yet *The Waste Land* produces an ideology, as well as being

produced by one. It is not in the first place an ideology of 'cultural disintegration'; it is an ideology of *cultural knowledge*. What the poem signifies, indeed, is not 'the decay of Europe' or fertility cults but its own elaborate display of esoteric allusion – a display *enabled* by such arcane or panoramic motifs. The reader who finds his or her access to the poem's 'meaning' baulked by its inscrutable gesturing off-stage is already in possession of that 'meaning' without knowing it. Cultures collapse, but Culture survives, and its form is *The Waste Land*: this is the ideological gesture of the text, inscribed in the scandalous fact of its very existence. It is in this sense that the poem's signifying codes contradict their signifieds: for if history is indeed sterility then the work itself could not come into being, and if the work exists then it does so only as an implicit denial of its 'content'. The self-cancelling status of *The Waste Land* is the index of an ideological riddle of origins to which there is no material answer: if history is futile and exhausted, where does Culture come from? One may rephrase the riddle differently: if poetic signs have ideological potency only by virtue of being crammed with sensory experience, how are they to fulfil the ideologically vital role of *commenting* on the experience they enact? It is the same question in a different guise: where *within* the sphere of experience is the source of the discourse (Culture, ideology) needed to redeem it? It cannot be inside that sphere, for this would be to level its transcendental status; but it cannot be outside of it either, for this would be to rob it of 'experiential' force, rendering it as impotent as the spectatorial Tiresias. If, then, positive value can lie neither inside nor outside the poem, it must reside instead in the very limits of the text itself – in that which gives it its form. It must lie in that which can be shown but not spoken, which is nothing less than the 'fact' of the poem itself. The 'fact' of the poem is constituted by a set of 'progressive' devices which articulate discourse with discourse, refusing the allure of organic closure; the text's partial dissolution of its signs to its fragmentary situations, its mimetic denial of a 'totalising' overview, *is* its ideological affectivity. Such partial dissolution, however, is in no sense a 'naturalising' of the sign: in its *articulated* discourses, the poem parades itself as a thoroughly constructed text, tempting a 'representational' reading which it simultaneously subverts by its exposed productive mechanisms. Yet this subversion turns out to be merely phenomenal: for behind the back of this ruptured, radically decentred poem runs an alternative text which is nothing less than the closed, coherent, authoritative discourse of the mythologies which frame it. The phenomenal text, to use one of Eliot's own metaphors, is merely the meat with which the burglar distracts the guard-dog while he proceeds with his stealthy business. The ideology of the text lies in the distance between these two discourses – in the fact that the 'phenomenal' text is able to 'show', but not *speak of*, the covert coherence which sustains it. For if that coherence is directly articulated, an ideological impact gained only through indirection is lost; yet it is important, none the less, that such impact should not be wholly dispersed to its phenomenal effects. It is for this reason that at the end of the poem the 'covert' text does, for once, speak, in the cryptic imperatives delivered by the voice of the thunder. It is not T. S. Eliot, or a character, or the 'phenomenal' text who speaks; it can only be an anonymous, conveniently hypostasised absolute. What the thunder enunciates is a withdrawn ascetic wisdom whose ideological implications are at odds with the 'progressive', pioneering, typographically-conscious forms of the poem itself; but it is precisely in this conjuncture of 'progressive form' and 'reactionary content' that the ideology of *The Waste Land* inheres. Both elements are united by a certain 'élitism': the *'avant-garde'* experiments of a literary côterie match the conservative values of a ruling minority. The purpose of those experiments is precisely to put such values 'in train'; yet the effect of this is nothing less than a questioning of their efficacy, as the thunder's Olympian *fiats* are shown up for the hollow booming they are.

Eliot's early espousal of F. H. Bradley's neo-Hegelianism, with its insistence on the non-relational unity of immediate experience, provided him with a partial solution to his search for organic wholeness. But Bradley's dissolution of the self to the relations between its experiences, while counteracting that puritan individualism which was for Eliot the ideological enemy, by the same token merely confirmed the exile's sense of ruptured, deracinated identity. Similarly, though in Bradley the unity of immediate experience prefigures the supra-rational unity of an Absolute for which the early Eliot hungers, in practice all standpoints are reduced by that doctrine to total relativism. Eliot's Tradition 'historicises' Bradleyan organicism, as Bradley had dehistoricised Hegel; but in doing so it extends rather than escapes from a sealed, intersubjective circuit, replacing real history with a self-evolving idealist whole in which all time is eternally present, and so unredeemable. The purely phenomenological totality offered by Bradley is ideologically insufficient: Eliot moves beyond it to the royalist Anglican conservatism which will provide a social locus for such organicism. Ideally, that is; in fact, his pathetically nostalgic fantasies of a hierarchical Christian order, organically interfusing a devout populace with a clericist élite, are as historically obsolescent as Conrad's romanticising of the merchant code. 'Spiritual' wholeness must find its social correlative, yet in doing so merely reveals its social impotence. *Four Quartets* offers a spiritual totality which transcends a nugatory phenomenal world, yet must lefthandedly imbue it with begrudged significance – a contradiction which will dislocate the very formal structures of Eliot's later drama, with its incongruous crossing and counterpointing of metaphysics and drawing-room comedy. Eliot 'advances' beyond Conrad and James to the point of locating the organic ideal in a concrete social institution, the Christian church;[65] if he could advance no further, it was because his solution was part of the problem.

7. W. B. Yeats

While Eliot, Pound, T. E. Hulme and the Imagists are turning in England from the dwindling resources of Romantic individualism towards forms of classical or symbolist impersonality, W. B. Yeats reaches back in Ireland to Celtic mythology and the early English Romantic heritage, defiantly opposing style, passion and personality to the 'hot-faced bargainers and the money-changers', the encroaching world of the Irish bourgeoisie. Whereas in England Romantic individualism is an ideological component of a long-established bourgeois class, that class in imperially subjugated Ireland is still nascent; Yeats therefore has to hand, in his struggle against bourgeois hegemony, the resources of an *aristocratic* Romanticism long since moribund in bourgeois England – the idealised cavalier, ceremonious lineage of the Anglo-Irish Ascendancy.

Yet Yeats's relation to that heritage, and through it to Irish

65. An institution which, incidently, exerted a significant fascination for both James and Conrad.

society as a whole, is markedly contradictory. He belonged by birth not to the Ascendancy class but to the Protestant bourgeoisie; and as such he was doubly dislocated within Irish society, both from the class with whom he identified and from the Catholic nationalist movement whose poetic mythologer he attempted to become. As the leader of the cultural wing of the nationalist movement in the 1890s, Yeats recoiled from the very Catholic bourgeoisie who formed the nationalist movement's mass social basis; the Land League, with its strategy of transferring economic power from Protestant to emergent Catholic bourgeoisie by organised boycott, had weakened the influence of both Yeats's own class and the Ascendency to which he spiritually belonged. Yeats accordingly committed himself to the Romantic nationalism of John O'Leary's Fenian Brotherhood, which rejected the Land League's agrarian agitational tactics, and so refused one of the most effective weapons against English imperialism. Yeats's cultural project was to replace the threadbare patriotic jargon of the Young Ireland poetic movement with a richer symbology of nationalist aspirations, nurtured by aristocratic Romanticism and traditional mythology; yet that commitment to the Anglo-Irish Ascendancy, who had never occupied a role of active popular leadership, threw him into contradiction with the real history and basis of the nationalist movement. His cultural nationalism, itself a displacement and appropriation of the political energies temporarily diffused by the Parnell affair, moves into deepening conflict with the realities of nationalist politics – a conflict poetically focused in Maud Gonne, for Yeats at once symbol of Ireland's eternal beauty and rancorous political demagogue. The oxymoronic double-vision of *Easter 1916* reveals well enough Yeats's difficulties in trying to reconcile the Romantic heroism of the uprising with the despised ideology and social class of its leaders.

Yeats's consciousness of his social disinheritance is precisely what fuels the process of his poetic maturation, as his poetry turns in the early years of this century from narcotic fantasy to the stripped, toughened forms of a bitter yet defiant disillusion. *Fin-de-siècle* languour is transformed into combative oratory as the historical contradictions sharpen, forcing the progressively displaced Yeats into a compensatory ideology of aggressive poetic activism. The theory of the poetic mask is accordingly developed, as a projection of Romantic 'personality' into impersonal, socially representative form; the mask protects the poet within a spiritually alien society, but also enacts the organic unity of personal identity and social function which that society has destroyed. Similarly, Yeats moves his poetry closer to common speech at the very point where his aristocratic values are being most scornfully flouted by bourgeois philistinism, and in doing so reactivates a crucial contradiction of early Romanticism – the poet's need to claim centrally 'representative' status at precisely the point where he is being relegated to an historically peripheral role.

It is to that early English Romanticism that Yeats returns, in his attempt to mediate turbulent individualism into historically 'representative' terms. In his drive to 'hammer (his) thoughts into unity', to counter bourgeois power with a cohesive, elaborate symbology less vulnerable to collapse than the vagaries of purely individualist impulse, Yeats reaches back to rework and relive the massive symbolic totalities of that earlier mythologer of bourgeois revolution, William Blake, whose poetry he edits in the early 1890s. Blake, too, marks an ideological conjuncture at which Romantic individualism must be raised to an elaborate mythological system if it is to survive and illuminate the real history which produces it. And as Yeats must come to terms with Blake, so Blake, in his major poem *Milton*, must engage in turn with his own bourgeois revolutionary predecessor. All three poets construct 'cosmic' symbologies which, in mythologising bourgeois revolution, can assess its historical limitations from the visionary vantage-point of an absolute idealism. The culmination of that process in the case of Yeats is the extraordinary cosmology of *A Vision*, the first draft of which was completed in 1917 in the throes of Irish nationalist and world imperialist crisis. The esoteric theosophical symbolism of that work, with its image of reality as a cyclical interpenetration of antinomies, signifies Yeats's most ambitious attempt to 'resolve the deep enmity between man and his destiny' – to reduce the contingencies of a recalcitrant history to the controlling order of myth.

From the outset, Yeats's search was for a mythology which would restore the organic unity of Irish society ('Have not all races had their first unity from a mythology, which marries them to rock and hill?'[66]). The organising symbols of his verse – tree, dancer, tower – are the poetic nodes of such organic wholeness. As that ideal unity

66. *Autobiographies* (London, 1966, p. 194.

became progressively unrealisable in bourgeois Ireland, it was forced into the political mould of fascism. His admiration for Mussolini and the extreme right-wing Free State Senator Kevin O'Higgins, his commitment to O'Duffy's Irish fascist movement in the 1930s, his advocation of 'force and marching men' to break the 'reign of the mob', his dream of a new European civilisation based on despotic élitist rule – in these political doctrines of the ageing Yeats, one destination of the organic ideal in literature stands starkly revealed.

8. James Joyce

There is a sense in which James Joyce's relation to W. B. Yeats is analogous to Henry James's relation to Joseph Conrad. Both Joyce and James displace into the devotional realm of art itself the unity which the two other writers still struggle to locate in a social tradition. Born into the Catholic petty bourgeoisie, Joyce rejected the Romantic Anglo-Irish tradition as bankrupt (he thought Yeats 'a tiresome idiot... quite out of touch with the Irish people'),[67] and its mystificatory aesthetic of inspirational spontaneity; art instead was a productive *labour*, a massive, life-consuming substitute for the social identity denied by a stagnant, clericist, culturally parochial Ireland. From his different class-standpoint, Joyce was as ambiguously related to Irish nationalism as Yeats: he supported Sinn Fein from his self-imposed European exile, comparing (deludedly enough) the socialism of its leader Arthur Griffiths to Labriola's Marxism; yet his abandonment of Ireland was in part a protest against the bourgeois limitations of nationalism, a decisive rupture with its sentimental patriotism, superstitious religiosity and cultural philistinism. If Yeats was historically isolated from nationalism by his identification with Ascendency reaction, Joyce's dissociation from it involved an opposing commitment. Writing to his brother from Trieste, where his friends were mostly workers and socialists, he insists that 'a deferment to the emancipation of the proletariat, a reaction to clericism or aristocracy or bourgeoisism would mean a revulsion to tyrannies of all kinds'.[68] In the determinate absence of such emancipation in Ireland, Joyce's painful self-liberation from

67. Quoted by Richard Ellmann, *James Joyce* (London, 1966), p. 248.
68. Quoted by Ellmann, *op. cit.*, p. 204.

clericism and imperialism had to be achieved, materially and spiritually, through his art.

Yet that art is not to be seen as the 'expression' of the contradictions of Joyce's own 'class-situation'. For the internal contradictions of his texts are a *production*, not a reflection, of the ideological formation into which Joyce as historical subject was ambivalently inserted – a production which, by putting that ideology to work, exposes its framing limits. Nor is the 'aesthetic ideology' to which Joyce's work relates a simple 'reflection' of the ideological formation as a whole. Joyce was born into an ideological sub-ensemble of petty-bourgeois Catholic nationalism – a sub-ensemble which formed a contradictory unity with the dominant ideology. That relation was then overdetermined by his expatriatism, which reproduced that initial contradictory unity in quite different terms. The complexity of this formation is 'produced' at the level of Joyce's aesthetic ideology. For if his espousal of literary naturalism is in one sense a fidelity to the 'realities' of petty-bourgeois Dublin, it is also a commitment to a cosmopolitan perspective within which those 'realities' could be critically distanced. Europe provided Joyce with a means of transcending Irish cultural provincialism, but European *naturalism* reinforced the obsessive petty-bourgeois preoccupation with material routine of a man who attributed to himself the mind of a grocer. Naturalism for Joyce signifies petty-bourgeois paralysis, but is also contradictorily unified with the serene realism of classical epic and the 'realist' scholasticism of the hegemonic Irish order. In *Ulysses*, accordingly, a pedantically 'scholastic' and 'materialist' mythology is used to situate materially-bound society. Conversely, Joyce's commitment to a transcendence and recuperation of Irish society through art links him with certain Romantic and aestheticist aspects of the hegemonic aesthetic ideology; but the idealist notion of the 'Romantic artist', supposedly inimical to naturalism, is seen in *Stephen Hero* as a characteristically *petty-bourgeois* ideology of artistic production.

These complex transactions overdetermine the crisis of literary discourse to which Joyce belongs. It is a crisis apparent in *Dubliners*, in which frustrated desires, fading memories and impotent dreams play listlessly within a drably naturalistic context, to encapsulate the spiritual inertia of contemporary Ireland. The detailed naturalistic 'content' implies an intimacy with Dublin life simultaneously undercut by the resolutely uncommitted, blankly self-effacing style — a style resonant with absences with embody themselves in the calculatedly meagre, inconclusive quality of the narratives themselves. Organic closure is defiantly withheld, as it is in a different way by *Ulysses*. *Ulysses* 'resolves' the contradiction between 'alienated' artistic consciousness (Stephen Dedalus) and material existence (Leopold Bloom) in its *formal* tressing of naturalist and mythological codes, just as Joyce himself surmounts this duality in his 'author-as-producer' aesthetic. He rejects the Romantic subjectivism of Stephen, while preserving (unlike Bloom) the essentially Romantic creed of total self-dedication to art. But this formal interpenetration in *Ulysses* is an immense, self-flaunting structural irony, so elaborately and exhaustively achieved that it draws attention to its flagrantly synthetic basis in Homeric myth. Indeed the factitiousness of that formal 'resolution' is satirically revealed in the novel's *content* — in the unepiphanic non-event of the meeting of Stephen and Bloom, the central absence around which the text's conflicts and complexities knot. The unity of material life and self-exiled artistic consciousness which Joyce seeks is achieved not *in* the work but *by* it: *Ulysses* is a novel about the conditions of its own production, subsisting in its ironic identity with and dissonance from the Homeric myth which provides its 'raw materials'.[69] Its seamless, organic composition of those materials is a phenomenon of the text as autonomous *product*, which by the very completeness of its closure invites the reader to deconstruct the text into the contradictions of its process of production. If its intricate mythologising represents an artistic vengeance wreaked on the miserableness of petty-bourgeois Dublin, its undauntedly veridical naturalism ceaselessly subverts such idealisations. In its partial, parodic resemblance to a conventional naturalistic novel, *Ulysses* offers itself to the reader as a familiar commodity only to undercut that transaction by its difficulty and self-absorbedness, refusing commodity-status while paradoxically parading, in the crafted, compacted involutions of its every phrase, the intensive labour which went into its production. By virtue of its status as self-parodic product, the novel struggles to escape the degradation

69. Georg Lukács speaks in *The Theory of the Novel* of Homeric myth as a world in which objects and meanings are spontaneously integrated, form and content united. For Joyce, that spontaneous integration can be achieved only sporadically and unpredictably: this is the basis of the 'epiphany' doctrine.

of becoming a commodity; its author consequently becomes a producer without consumers.

In *Ulysses*, then, Joyce produces a work which is at once 'closed' and 'open'; and something similar can be said of *Finnegans Wake*. The *Wake* is on the one hand an enormously elaborate, self-sealing system, powered by the 'totalising' drive which Joyce inherited from the scholasticism to which he declared himself committed in everything but the premises. Yet such a 'closed' text, by attempting to absorb the whole of reality into itself, becomes coterminous with the universe, and so an 'open' play of codes, differences, transformations. For Joyce, reality itself is one immense organic artefact, a sealed, interpenetrative system powered by its own laws, ceaselessly in flux yet fundamentally stable. The organic literary work thereby becomes a 'scientific' model of the world itself, enacting in the laws of its structure the dynamic stasis of the cosmos itself. Human societies are specific sectors of that cosmic process, determined by its unalterable laws, moving inexorably through their Viconian cycles to provide the spectatorial artist with his classical vision of 'security and satisfaction and patience'. In this sense, Joyce's aesthetic ideology, like that of the mature Yeats, marks a retreat from a history in crisis. Yet while Yeats, Eliot and Lawrence turn distastefully from the city, Joyce remains a progressive, prototypically urban producer, exploiting difference, disconnection, splitting, permutation and simultaneity as the very forms of his art.

9. *D. H. Lawrence*

Of all the writers discussed in this essay, D. H. Lawrence, the only one of proletarian origin, is also the most full-bloodedly 'organicist' in both his social and aesthetic assumptions. As a direct twentieth-century inheritor of the 'Culture and Society' Romantic humanist tradition, Lawrence's fiction represents one of the century's most powerful literary critiques of industrial capitalism, launched from a deep-seated commitment to an organic order variously located in Italy, New Mexico, pre-industrial England and, metaphorically, in the novel-form itself. The novel for Lawrence is a delicate, labile organism whose elements are vitally interrelated; it spurns dogma and metaphysical absolutes, tracing instead the sensuous flux of its unified life-forms.[70] Yet Lawrence is also a dogmatic, metaphysically absolutist, radically dualistic thinker, fascinated by mechanism and disintegration; and it is in this contradiction that much of his historical significance lies.

What Lawrence's work dramatises, in fact, is a contradiction within the Romantic humanist tradition itself, between its corporate and individualist components. An extreme form of individualism is structural to Romantic humanist ideology – an application, indeed, of organicism to the individual self, which becomes thereby wholly autotelic, spontaneously evolving into 'wholeness' by its own uniquely determining laws. This ideological component – at once an idealised version of common place bourgeois individualism and a 'revolutionary' protest against the 'reified' society it produces – is strongly marked in Lawrence's writing, and enters into conflict with the opposing imperatives of impersonality and organic order. His social organicism decisively rejects the atomistic, mechanistic ideologies of industrial capitalism, yet at the same time subsumes the values of the bourgeois liberal tradition: sympathy, intimacy, compassion, the centrality of the 'personal'. These contradictions come to a crisis in Lawrence with the First World War, the most traumatic event of his life. The war signifies the definitive collapse of the liberal humanist heritage, with its benevolistic idealism and 'personal' values, clearing the way for the 'dark gods' of discipline, action, hierarchy, individual separateness, mystical impersonality – in short, for a social order which rejects the 'female' principle of compassion and sexual intimacy for the 'male' principle of power. 'The reign of love is passing, and the reign of power is coming again.'[71]

In this sense Lawrence was a major precursor of fascism, which is not to say that he himself unqualifiedly accepted fascist ideology. He unequivocally condemned Mussolini, and correctly identified fascism as a spuriously 'radical' response to the crisis of capitalism.[72] Lawrence was unable to embrace fascism because, while it signified a form of Romantic organistic reaction to bourgeois liberalism, it also negated the individualism which was for him a crucial part of

70. See 'The Novel', *Phoenix II* (London, 1968).
71. 'Blessed are the Powerful', *Phoenix II*.
72. See his comment in *St. Mawr*: 'Try fascism. Fascism would keep the surface of life intact, and carry on the undermining business all the better.' Lawrence was not a fascist rather perhaps in the sense that he was not a homosexual. He thought both fascism and homosexuality immoral, but was subconsciously fascinated by both.

the same Romantic heritage. This is the contradiction from which he was unable to escape, in his perpetual oscillation between a proud celebration of individual autonomy and a hunger for social integration; he wants men to be drilled soldiers but *individual* soldiers, desires to 'rule' over them but not 'bully' them.[73] To 'resolve' this contradiction, Lawrence had recourse to a metaphysic which dichotomised reality into 'male' and 'female' principles and attempted to hold them in dialectical tension. The male principle is that of power, consciousness, spirit, activism, individuation; the female principle that of flesh, sensuality, permanence, passivity.[74] The male principle draws sustenance from the female, but must avoid collapsing inertly into it. Yet Lawrence's dualist metaphysic is ridden with internal contradictions, for a significant biographical reason: his mother, symbol of primordial sensual unity, was in fact petty-bourgeois, and so also represented individuation, aspiring consciousness and active idealism in contrast to the mute, sensuous passivity of his working-class father. This partial inversion of his parents' sexual roles, as defined by Lawrence, contorts and intensifies the contradictions which his metaphysic tries to resolve.[75] The mother, as symbol of the nurturing yet cloying flesh, is subconsciously resented for inhibiting true masculinity (as is the father's passivity), yet valued as an image of love, tenderness and personal intimacy. Conversely, her active, aspiring consciousness disrupts the mindless unity of sensual life symbolised by the father, but is preferred to his brutal impersonality. *Sons and Lovers* takes these conflicts as its subject-matter, on the whole rejecting the father and defending the mother; yet as Lawrence's fiction progresses, moving through and beyond the First World War, that priority is partly reversed. *Women in Love* struggles to complement a potentially claustrophobic sexual intimacy with the 'liberating' effect of a purely 'male' relationship; and the hysterical male chauvinism of the post-

73. *Fantasia of the Unconscious* (London, 1961), p. 84.
74. This duality is imaged in Lawrence's work in a whole gamut of antinomies: love/law, light/dark, lion/unicorn, sun/moon, Son/Father, spirit/soul, sky/earth, and so on.
75. A contortion evident in the *reversibility* of some of Lawrence's symbolic antinomies: the Father, symbol of sensual phallic consciousness, is identifiable with the *female*; the lion may signify both active power and sensuality; the sun is sometimes male intellect and sometimes sensuous female warmth, while the moon may suggest female passivity or the cold abstract consciousness of the male.

war novels (*Aaron's Rod*, *Kangaroo*, *The Plumed Serpent*) represents a strident rejection of sexual love for the male cult of power and impersonality. Lawrence's deepening hatred of women is a reaction both against bourgeois liberal values and the snare of a sensuality which violates individual autonomy; yet his commitment to sensual being as the source of social renewal contradictorily persists. In *Lady Chatterley's Lover*, the image of the father is finally rehabilitated in the figure of Mellors; yet Mellors combines impersonal male power with 'female' tenderness, working-class roughness with petty bourgeois awareness, achieving a mythical resolution of the contradictions which beset Lawrence's work.

Lawrence's particular mode of relation to the dominant ideology, then, was in the first place a contradictory combination of proletarian and petty-bourgeois elements – a combination marked by a severe conflict between alternative ideological discourses which becomes encoded in his metaphysic. Yet this fact is of more than merely 'biographical' interest: for the ideological contradictions which the young Lawrence lives out – between power and love, community and autonomy, sensuality and consciousness, order and individualism – are a specific overdetermination of a deep-seated ideological crisis within the dominant formation as a whole. Lawrence's relation to that crisis is then doubly overdetermined by his expatriatism, which combines an assertive, deracinated individualism with a hunger for the historically mislaid 'totality'. The forms of Lawrence's fiction produce this ideological conjuncture in a variety of ways. The 'symptomatic' repressions and absences of the realist *Sons and Lovers* may be recuperated in the ultra-realist forms of *The Rainbow* – a text which 'explodes' realism in its letter, even as it preserves it in the 'totalising' organicism of its evolving generational structure. After the war, Lawrence's near-total ideological collapse, articulated with the crisis of aesthetic signification, presents itself in a radical rupturing and diffusion of literary form: novels like *Aaron's Rod* and *Kangaroo* are signally incapable of evolving a narrative, ripped between fragmentary plot, spiritual autobiography and febrile didacticism. But between these texts and *The Rainbow* occurs the unique moment of *Women in Love*. That work's break to synchronic form, away from the diachronic rhythms of *The Rainbow*, produces an 'ideology of the text' marked by stasis and disillusionment; yet it is precisely in its fissuring of organic form, in its 'montage' techniques of symbolic juxtaposition, that the novel enforces a 'progressive' discontinuity with a realist lineage already put into profound question by *Jude the Obscure*.

10. *Conclusion*

That the fissuring of organic form is a progressive act has not been a received position within a Marxist aesthetic tradition heavily dominated by the work of Georg Lukács. Yet to review a selection of English literary production from George Eliot to D. H. Lawrence in the light of the internal relations between ideology and literary form is to reactivate the crucially significant debate conducted in the 1930s between Lukács and Bertolt Brecht.[76] Brecht's rejection of Lukács's nostalgic organicism, his traditionalist preference for closed, symmetrical totalities, is made in the name of an allegiance to open, multiple forms which bear in their torsions the very imprint of the contradictions they lay bare. In English literary culture of the past century, the ideological basis of organic form is peculiarly visible, as a progressively impoverished bourgeois liberalism attempts to integrate more ambitious and affective ideological modes. In doing so, that ideology enters into grievous conflicts which its aesthetic forms betray in the very act of attempted resolution. The destruction of corporate and organicist ideologies in the political sphere has always been a central task for revolutionaries; the destruction of such ideologies in the aesthetic region is essential not only for a scientific knowledge of the literary past, but for laying the foundation on which the materialist aesthetic and artistic practices of the future can be built.

76. See 'Brecht Against Lukács', *New Left Review* 84, March/April, 1974.

Marxism and Aesthetic Value

The authors I have discussed in the previous chapter are all ranked by conventional estimation as 'major'. If the issue of literary value is indeed a legitimate component of Marxist criticism, should not such a criticism be devoted to *transvaluating* received assumptions, rather than merely reproducing them? It depends, naturally, on the valuations in question. Marxist criticism should indeed decisively intervene in the 'value-problem'; but nothing is to be gained by that form of literary ultra-leftism which dismisses received evaluations merely because they are the product of bourgeois criticism. The task of Marxist criticism is to provide a materialist *explanation* of the bases of literary value – a task which Raymond Williams, in his discussion of the English novel, seems to me to have left largely unachieved. It should not, then, be a matter of embarrassment that the literary texts selected for examination by Marxist criticism will inevitably overlap with those works which literary idealism has consecrated as 'great'; it is a question of challenging the inability of such idealism to render more than subjectivist accounts of the criteria of value.

It would seem absurd for Marxist criticism to be silent on the qualitative distinction between, say, Pushkin and Coventry Patmore. Yet such a theoretical prudery is in vogue within Marxist aesthetics. At its simplest level, it appears as an egalitarian unease about the 'élitism' of assigning certain works to second-class status: how patrician to prefer Blake to Betjeman. In its more sophisticated form, it presents itself as a rigorous scientificity hostile to the idealism of 'normative' judgement. The critic's task is not to range works upon an evaluative scale but to achieve scientific knowledge of the conditions of their historical possibility. Whether the work in question is to be approved or censured is irrelevant to that end; evaluation is thus evacuated from the realm of literary science, to be furtively cultivated, perhaps, as a private pleasure.

There is a parallel between this particular ideology of literary science and the notorious dichotomy enforced by Rudolf Hilferding in the Preface to his *Finance Capital*:

'It has been said that politics is a normative doctrine ultimately determined by value judgements; since such value judgements do not belong within the sphere of science, the discussion of politics falls outside the limits of scientific treatment... According to the Marxist viewpoint, the task of a scientific politics is to discover the determination of the will of classes; hence a politics is scientific when it describes causal connections. As in the case of theory, Marxist politics is exempt from value judgement... It is therefore incorrect, though widely diffused both *intra* and *extra mures*, simply to identify Marxism and socialism... To recognise the validity of Marxism (which implies the recognition of the necessity of socialism) is by no means a task for value judgements, let alone a pointer to a practical line of conduct. It is one thing to recognise a necessity, but quite another to place oneself at the service of that necessity.'

If it is possible to be a Marxist without being a revolutionary socialist, it seems equally possible to study literature without in the least valuing it. The positivism/idealism couple of the Second International is merely reproduced in the aesthetic sphere: 'economic law' is to political class struggle as textual 'fact' is to textual 'value'. The scepticism of the 'anti-élitist' critic, however, is not precisely of this kind. His demotic protest against literary league-tabling is aimed at the enshrinement of Literature itself as reified value; his posture – pluralist, humanist, egalitarian – is an opening to the value of 'cultural studies', within which traditionally consecrated literary texts must discover their subordinate, transvaluative status. He is disturbed by the question of value, and wishes to re-locate it. The literary positivist, by contrast, pursues his sealed enquiry into such consecrated texts because the question of value does not engage him in the least, other than as an instinctual reflex of bourgeois ideology still to be combated. Whereas the first critic reproduces bourgeois ideology in his abstract egalitarianism, the second reproduces it in his 'value-free' theoreticism.

164

Politically counterproductive though both positions undoubtedly are, they are none the less considerably more valuable than the bourgeois aesthetics they oppose. For there is no question that the instalment of the 'value-question' at the heart of critical enquiry is a rampantly ideological gesture. The ideological unity between the old-fashioned school of 'appreciation', and the anti-academicist school of 'relevance', is nowhere more clearly revealed than in the priority they assign to problems of value, on which all else is made to turn. Whether it is translated as 'taste' or metaphysical commitment, private predilection or public conviction, intuitive sympathy or moral allegiance, the ideological function of the 'value-question' is to dissolve the materialist analysis of literary texts into abstract moralism, or into the existential moment of individual consumption. (We may leave aside the reformist moves towards 'readers' participation' predictable within such a problematic.) Criticism becomes a mutually supportive dialogue between two highly valorised subjects: the valuable text and the valuable reader. We do not need to ask how the value of each of these privileged subjects is established, any more than we need to ask how the value of a commodity is sealed. It is sealed by exchange: by that alienation of the historically specific which permits one lonely abstraction to encounter, and be equalised by, another, in a self-closing circle from which the material has been abolished. Valuable text and valuable reader are reversible: in a mutual complicity, such a text writes its reader and such a reader writes the text. The valuable reader is constituted as valuable by the texts which he constitutes as such; ideological value is projected into the Tradition to re-enter the present as metaphysical confirmation or critique. The name of this tautology is Literature – that historical invention whose ideological tyranny is more supple and deep-seated for us than that of any other art-form. For the art gallery, concert hall and opera house are flagrantly privileged spaces which flaunt themselves as such: the demarcation between initiate and ignorant is here taut and unmistakeable. This is not so of literature, for two reasons. First, the character of literary production in advanced social formations is such that it ceaselessly surpasses such cloistered, isolable spheres: literature is multiple and polycentric, saturating the very textures of our social life, pervasively present as consolation, information, persuasion, infatuation. Second, an advanced social formation demands that literacy also should be widely diffused, so that today its relatively marked absence even in such conditions is inevitably scandalous, signifying a loss of full humanity. In such a situation, Literature presents itself as threat, mystery, challenge and insult to those who, able to read, can nonetheless not 'read'. To be able to decipher the signs and yet remain ignorant: it is in this contradiction that the tyranny of Literature is revealed. Reading is at once the most natural and esoteric of acts, spontaneous and sacred, public facility and privileged cult. Its unnaturalness is thus enforced by its very naturalness, which is not the case with opera houses and concert halls. Whereas they are in principle out of reach, Literature is always that which can be reached for – an 'ordinary' phenomenon which is always alien. Sited somewhere on the ground of familiar language, Literature entices only to refuse, appears complicit only to cold-shoulder. Literature is always somewhere else: that which, being literate, we have not read or cannot read. Literacy admits us to reading so that we can take the full measure of our exclusion: its effect is to display the secretive knowledge which is always possible but never possessed.

It can be argued, of course, that the unreadability of Literature is precisely its radicalism – that the 'readable' text, in naturalising its signs, operates upon the reader an insidious mystification subverted by the modernist text which puts its modes of sense-production archly or candidly on show. Yet that 'radical' case has rarely been coupled with a critique of the social determinants which allow a mere few thousand access to such writing. It is then predictable that such purely gestural, shamefaced materialism will provoke its angry reaction – the reaction of those who press their questioning of the intrinsic élitism of Literature and its aesthetics to neo-*proletkult* limits. And it is certainly true that there is little theoretical work in materialist aesthetics which one would choose to preserve over Trotsky's writings on practical problems of revolutionary culture – writings which range from the need to eradicate cursing and incivility from Russian speech to the role of cinema in providing more productive illusions for the masses than vodka and the church. Marked by a grim realism about the cultural devastation of the Soviet masses, Trotsky's work outlines ambitious strategies (co-operation between demobbed, newly literate Red Army soldiers, library workers and newspaper worker-correspondents in raising the cultural standards of the countryside), yet deems no cultural detail too low for scrutiny (why does a certain revolutionary newspaper fold so awkwardly?). Yet it is not only that the populism of the neo-*proletkult* is inimical to Trotsky's aesthetics (to say nothing of Marx and Lenin); it is also that it aims an unintended insult at – to choose merely one example – those Lancashire mill-girls of early Victorian England who rose an hour before work to read Shakespeare together. It would be a curious kind of materialistic critic who would now wish to inform those women, in wise historical retrospect, that they were wasting their time over a reactionary hack. Literature must indeed be re-situated within the field of general cultural production; but each mode of such production demands a semiology of its own, which is not conflatable with some universal 'cultural' discourse.

Populism and theoreticism, in aesthetics as in politics, are familiar deformations of Marxist-Leninism, and the question of literary value is a crux of this debate. Yet if there can indeed be a 'science of value', it must differ from those familiar forms of historicism which regard the work as the 'expression' of a 'world view' which in turn expresses a privileged 'class-position' occupied by the individual or 'transindividual' author at a particular historical point. Such a conception merely dissolves the materiality of the text to the transparency of historical 'consciousness' or 'praxis'. Conversely, if the varieties of formalism have insisted that value (where they have admitted it) is the product of a certain play of significations, they have tended to isolate that process from the material matrix within which historicism, in however idealist a form, has tried to place it. A materialist approach to the problem of value must therefore appear as a double-refusal: of the expressive models of historicism, and of the reductive operations of formalism.

Moreover, in opposition to certain trends within bourgeois and even materialist criticism, such a method must re-enact the founding gesture of Marxist political economy and re-consider the question of value on the site of literary *production*. This is not, need one say, to ignore the spheres of textual circulation and consumption – to fetishise value as an immanent quality of the product, sublimely untainted by the ideological practices of literary reception. For there is no 'immanent' value – no value which is not *transitive*. Literary value is a phenomenon which is *produced* in that ideological appropriation of the text, that 'consumptional production' of the work, which is the act of reading. It is always *relational* value: 'exchange-value'. The histories of 'value' are a sub-sector of the histories of literary-ideological receptive practices – practices which are in no sense a mere 'consumption' of a finished product, but which must be studied as a determinate (re)production of the text. We read ('consume') what an ideology reads ('produces') for us; to read is to consume the determinate material of a text in a specific ideological production of it. For the literary text is always the text-for-ideology, selected, deemed readable and deciphered by certain ideologically governed conventions of critical receptivity to which the text itself contributes. Those conventions are embedded in the material apparatuses of 'culture' and education, and represent a conjuncture of 'general' ideological discourses and that specific, overdetermined instance of them which is the literary-aesthetic. If the text itself is the overdetermined product of a structural conjuncture, so indeed is the practice of reading; the problems of textual meaning and value pose themselves precisely in the series of historical conjunctures between these two moments. Reading is the operation whereby a particular historical ideology so puts to work the materials of the text as to fashion it into a readable product, an ideological object, a text-for-ideology. And as the text is itself a production of ideology, working now athwart, now in complicity with it, so reading, as an ideological production of the production of ideology, works now 'with', now 'athwart' the lines of the text, in a double-movement determined by its relation to the textual production of ideology ('textual ideology') and to the extra-textual ideology thus produced.

To re-consider the point of textual production, then, is not to surrender to some immanentist theory of value. As a determinate product, the text naturally presses its own modes of producibility upon the recipient, and in this sense may be said to produce its own consumption – not that it dictates a single sense to the reader, but that it generates a field of possible readings which, within the conjuncture of the reader's ideological matrix and its own, is necessarily finite. The text, it can be claimed, produces its own reader, even if only to be misread. But the text's own proffered modes of producibility are naturally constructed by the ideological act of reading; and there is no way out of this hermeneutical circle at the level of empirical reception. The theoretical importance of production for the value-question lies not at this level, where text and reading mutually produce each other in ideological complicity, but at the level of the text's own historical self-production in relation to its ideological environs. It is because this process can be scientifically analysed (rather than confined to some mythical limbo of lost origins) that a knowledge of the text is possible – a knowledge which, as I shall argue, embraces as one of its facets the question of value. Only by posing the problem in this way can we avoid at once that form of empiricism whereby the text naturalistically reproduces its meaning within the reader, and those modes of voluntarism in which the reader arbitrarily projects his meaning upon the text. Just as the relations between text and the ideology it produces are neither mechanistic nor gratuitous, so the same can be maintained for the relations between the text and a knowledge of it. If the text does not spontaneously enforce its immanent meaning on the reader, neither is it a mere gestural cue, a set of empty notations to be filled. The text is indeed irreducible to some single privileged significance intuitable across history; but it is equally indissoluble to a random splay of pluralist sense. For it is the determinations of that pluralism which count: this *découpage* of meaning rather than another, constituted by a determinate set of distances, breaks and redoublings whose source is to be found in its ideologically governed process of self-production. Both transcendentalist and pluralist cases end in mysticism: in the enigma of the concealed essence of meaning, or in the profound mystery of the purely phenomenal. The one is no more than the obverse of the other, in a shared problematic of essence/phenomenon, a coupling of idealism and empiricism. The critical sceptic sensually thrilling to the unfounded play of signs is the son of the metaphysical father rapt before the ritual of ultimate meaning.

If, then, a 'science of literary value' is an element of the science of ideologies, is value to be abandoned to some mere ideological relativism, some 'solipsism of the citizen' in which any discourse of 'objective merit' or 'false estimation' is to be jettisoned as immanentist and idealist? It is at this point that we need to re-open the question of textual production in relation to the problem of value. For if there can be a science of the ideologies of value, there may also be a science of the ideological conditions of the production of value. Such a science would not reinsert value 'within' the product, but would rather reinsert the conditions of textual production within the 'exchange relation' of value. On the question of aesthetic value, one must surely agree with Brecht:

'Anything that was worn out, trivial, or so commonplace that it *no longer made one think*, they did not like at all ('You get nothing out of it'). If one needed an aesthetic, one could find it here.[1]

When Shakespeare's texts cease to make us think, when we get nothing out of them, they will cease to have value. But *why* they 'make us think', why we 'get something out of them' (if only for the present) is a question which must be referred at once to the ideological matrix of our reading and the ideological matrix of their production. It is in the *articulation* of these distinct moments that the question of value resides.

Speaking before a critical audience of fellow-Bolsheviks in 1924, Leon Trotsky attempted to rescue the concept of the aesthetic from the grip of historical reductionism:

'In works of art (Raskolnikov) ignores that which makes them works of art. This was most vividly shown in his remarkable judgement on Dante's *Divine Comedy*, which in his opinion is valuable to us just because it enables us to understand the psychology of a certain class at a certain time. To put the matter that way means simply to strike out the *Divine Comedy* from the realms of art. If I say that the importance of the *Divine Comedy* lies in the fact that it gives me an understanding of the state of mind of certain classes in a certain epoch, this means that I transform it into a mere historical document, for, as a work of art, the *Divine Comedy* must speak in some way to my feelings and moods... Nobody, of course, forbids a reader to assume the role of a researcher and approach the *Divine Comedy* as merely an historical document. It is clear, though, that these two approaches are on two different levels, which, though connected, do not overlap. How is it thinkable that there should be not an historical but a directly aesthetic relationship between us and a medieval Italian book? This is explained by the

1. 'Brecht Against Lukács', *New Left Review* 84, March/April, 1974.

fact that in class society, in spite of all its changeability, there are certain common features.[2]

The particular feature which Trotsky proceeds to single out is not, in fact, common only to class-societies: it is death. Death, he concedes, is of course experienced differently in different social milieux; nevertheless, what was said of it by Shakespeare, Byron, Goethe and the Psalmist (an exclamation at this point from Comrade Libedinsky) can still move us. The historical approach to Dante affects our aesthetic attitude to him, but 'one can't substitute one for the other': 'art has to be approached as art, literature as literature, that is, as a quite specific field of human endeavour. Of course we have a class criterion in art too, but this class criterion must be refracted artistically, that is, in conformity with the quite specific peculiarities of that field of creativity to which we are applying our criterion'.[3] Mayakovsky produced his powerful *The Thirteen Apostles* in his politically ambiguous day, and his arid *150 Million* from a proletarian standpoint.

Trotsky's fight to preserve the relative autonomy of the aesthetic from the abstract dogmatism of *proletkult* is at its sharpest in *Literature and Revolution*. There too he insists that art must be judged in the first place by its own autonomous laws – that artistic creation is a 'deflection, a changing and a transformation of reality, in accordance with the peculiar laws of art'.[4] The historical and the aesthetic are not synchronous systems, faces of the same phenomenon; history does not present itself as a unified formation through which a 'clean' cross-section can be made, displaying each of its levels as harmoniously co-temporal with the other, When such a cross-section is made by the act of revolutionary rupture, the strata of history are revealed as temporally disjunct – as different *histories*:

'When one breaks a hand or a leg, the bones, the tendons, the muscles, the arteries, the nerves and the skin do not break and tear in one line, nor afterwards do they grow together and heal at the same time. So, in a revolutionary break in the life of society, there is no simultaneousness and no symmetry of process either in the ideology of

2. *Class and Art: Problems of Culture under the Dictatorship of the Proletariat* (London, 1974), pp. 7–8.
3. *ibid.*, p. 17.
4. *Literature and Revolution* (Ann Arbor, 1971), p. 175.

society, or in its economic structure. The ideological premises which are needed for the revolution are formed before the revolution, and the most important ideological deductions from the revolution appear only much later. It would be extremely flippant to establish by analogies and comparisons the identity of Futurism and Communism, and so form the deduction that Futurism is the art of the proletariat.'[5]

But if Trotsky is acutely conscious of the asymmetries of the aesthetic and historical, he lacks the theoretical instruments to define them precisely. *Literature and Revolution* affirms the relative autonomy of art, but struggles painfully towards the categories in which it might be theorised. Its superb local criticism grasps the *unity* of aesthetic and ideological with fine intuitiveness – as when it argues of a Mayakovsky poem, for example, that its isolated, colliding images reflect contradictions which spring not from its historical materials but from its ideological conflicts. But in the absence of a theory of the articulations of the historical, ideological and aesthetic, it is condemned for the most part to a brilliant, unerring impressionism of response. The main form that impressionism assumes is one identified by Theodor Adorno in the *Passagenarbeit* of Walter Benjamin, and which we might term 'adjacentism'. Adjacentism – that critical method which lifts an isolated detail from the 'base' and places it in metaphorical relationship to a literary fact – is a marked characteristic of Trotsky's text. '(Kliuev) has brought his new poetic technique from the city, as a neighbouring peasant might bring a phonograph; and he uses poetic technique, like the geography of India, only for the purpose of embellishing the peasant framework of his poetry. He is many-coloured, often bright and expressive, often quaint, often cheap and tinsel-like – and all this is on a firm peasant basis'.[6] Or again, on the Imagist Yessenin: 'His verses are weighted down with an imagery which is. . . isolated and immobile. At bottom, this is not an individual, but a peasant aesthetics. The poetry of the repetitive forms of life has at bottom little mobility and seeks a way out in condensed imagery.'[7] Mode of production, ideology and aesthetic technique are swept masterfully

5. *ibid.*, p. 159.
6. *ibid.*, p. 63.
7. *ibid.*, pp. 67–8.

together in a rhythm of relentless conflation. A parallel adjacentism (this time political rather than social) marks Trotsky's more general aesthetic pronouncements: 'But for art to be able to transform as well as to reflect, there must be a great distance between the artist and life, just as there is between the revolutionist and political reality.'[8] The specific autonomy of art is insisted upon at the very moment when art is being offered as a simile of political practice.

It is worth looking more closely at Trotsky's argument over the *Divine Comedy*, for it contains in microcosm many of the elements of this fraught issue in Marxist criticsm. Trotsky first distinguishes the 'aesthetic' from the 'historical' approach to Dante's text by a naïvely affective claim: 'as a work of art, the *Divine Comedy* must speak in some way to my feelings and moods. Dante's work may act on me in a depressing way, fostering pessimism and despondency in me, or, on the contrary, it may rouse, inspire, encourage me... This is the fundamental relationship between a reader and a work of art'.[9] The crucial distinction between aesthetic and scientific cognition which he enforces in *Literature and Revolution* ('In the field of poetry we deal with the process of feeling the world in images, and not with the process of knowing it scientifically')[10] is reduced to the banalities of bourgeois subjectivism. Having then asserted that the aesthetic and historical 'though connected, do not overlap', the affectivity of historically remote art is accounted for in terms of historical transcendence and individual 'genius':

'Works of art developed in a medieval Italian city can, we find, affect us too. What does this require? A small thing: it requires that these feelings and moods shall have received such broad, intense, powerful expression as to have raised them above the limitations of the life of those days. Dante was, of course, the product of a certain social milieu. But Dante was a genius. He raised the experience of his epoch to a tremendous artistic height. And if we, while today approaching other works of medieval literature merely as objects of study, approach the *Divine Comedy* as a source of artistic perception, this happens not because Dante was a Florentine petty

8. *ibid.*, p. 139. Or again: 'A sense of measure in art is the same as having a sense of realism in politics.'
9. *Class and Art*, p. 8.
10. *Literature and Revolution*, p. 147.

bourgeois of the 13th century but, to a considerable extent, in spite of that circumstance.[11]

The final part of the statement partly retracts what the first part has offered: historical transcendence is seen first as an intensive universalising of historically specific experience, then as almost wholly independent of such experience. Aesthetic and historical are first of all severed by subjectivism, then briefly unified, and finally sundered once again. Uncertain of its notion of the 'historically universal', the argument then shifts to the biological universal of death.

There was little in the annals of Marxist aesthetics to rescue Trotsky from his dilemma. Franz Mehring and Georgy Plekhanov had 'resolved' the problem of aesthetic value by that incongruous amalgam of Kantianism and materialism characteristic of the theorising of the Second International. If a positivistic materialism expelled value from history, the free-wheeling concepts of a contemplative neo-Kantianism lay in wait to smuggle it in by the backdoor. The sphere of utility accounts for art's historical development; the disinterested enjoyment of beauty explains its aesthetic power. Nor could Trotsky learn much in this respect from Lenin. Lenin's engagment with aesthetics, while in no sense comparable to Trotsky's, was deep and active: his philological interests alone ensured his attention to formal structures rather than abstractable content. And the celebrated master-text of his aesthetics – the articles on Tolstoy – is alert enough to the complex articulations of the aesthetic and ideological. Yet for all that, Lenin's aesthetic predilections ran remarkably parallel to his theoretical priorities. One might say of Lenin (to draw an incongruous parallel) as one might say of Samuel Johnson, that for him personally the problem of the relation between aesthetic and ideological did not arise, since he was for the most part simply incapable of enjoying art which he found theoretically unsympathetic. One has only to review a selection of his favourite authors – Chernyshevsky, Gorky, Rolland, Barbusse, Sinclair, Wells, Shaw – to take the point of his self-confessed incomprehension of less socially conscious literature. The point should be taken with care: the man who admired Turgenev and Chekhov, defended the heritage of traditional culture against Bogdanov and the Futurists, personally initiated and supervised the

11. *Class and Art*, p. 8.

ninety-volume Soviet edition of Tolstoy's works and encouraged the dissemination of cheap editions of the classics to the masses, was the very reverse of a philistine. Yet when Lenin is called upon to analyse the specificity of the aesthetic in Tolstoy's fiction, he is ready, as with Trotsky on Dante, to fall back upon the Romantic category of individual 'greatness'.

There is a parallel between the Marxist tradition's embarrassment over the question of aesthetic value and its embarrassment over the problem of morality. Indeed it is hard to resist the temptation of placing that last term in quotation marks, since it can now hardly be used without the contaminating implications of moralism. Moralism eschews scientific analysis of its object for an irrational appeal to subjective or 'universal' ethical values; aestheticism, similarly, discards rational enquiry into the artefact for a 'universalising' discourse or a subjective savouring of its flavour. But it is not only that the 'moral', thus conceived, has nothing in common with historical materialism; it is also that it has nothing in common with many traditional conceptions of morality.[12] The moral systems of Plato and Aristotle turn on an investigation of the social order which can generate norms for action; the 'moral' question of how one is to act is inseparable from an enquiry into the character of the *polis* to which one does or should belong. That enquiry, for Plato, cannot be satisfied merely by examining *doxa* (opinion, ideology), for this will simply render the structure of a society's illusions, which is quite distinct from knowledge. This notion of morality conflicts with the stance of the Sophists, for whom social and moral knowledge were mutually independent: moral knowledge equipped an individual for membership, not of an actual or ideal *polis*, but of any *polis* at all. It is this purely prescriptivist morality, a formalist discourse untrammelled by the determinants of any specific contents established by social enquiry, which finds a later echo in the moral ideology of Kant. The moral 'ought' is severed from those historical interests and needs determinable by scientific analysis: one should act morally, independently of one's objective needs and interests, because it is moral to do so.[13]

12. I am endebted for this brief discussion of 'traditional' moralities to Denys Turner's article 'Morality is Marxism' (*New Blackfriars*, February and March, 1973).

13. Lucio Colletti points out how Rousseau also rejects the distinction

When Marx transforms his initially ideological concept of alienation into a scientific category, replacing the essentialist notion of
Gattungswesen with a theory of the mechanisms of the objective
divorce of the proletariat from the capitalist mode of production, it
is not that he is ceasing to speak 'morally'. Only a bourgeois conception of morality could produce such a conclusion. It is rather
that he has returned the idea of the 'moral' to its proper basis in a
scientific enquiry into the historical facts. The morality of *capital*
does not lie in the fine pages of passionate indignation directed
against the bestialities of capitalism; it lies (among other things) in
the laying bare of the mechanisms whereby surplus-value is extracted
from labour-power. And yet Marx certainly does not intend such
analysis to evoke the reader's 'moral protest', as though exploitation
signified 'denying human dignity', or some such formula. That this
is so is apparent from the fact that it is possible to understand and
endorse the theory of surplus value without holding that it entails
'immorality'. Is Marxism, then, merely a positivism, and 'morality'
merely a question of the private attitude one takes up to its neutral
scientific findings? No, because the moral significance of the theory
of exploitation can be discovered only by re-inserting this concept into
the matrix of Marx's revolutionary theory as a whole. The founding
concept of historical materialism is the contradiction between the
forces and social relations of material production; the theory of
surplus value instructs us in the mechanisms of that contradiction
in a particular epoch of class-society. A man might endorse that
theory in isolation, without feeling in the least constrained to change
his historical behaviour; but he could not consistently recognise a
contradiction between the forces and social relations of production
and remain similarly unaffected. For Marx writes in *The German
Ideology* that 'every development of a productive force is a development of the capacities of men'; individual subjects, distributed into
social classes, *are* productive forces. What distinguishes men from
the other animals, for Marxism, is that they are capacity-producing
and reproducing creatures, and are so because of the structure of
their bodies. What is 'absolute' about men is that they consistently
produce, reproduce and transform their living capacities in the

---

between the 'virtuous man' and the 'good citizen' for an identification of
morality and politics (*From Rousseau to Lenin*, London, 1972, pp. 144-5).

process of producing their material existence. The specificity of historical *materialism* is not an historicism – that men 'create their own history', or that their 'nature' is 'culture', propositions with which many a reactionary idealist would concur. The specificity of the science lies in the internal relation it proposes between the production of historical capacities and the production of material life. The concept of a productive force is itself for Marx such a unity of 'fact' and 'value'. A capacity-producing animal (like Rudolf Hilferding) who refused to recognise the relevance to his course of action of a condition in which the productive forces were inhibited would in this sense stand convicted of inconsistency. In failing to articulate his scientific knowledge with the question of the determinate action to which it led, he would cease to behave 'morally', and would behave instead in moralist and idealist fashion. The 'moralities' of a social formation – the ethical region of its ideology – exist to conceal the contradictions of its material 'base' – contradictions between the character of the social relations and the organised social capacities whose development they impede. To destroy the ethical region of ideology is to return the 'moral' to its proper basis in a scientific examination of the facts: to pose the question of the necessary bearing of those facts upon an historical course of action. It is therefore to abolish 'morality' as an autonomous discourse – to identify it as a product of class-society. The notion that there is a privileged 'moral level' at which the object is to be evaluated disappears: the moral becomes coterminous with the political.

If moralism holds that there is an autonomous 'moral level' at which the object is to be judged, aestheticism holds that there is an autonomous 'aesthetic level' for examining artefacts. This statement is in one sense false, and in another sense banal. If the level in question is seen as a level *within* the artefact, it is false: for everything in the artefact is 'aesthetic'. It is not that we object to the 'ideology' of the *Divine Comedy* but admire its 'technique': the 'ideology' of the poem is the effect of certain aesthetic mechanisms. To speak of approaching the *Divine Comedy* as historical documentation is curious: for it is certainly a very peculiar kind of historical documentation. Its peculiarity is that of the aesthetic. This is the sense in which it is banally true to say that we should approach artefacts 'at the aesthetic level': we should approach *them*, not something else. The relative autonomy of the aesthetic is not a question of some hierarchical division of levels within the work; it is a matter of the work's irreducibility to the historico-ideological of which it is the product. It is not that reductionism gives us a merely partial view of the artefact: it is that it abolishes it as an object and puts another in its place. It is not a question of 'suspending' the work's historical conditions of possibility, placing them in brackets (as Trotsky suggests) to attend to its 'aesthetic effect'; it is rather that its aesthetic effect is itself the index of a certain bracketing, whereby the work dissolves and distantiates the real to produce it as signification. The aesthetic is that which speaks of its historical conditions by remaining silent – inheres in them by distance and denial. The work 'shows' rather than 'states' those conditions in the nature of the productive relations it sets up to the ideological significations which found it. 'Real' history is cancelled by the text, but in the precise modes of that cancellation lies the text's most significant relation to history. The relation between 'aesthetic' and 'historical' is neither one between 'levels' within the text, nor between the work as aesthetic fact and its encircling historical conditions; it is rather that those historical conditions, in the form of the ideological, become the very determinant structure of that process of textual self-production which is, in its entirety, 'aesthetic'. We are concerned, in other words, with the specific operations whereby the ideological produces within itself that internal distantiation which is the aesthetic. It is not, *pace* Trotsky, a question of suspending the fact that Dante was a petty-bourgeois medieval Florentine; it is a matter of taking Trotsky's pertinent comments together with Engels's remarks in his Preface to the 1892 Italian edition of *The Communist Manifesto*:

'The close of the feudal Middle Ages and the onset of the modern capitalistic era are marked by a figure of grandiose stature: it is an Italian, Dante, who is both the last poet of the Middle Ages and the first modern poet. Today, just as it was around 1300, a new historical era is in the making. Will Italy provide us with a new Dante who will announce the birth of this new proletarian era?'

It is not that Dante's work is valuable because it 'speaks of' an important historical era, or 'expresses the consciousness' of that epoch. Its value is an effect of the process whereby the complex ideological conjuncture in which it inheres so produces (internally distantiates) itself in a play of textual significations as to render its depths and intricacies vividly perceptible.

The distinction between the 'aesthetic' and 'ideological' elements of the text, then, is methodological rather than real. It is not a question of grouping diverse textual elements under either heading; it is a matter of analysing how the text constructs itself as a wholly 'aesthetic' product on the basis of its internal relations to the ideological. To argue that *The Divine Comedy* survives its historical moment because of its 'aesthetic' effect is finally tautological: it is to claim, in effect, that a work of art survives because it is a work of art. Some works of art certainly survive their contemporary moment and others do not; but this is not determined by something called their 'aesthetic level'. It is determined, as I have suggested, by the aesthetic 'producibility' of the concrete ideological conjunctures in which they inhere – conjunctures of which the available, relatively autonomous lineages of literary forms are a crucial structure. 'Survivability', as Brecht saw, is in any case a profoundly suspect criterion of literary value: the history of the life, death and resurrection of literary texts is part of the history of ideologies. But even where literary science would deem a work to have 'justly' survived, there is no call for materialist embarrassment about the 'metaphysical' quality of such transhistorical status. The question of why we still respond to *Beowulf* or Villon seems in principle no more perplexing than the question of why we still respond to the Lollards or the Luddites. Literary works 'transcend' their contemporary history, not by rising to the 'universal', but by virtue of the character of their concrete relations to it – relations themselves determined by the nature of the historical conditions into which the work is inserted. The 'history' to which an artefact belongs is by no means necessarily reducible to its contemporary moment; indeed it may not 'belong' to that contemporary moment at all. *The Divine Comedy*, as Engels implies, belongs to the general history of class-society *by virtue* of occupying a particular moment in medieval Italy. And even an historically alien work may 'speak' to us in the present, for human animals (as Sebastiano Timpanaro has reminded us[14]) share a biological structure even where they do not share a direct cultural heritage. Birth, nourishment, labour, kinship,

14. 'Considerations on Materialism', *New Left Review* 85 (May/June, 1974).

sexuality, death are common to all social formations and to all literature; and it is no rebuttal of this to insert the correct but commonplace caveat that this biological 'infrastructure' is always historically mediated. So indeed it is; one merely repeats that what is variably mediated is a common biological structure.

It is not, of course, that art is necessarily more valuable when it evokes such transhistorical themes, any more than it is the case that only 'world-historical' conjunctures of the kind Engels identifies in Dante form the basis of literary achievement. Trotsky speaks of art as raising historically relative 'feelings and modes... above the limitations of the life of those days'; and this displaced 'universalism' can be traced throughout Marxist aesthetics as far as the later Lukács, who speaks in *The Peculiarity of the Aesthetic* of art as a suspension of heterogeneous life through which men enter momentarily into truly 'generic' being. What this 'materialist' position overlooks is that valuable art comes into being not *despite* its historical limitations (in some mystified Marcusean idealism) but *by virtue of* them. It is precisely this attitude which Marx adopts in his discussion of ancient Greek art in the *Grundrisse*; and it is not difficult to see in English literature how the value of, say, Jane Austen's fiction is indissociable from the dominative, drastically constricted class-practices and class-ethics which provide its problematic. The literary achievement of an Austen or a James is based on its reactionary conditions of class-formation, not a miracle which escapes them. Or let us take the instance of W. B. Yeats: what is meant by the claim that Yeats is a 'great' poet? Bourgeois criticism has, characteristically, no convincing answer to this question beyond intuitionist rhetoric. Nor does a certain style of 'materialist' criticism feel wholly unembarrassed by the celebration of an extreme right-wing, sporadically fascist writer. But it is precisely Yeats's ideological limitations which lay the basis for the value of his aesthetic achievement. Like Eliot, Pound, Joyce and Lawrence, Yeats was *tangentially* related to the hegemonic bourgeois ideology of his era, so situated as to have at his disposal certain mythologies alternative and antagonistic to it.[15] Nurtured by the partial, nascent state of capitalist

15. I leave aside here Matthew Arnold, a writer I examine as an ideologue; but his place may be filled by the Brontë sisters, whose work I have discussed separately in these terms in my *Myths of Power: a Marxist Study of the Brontës* (London, 1975).

development in Ireland and the prolonged influence of pre-capitalist modes, those mythologies were able, in their arcane metaphysical sweep and intensely mystified modes, to penetrate to certain sensory and emotional capacities necessarily banished by bourgeois empiricism. In twentieth-century English literature, given the absence of a revolutionary tradition, it was only from the 'radical right' that such a critique could be launched – a critique which is thereby warped, corrupted and disabled by the idealist moulds in which it is inevitably cast. But it is not only that Yeats has at his disposal alternative ideological resources; it is not merely a matter of his art 'expressing' certain censored capacities. For Yeats's access to such resources is simultaneously an access to certain literary forms and discourses – to modes of signification which (unlike those of the Rhymers' Club) are able to *rewrite* contemporary history in ideologically oppositional terms. The producing of such significations, in turn, has its root in the Yeatsian ideology of the literary mode of production, in which a certain idealised transparency of author to reader licenses a peculiar complex concretion of poetic utterance.

If Yeats was significantly displaced from the hegemonic bourgeois ideology, so also were all the agreed 'major' authors of the nineteenth and twentieth centuries with whom I have dealt in the previous chapter.[16] By some conjuncture of elements (class, sexuality, region, nationality and so on), these writers were contradictorily inserted into an hegemonic bourgeois ideology which had passed its progressive prime; and the relations here between historical fact and aesthetic value, overlooked by both formalist and sociologist, need to be enforced. Once more, it is not a question of some historicist 'expression' of certain privileged ideological sub-ensembles – an expression which bursts triumphantly through the fault-lines of 'orthodox' aesthetic and ideological modes to herald a new creation. It is a matter of a certain curvature in the ideological space in which the texts play – a curvature produced by the impaction of value upon value, signification upon signification, form upon form. It is not that a 'progressive' ideology thrusts through the constrictions of the hegemonic formation; there is little historically

16. I do not intend to suggest that literary value is produced *only* by such obviously tangential relations, as the case of Jane Austen would itself suggest. It is rather a question of a certain ideological complexity, range, obliquity and ambivalence, in which the character of a dominant ideology *and* the precise nature of the text's insertion into it must be examined simultaneously.

progressive about the ideological worlds of those major authors. It is rather that the hegemonic formation is produced from a particular dissentient conflictual position within it, and that the resulting problematic throws the 'fault-lines' of that formation into partial relief. One must examine this process simultaneously from the standpoint of textual production. In producing its meanings, such a text *produces* the ideological curvature of which I have spoken, inscribes it in its very substance. A particular line of sense, in order to preserve 'aesthetic' impact and consistency, will invert or modulate itself into an alternative 'ideological' register; or, to preserve 'ideological' purity, will be refracted into alternate forms of signification. It can be seen how the complex, intensive, pluralist play of senses thus constituted is relevant to the 'value-question' if one thinks of the work of a Trollope: work which bathes in a self-consistent, blandly undifferentiated ideological space. In much of Trollope's fiction, 'ideology' produces 'sign' and 'sign' produces 'ideology' in simple, mutually reductive exchange; and this, indeed, could not be different. For the ideological matrix of Trollope's fiction (as with all writing) includes an ideology of the aesthetic – in Trollope's case, an anaemic, naïvely representational 'realism' which is merely a reflex of commonplace bourgeois empiricism. For Eliot, Hardy, Joyce and Lawrence, by contrast, the ideological question is implicit in the aesthetic *problem* of how to write; the 'aesthetic' – textual production – becomes a crucial, overdetermined instance of the question of those real and imaginary relations of men to their social conditions which we name ideology.

In most of the texts I have examined, then, it is a production of the hegemonic ideological formation from a particular *regressive* standpoint within it which lays the basis for literary value. And this is to say no more of George Eliot's nostalgic pastoralism, Conrad's romantic nationalism or Yeats's aristocratic reaction than Marx says of the ancient Greeks in the *Grundrisse*: that the ideologies proper to certain restricted stages of material development are capable of producing aesthetic significations whose power thrives precisely on such limits. There is no simple homology between material and aesthetic development: art does not get better and better as men get richer and richer. But this does not mean on the other hand that the relations between the stage of development of the productive forces, and the possibilities of producing aesthetic value, are merely fortuitous,

If material wealth and aesthetic value do not intertwine in an ascending graph, it is possible to say why not – just as it is possible to say why men do not become more and more 'morally' admirable as their material abundance increases. In an undeveloped social formation, it is possible to a degree for certain individuals to experience the articulation of their personal behaviour with their social functions as relatively unproblematical. 'Morality' fully emerges as a distinct mode of discourse when historical contradictions sharpen to the point where such relative 'transparency' is unattainable – where the question of the ideological criteria which should govern individual behaviour becomes vexed and recalcitrant, the relations between individual behaviour and social function indecipherable and opaque. 'Moral' discourse then enters into its ideological sovereignty, to await its historical resolution at the hands of revolutionary politics. Such a development is, of course, progressive: 'morality' is an aspect of the 'bad side' by which history develops. It is in some such terms that Marx appraises the aesthetic achievements of ancient Greece, whose 'measure', symmetry and sensuousness thrive precisely upon the restrictions of the classical mode of production. The subsequent history of art is not the history of 'material abundance', but of the uneven development of the forces of production within certain specific class-relations and ideological forms – forms and relations which, in the case of capitalism, are (as Marx comments) 'actually inimical' to artistic production.

Yet this hostility is historically progressive. Capitalism destroys, cripples or suppresses certain historically produced capacities in the process of developing others; and it is on the basis of the revolutionary transformation of these other capacities that what Marx indirectly refers to in *The Eighteenth Brumaire* as 'the poetry of the future' will become possible. The regressive ideological sub-ensembles I have remarked on act *inter alia* as 'custodians' of historically threatened values: and their role in the production of aesthetic value must not be undialectically assessed. If they cannot simply be rejected as reactionary (on the vulgar assumption that only progressive classes and ideologies produce significant literary texts), neither can they merely be seen as awaiting their harmonious 'integration' into the fully-rounded individual of the future. For the 'poetry of the future' will be characterised precisely by a ceaseless surpassing of such fixed and known historical values:

'Camille Desmoulins, Danton, Robespierre, Saint-Just, Napoleon, the heros as well as the parties and the masses of the old French Revolution, performed the task of their time in Roman costume and with Roman phrases, the task of unchaining and setting up modern *bourgeois* society... unheroic as bourgeois society is, it nevertheless took heroism, sacrifice, terror, civil war and battles of peoples to bring it into being. And in the classically austere traditions of the Roman republic its gladiators found the ideals and the art forms, the self-deceptions that they needed in order to conceal from themselves the bourgeois limitations of the content of their struggles and to keep their enthusiasm on the high plane of the great historical tragedy. Similarly, at another stage of development, a century earlier, Cromwell and the English people had borrowed speech, passions and illusions from the Old Testament for their bourgeois revolution. When the real aim had been achieved, when the bourgeois transformation of English society had been accomplished, Locke supplanted Habakkuk...

The social revolution of the nineteenth century cannot draw its poetry from the past, but only from the future. It cannot begin with itself before it has stripped off all superstition in regard to the past. Earlier revolutions required recollections of past world history in order to drug themselves concerning their own content. In order to arrive at its own content, the revolution of the nineteenth century must let the dead bury their dead. There the phrase went beyond the content; here the content goes beyond the phrase.'[17]

The 'poetry' of previous revolutions, the symbologies by which they lived themselves, was opiate and inauthentic – an artificial engraftment of past forms onto historical circumstances too constricted to produce their own adequate significations. Marx's comments here may be taken along with his *Rheinische Zeitung* articles of 1842, in which he castigates German Romanticism as a vacuously elaborate form of concealing a sordidly prosaic substance, reflecting the liberal face put upon reactionary politics. They also relate to his sardonic remarks in the *Grundrisse* about the absurdity of imagining an Homeric epic produced in the conditions of capitalist technology. What he criticises, in fact, is a kind of historical aestheticism – an incongruous, extrinsic appropriation of ready-

17. *The Eighteenth Brumaire of Louis Bonaparte*, in *Marx and Engels: Selected Works* (London, 1968), pp. 97–9.

fashioned symbolic forms to grace an impoverished content. It is on the necessarily *internal* relations between historical 'fact' and aesthetic 'value' that his argument closes. Yet this enigmatic passage also contains a further layer of insight, summarised in its final sentence. The 'poetics' of previous revolutions have been of an 'expressive' or 'representational' kind: it was a matter of the content discovering a form. But the 'form' of the future society is that of a ceaseless self-surpassment of 'content', grounded in the limitless non-contradictory development of the productive forces. The symbolic forms of the bourgeois revolutions inflated their social contents to grandiose proportions, but in doing so shored up their true constrictedness, deflecting a perception of their real paucity. Marx appears here to be simply *inverting* this problematic – stressing the dynamism of revolutionary content against the reifications of form. But the deeper implication of the passage, not least when taken together with elements of the *Grundrisse*, suggests the need to re-think this whole form/content problematic from a materialist standpoint. For the *Grundrisse*, the restricted 'measure' of ancient art and society is not to be 'sublated' by socialism to some 'higher' measure; on the contrary, this very concept of 'measure' – of a rounded proportionality consequent upon constriction – must be rejected for a way of thinking that form of productivity whose mark is, precisely, measurelessness. Similarly, for *The Eighteenth Brumaire*, it is not simply a matter of discovering the expressive or representational forms 'adequate to' the content of the socialist revolution. It is a question of rethinking that opposition – of grasping form no longer as the symbolic mould into which content is poured, but as the 'form of the content': which is to say, grasping form as the structure of a ceaseless self-production, and so not as 'structure' but as 'structuration'. It is this process of continual self-excess – of 'the content go(ing) beyond the phrase' – which is for Marx the poetry of the future and the sign of communism, as it is for us the secret of a materialist analysis of the literary text.

To claim, then, that (say) Yeats's anti-rationalist reverence for concrete qualities of experience is a value to be integrated into the post-revolutionary future is in one sense to derive one's poetry from the past. Yet Yeats, nevertheless, has his value. It is not a value which can be 'read back' from some imaginary construct of the future: the value is a function of a specific relation to a concrete ideological formation. More precisely, its value is the function of a particular process of textual production which is itself a sustained relation (overdetermined by the ideological sub-ensemble within which the texts are held) to such an ideological formation.

Trotsky's risposte to Raskolnikov is certainly correct: literature is not just some form of documentary access to ideology. Literature is a peculiar mode of linguistic organisation which, by a particular 'disturbance' of conventional modes of signification, so foregrounds certain modes of sense-making as to allow us to perceive the ideology in which they inhere. Such foregrounding is at once constructed artifice and experiential enticement swallowing the reader into a play of signs which is seductive in proportion to its 'unnaturalness'. The text is a theatre which doubles, prolongs, compacts and variegates its signs, shaking them free from single determinants, merging and eliding them with a freedom unknown to history, in order to draw the reader into deeper experiential entry into the space thereby created. There are, of course, polar extremes here: the text which deliberately estranges by its 'excessive' parading of devices, and the text which woos us by a form of 'natural', 'innocent' writing with the seeming transparency of experience itself. But the literary work is more typically reducible to neither: it engages sympathy in proportion to its unreality. It is because its 'unreality' licenses a more-than-'natural' flexing and compacting of senses that we are made to see (and tempted to accept) the versions of historical reality it offers.

Yet it is precisely here that the question of value is engaged. For not every text 'flexes and compacts its senses' in the same mode or to the same degree as every other; nor does every text's 'versions of historical reality' count for much. All texts signify, but not all texts are significant. It is possible for a literary work so to produce a constricted ideology as to 'renew' it — so to 'estrange' its staled, threadbare significations, by virtue of its own 'second order' signifying labour, as to revivify the values and perceptions that ideology proffers. The converse is also familiar: a work may occlude and impoverish the elements of a positively enabling ideology by its textual operations. And there are, of course, other possibilities: we speak of the average love-story in a teenage magazine as 'inferior' literature because the withered ideological matrix within which it moves simply precludes that transformative textual production of such myths which might alone 'redeem' them. Yet it is too simple to speak of a 'first' and 'second' order of significations (ideology and text), as though these were both monistic systems. For each order is typically constituted by a complex ensemble of signs which belong to distinct ideological spheres; and the study of textual production, from the viewpoint of both meaning and value, is the study of the complex transactions between these sub-ensembles.

The value of a text, then, is determined by its double mode of insertion into an ideological formation and into the available lineages of literary discourse. It is in this way that the text enters into relation with an always partial range of the historically determined values, interests, needs, powers and capacities which surround it: not that it 'expresses' or 'reproduces' such things (for a text is made of words, not needs), but that it constructs itself in relation to the ideological signs which encode them. This is not to say, however, that the valuable text is always the bearer of 'progressive' values and capacities, or that it is the mere reflex of a progressive 'class-subject'. Take the contrast between Ben Jonson and Walter Savage Landor. Incongruously diverse as those writers are, they have in common a certain tradition of conservative classical humanism; but the positively enabling nature of that ideology in the first could not be in sharper contrast with its tepid, synthetic lifelessness in the second. By the time of Landor, such classical humanism has become a decorous academic withdrawal, an elaborate shell sucked of substance. In Jonson, however, such classicism combines with other elements to create a complex ideological space in which the experience of a limited but significant dialectic of historical interests is brought into sharp focus. It is not at all that Jonson's texts display a 'progressive class-ideology'; nor is it simply a matter of the ideological materials which those texts work. For classical humanism is an active determinant of the forms and significations of Jonson's drama, part of the aesthetic tradition into which his texts are inserted. In conjuncture with other traditions, it becomes the productive instrument by which a resourceful ideological world is so 'internally distantiated' as to yield up the wealth of its prejudices and perceptions. It is not that Jonson is 'exposed to history', and Landor is in flight from it – not that Jonson's texts resonate with 'real life', while Landor's smell of the study. While Landor was in full flight from history on the back of his bizarre epics, *The Prelude* was moving in a similar direction; but the contradiction and complexity of that movement in Wordworth's case are a condition of superior value. It is a contradiction inscribed in the very form of Wordsworth's text: *The Prelude* is a poem about the poet's preparation to write an epic which turns out to be *The Prelude*. While Landor launches his exotic verse-tragedies and outlandish epics in cavalier disregard of the most basic question – how could such forms at such an historical conjuncture be anything but worthless? – *The Prelude* is creased and haunted by the aesthetic and ideological ambiguities of its moment. It is haunted by certain spiritual and historical possibilities, by the ghost of certain powers and values which its formal ideology is forced to censor; and it is in the rifts created by this radical lack of unity with itself that its play of meanings becomes most fertile. The work of a Landor or a Lamb, lacking for the most part access to such possibilities, relegates itself to irretrievably minor status.

It is necessary, then, to refuse a 'moralism' of literary value: to reunite the question of a work's quality with the question of its conditions of possibility. Men do not live by culture alone: far from it. But the claim of historical materialism is that, in effect, they will. Once emancipated from material scarcity, liberated from labour, they will live in the play of their mutual significations, move in the ceaseless 'excess' of freedom. In that process, the signs of sense and value by which previous societies have lived their life-conditions will still, no doubt, be relevant. Yet if Marxism has maintained a certain silence about aesthetic value, it may well be because the material conditions which would make such discourse fully possible do not as yet exist. The same holds for 'morality': if Marxism has had little to say directly about the 'moral', one reason for this obliquity is that one does not engage in moral debate with those for whom morality can only mean moralism. It is not a question of injecting a different content into these categories, but of transvaluating the categories themselves; and that cannot be done by a simple act of will. The 'aesthetic' is too valuable to be surrendered without a struggle to the bourgeois aestheticians, and too contaminated by that ideology to be appropriated as it is. It is, perhaps, in the provisional, strategic silence of those who refuse to speak 'morally' and 'aesthetically' that something of the true meaning of both terms is articulated.

Index of Names

Goethe, Wolfgang, 170
Goldmann, Lucien, 24, 26n, 32–3, 35, 83, 97
Goode, John, 112
Gramsci, Antonio, 32, 102–5
Griffiths, Arthur, 154

Habakkuk, 183
Hardy, Florence, 131n
Hardy, Thomas, 36, 52, 94–5, 125–6, 131–2, 181
Harrison, Frederic, 108, 118n
Hegel, Georg Wilhelm Friedrich, 26, 77, 82, 93, 98, 151
Hilferding, Rudolf, 163, 176
Hobsbawm, Eric, 103n
Hoggart, Richard, 34
Hulme, T. E.
Hume, David, 32
Hutton, R. H. 111

Ibsen, Henrik, 37

James, Henry, 16, 104, 126, 133n, 135, 141–6, 151, 154, 179
Jameson, Frederic, 84–5
Johnson, Samuel, 173
Jonson, Ben, 186
Joyce, James, 36, 82, 126, 136n, 154–7, 179, 181

Kant, Immanuel, 173–4
Kliuev, Nikolai, 171

Labriola, Antonio, 154
Lamb, Charles, 187
Landor, Walter Savage, 186–7
Lawrence, David Herbert, 15, 25–6, 32, 102, 127, 157–61, 179, 181
Leavis, F. R., 12, 22, 25–6, 36, 38–9, 103n, 136
Lenin, Vladimir Ilyich, 84, 166, 173–174
Locke, John, 183
Lukács, Georg, 24, 32, 36–7, 69, 156n, 161, 179

Lytton, Bulwer, 125

Macherey, Pierre, 83–4, 89–95, 97
Mallarmé, Stéphane, 81
Marcuse, Herbert, 179
Martin, Graham, 147
Marx, Karl, 22, 43, 64, 76, 166, 175–6, 179, 181–4
Mayakovsky, Vladimir, 84, 170–1
Mehring, Franz, 173
Mill, John Stuart, 103, 106–7
Milton, John, 56, 59, 148
Morris, William, 26, 63
Mulhern, Francis, 121n, 124n
Mussolini, Benito, 154, 158

Napoleon Bonaparte, 70
Nietzsche, Friedrich, 43
Norton, Grace, 143

O'Duffy, General Eoin, 154
O'Higgins, Kevin, 154
O'Leary, John, 152

Parnell, Charles Stewart, 152
Patmore, Coventry, 162
Pearson, Gabriel, 146n
Plato, 174
Plekhanov, Georgy, 173
Pope, Alexander, 63, 76, 87, 93
Poulantzas, Nicos, 14, 106n
Pound, Ezra, 126, 151, 179
Pushkin, Alexander, 162

Rousseau, Jean-Jacques, 174n
Ruskin, John, 25, 26, 102

Scrutiny, 13–16, 21–2, 24–5, 32, 38, 40
Shakespeare, William, 70, 96, 100, 166, 169–70
Shelley, Percy Bysshe, 121
Sidney, Sir Philip, 19, 75n
Solzhenitsyn, Alexander, 83
Steiner, George, 36
Strauss, David, 110
Strindberg, August, 37